Mainline Christian

Mainline Christianity

The Past and Future of
America's Majority Faith

Jason S. Lantzer

NEW YORK UNIVERSITY PRESS
New York and London

NEW YORK UNIVERSITY PRESS
New York and London
www.nyupress.org

References to Internet websites (URLs) were accurate at the time of writing.
Neither the author nor New York University Press is responsible for URLs
that may have expired or changed since the manuscript was prepared.

Library of Congress Cataloging-in-Publication Data

Lantzer, Jason S.
Mainline Christianity : the past and future of America's majority faith / Jason S. Lantzer.
    p. cm.
Includes bibliographical references (p.   ) and index.
ISBN 978-0-8147-5330-9 (cl : alk. paper)
ISBN 978-0-8147-5331-6 (pb : alk. paper)
ISBN 978-0-8147-5332-3 (ebook)
ISBN 978-0-8147-5333-0 (ebook)
    1. United States — Church history. I. Title.
BR515.L36 2012
277.3 — dc23
                            2011045381

New York University Press books are printed on acid-free paper,
and their binding materials are chosen for strength and durability.
We strive to use environmentally responsible suppliers and materials
to the greatest extent possible in publishing our books.

Manufactured in the United States of America
c   10 9 8 7 6 5 4 3 2 1
p   10 9 8 7 6 5 4 3 2 1

Contents

Acknowledgments

This book began life as an email exchange in 2006. After posting a reply to an online discussion forum about the use of terminology in describing various religious groups, I received an email from Jennifer Hammer of New York University Press asking if I had ever considered expanding my thoughts into something more. Intrigued by the idea, I sat out to do just that, with the end result being a discussion of the concept of the Mainline in American religious history. It was a process that, with some stops and starts, took longer than I expected, but it is better than I could have imagined back when the email was first composed. At the outset then, let me thank Jennifer and the staff at NYU Press (including the various reviewers during the writing process) for their patience and support over the past several years.

That I should undertake such a journey into the heart of American Christianity really did not surprise me. I was raised in a home where faith was a central part of life. From Sunday worship to Wednesday night activities to reading Bible stories, church and religious observance was constant. And so, I am thankful to my parents, Jack and Juanita Lantzer, for instilling and nurturing faith in God in me at a young age, a faith that I have relied on ever since. I am thankful for every moment spent in my various "home" congregations over the years, which have nurtured that faith even more. My pastors, teachers, and friends have also helped to shape the book as well. Likewise, I am grateful for the opportunities, both as a worshiper, visitor, and a historian I have had to visit a wide variety of congregations in eleven states across the country during the course of this project.

While I may have had the background that brought me to study American religious history, I would not have been able to do so without the support of the academic communities in which I am a part. This book benefited from the financial support of the Southern Baptist Library and Archives, and the Congregational Library, which allowed me to conduct research among primary sources. My students, both past and present, are also in order for thanks. I have taught American Religious History in a variety of formats over the years, and those students who made the journey with me deserve some recognition. My students at Butler University in particular helped me to undertake a fundamental revamping of an earlier draft, and I would like to single out Ali Sebald for her help in reading portions of the eventual manuscript.

As some of the information that follows appeared in an earlier form in previous published works, I am thankful for the opportunity to rethink and recalibrate it so that I can share it anew. Portions of chapter 2 are drawn from my book *Prohibition is Here to Stay*, published by the University of Notre Dame Press. Parts of chapter 3 appeared in the *Journal of Anglican and Episcopal History*. And portions of chapter 5 were first published by the *Journal of History and Computing*. The ability to bring much of my published body of work together within the new conceptualization of this book is exciting for me as an author and a privilege made possible by professional generosity.

There are a host of other people, largely friends, family, and colleagues, whom I should thank as well. Among them are Chad Parker and Scott Enbrecht who looked at early drafts. Both provided important insights, from very different perspectives, as did my old friends Jason VanHorn, PhD, and Jayson Hartman, PA, who shared their accounts of short-term missionary trips with me. Pat Harvey, of Indiana University-Purdue University Indianapolis (IUPUI) also offered comments as the project moved along. I am very thankful to Clark Hodgson, who not only provided insight on some of the court cases I discuss but also brought me into the world of Philadelphia lawyers for two years. I remain indebted to Professor Robert Barrows of IUPUI, who when I was working on my master's degree, helped bring me to the Polis Center, and to Professor James Madison of Indiana University, who directed my PhD dissertation. Both are now friends and colleagues as well as mentors. Likewise, Professor Stephen Stein helped nurture my understanding of American religious history while I was in graduate school. While I have already mentioned my parents, they deserve recognition along with my in-laws, Bill and Susan Hebert and the Honorable James Heuer and Kathy Heuer, for their efforts as grandparents (allowing me time to research and write kids-free). And those children, Kate and Nick, are sources of inspiration and distraction to their father. My first book was largely completed before either of them was born. This book, on the other hand, has been with them their entire lives.

Finally, I wish to thank my wife, Erin. She is my constant, a source of stability, consistency, and support in so many ways. When we were married, we selected for our scripture reading 1 Corinthians 13, and the words contained in that chapter remain as true today as they were then: "And now these three remain: Faith, hope, and love. But the greatest of these is love." It is to her, once again, that my work is dedicated, with all the love a husband can give to his darling wife.

The Mainline's Slippery Slope

An Introduction

"So, what is the Mainline?" Anyone who has taught a course on American religious history has heard this question numerous times, and usually more than once during the course of a semester. On the surface, this seems to be an easy question to answer. The Mainline is made up of the "Seven Sisters" of American Protestantism:[1] the Congregational Church (now a part of the United Church of Christ), the Episcopal Church, the Evangelical Lutheran Church, the Presbyterian Church (USA), the United Methodist Church, the American Baptist Convention, and the Disciples of Christ. The name itself derives from the formation of the Federal Council of Churches in Philadelphia in 1908, where the influence of the Pennsylvania Railroad helped give birth to the term.[2] As a group, these denominations represent a diverse Reformation Era heritage, have traditionally exhibited differing theological and liturgical emphasis and preferences, and, since the nineteenth century have been the dominant cultural representatives of how and where the majority of American Christians, the largest faith tradition in the United States, worships.

And yet, there is more to the question than the textbook answer will satisfy, a deeper concept and reality that students sense intuitively. For the majority of Americans in the twenty-first century, the Seven Sisters no longer reflect where *they* worship. After all, missing in the textbook definition are Roman Catholics as well as Protestant denominations such as the Southern Baptist Convention and Assemblies of God. According to the 77th Annual Yearbook of American and Canadian Churches in 2009, the Seven Sisters had a total membership of around 21.2 million (with the largest denomination being the United Methodist Church at 7.9 million members). By comparison, the Roman Catholic Church claimed a membership of 67.1 million; making it the largest church in the nation. The Southern Baptist Convention, the second largest denomination in the survey, had a membership of 16.2

million.[3] Simply put, the Seven Sisters, from a numerical standpoint, are no longer the majority denominations, and thus no longer the face of American Christianity.

How did this happen? The simple answer is Mainline decline, a topic that has received a good deal of scholarly attention. The thrust of most critiques is that the Seven Sisters, beginning in the early- to mid-twentieth century, began sacrificing doctrinal and theological orthodoxy in order to be more "appealing" and "relevant" to a changing and emerging "modern" American society and culture. In short, they stopped trying to shape culture via orthodox Christianity, and instead began to be shaped by it, liberalizing doctrine and theology in order to appear more welcoming. Christians in America, so the classic thesis goes, then began flocking to denominations and churches that were more orthodox or "conservative," prompting not just a short-term shift but a demographic one as well. Not only did these denominations attract more members but those members also tended to be younger and more apt to have larger families than those who remained in the Seven Sisters.[4]

The decline thesis is compelling. It surely captures many aspects of the dilemma in which the Seven Sisters find themselves as the twenty-first century begins, and it may even hold a warning for the larger denominations and congregations of the present. However, the theory raises as many questions as it answers. One of the problems with it is the use (while not wholly inappropriate) of political terms such as "liberal" and "conservative" to describe individual actors as well as entire denominations. If the Mainline is "liberal," and Roman Catholics are "conservative" theologically, then it would stand to reason that Methodists (for example) would be supporters of the Democratic Party, while Catholics would be the backbone of the Republican Party. And yet, what we find is a good deal of theological diversity within denominations, and thus a good deal of political diversity as well. Taking the above two denominations as examples, Hillary Clinton and George W. Bush are both United Methodists, while John Kerry and Bobby Jindal are both Roman Catholics. If anything, the inclusion of political terms obscures more than it illuminates, taking the focus off of other factors (ranging from congregational and pastoral preference, family membership traditions—which are compounded by cross-denominational marriage–and congregational availability/location), which are at least as important, if not more so, than denominational pronouncements and stances.[5]

Having offered this critique, this book is not just another chronicle of Mainline decline, though that is, to be sure, an issue discussed in the pages that follow. Rather, it is an attempt to capture the history of the Mainline. The

Seven Sisters were not the first nor are they likely to be the last "Mainline" in America's religious history. The Mainline is best viewed not as a single, solitary collection of denominations but as the most culturally influential and demographically representative group of denominations at a given historical moment. Such an understanding allows for continuity as well as change within that membership, and it also invites studies of American Christianity that avoid being saddled with debates over political terminology within doctrinal (both denominational and foundational) disputes, while respecting the diversity that theological discussion has produced. Understanding the history of the Mainline opens the door for a greater appreciation of the role of religion in American life and for new lines of study into its future.

If this historical insight is both evident from the record and even desirable as a tool of inquiry, then why has it been largely neglected? Even at the height of their power, some questioned the Seven Sisters' exclusiveness, arguing that other branches of Christendom, particularly Roman Catholics and Greek Orthodox Christians, needed to be included.[6] So, why are the Seven Sisters still widely counted as the Mainline if they no longer have the numbers (or clout) to back it up? There are several possible answers to these important questions, some of which will be explored in this book. But the crux of the answer centers on the concept of being a majority (or dominant cultural force), perceptions attached to that status, the coveted and comfortable place it became for its members, and what it means to lose that position, all of which is made more complex by the question of who gets to make such a categorization to begin with.

From an academic perspective, majority status is something of a double-edged sword. On the one hand, if a denomination is seen as part of the Mainline, there is little need (unless a scandal erupts) to spend time researching and writing about it because it is assumed that "everyone" already knows about or is a part of the denomination. If work is done, it is likely to focus on particular figures that helped form or influenced the denomination, or its rise to majority status, or even on important congregations within the denomination. In the American context, according to the historian Martin Marty, this has caused academics to slight Protestantism.[7] And while works of this type can all be important, insightful, and useful, they do not often get at what it means to be part of the Mainline. Perhaps the closest we have come to a study of the Mainline is David Sehat's recent work *The Myth of American Religious Freedom*. Sehat never engages the Mainline as the Mainline (indeed, he never invokes the term), though he does a fine job of discussing the interactions of religion, politics and the law in American life and culture.[8]

The other edge of majority status flows from the idea that the majority is of little interest, because it is the majority. Many academics, always on the lookout for new scholarship trends, have gravitated to studying groups or denominations on the margins of the Mainline. This includes works on New Religious Movements (NMRs), established denominations that are not part of the Mainline, and popular religious devotions, as well as sensational sects and cults. Like those who study the rise of Mainline denominations, these scholars are making important contributions to our knowledge about religion in America, including offering key insights as to why some people opt out of mainstream religious culture and expression. And yet, by not focusing on the majority, there is a failure to engage how most Americans have experienced and do experience religious life. Thus, readers will look largely in vain for discussion of the Church of Jesus Christ of Latter-day Saints, the Unitarians or their Universalist co-denominationalists, Christian Science, or "sects" of any kind in these pages.[9] Our focus here will be on the majority.

Because there is value in majority status, those who have once been a part of it are reluctant to give it up. Here then, is the reason why the Seven Sisters work so hard to remain considered as the Mainline, despite more than three decades of talking about Mainline decline and despite denominational membership figures that argue for a reconfiguration or reconceptualization.[10] Part of this is tradition; after all, they were *once* the Mainline, and some continue to lay claim to this position via nationally known leaders or by their prominence in certain areas of the country. That tradition also affords them a certain "bank of goodwill" in the larger public (including among journalists) memory.[11] They are, after all, the denominations from which people have "always" sought answers. And part of the Seven Sisters' appeal as the Mainline comes from their continued dominance of local, state, and national pandenominational groups, boards, and organizations that can speak officially to the press on an issue for all member denominations and congregations, no matter how controversial the issue or statement may be. This is a function usually reserved for the majority, and provides an easy way to "know" what Christians think.

The problem is that these organizations are vestiges of a different time, when the Seven Sisters *were* the Mainline. To say that the National Council of Churches (the successor to the Federal Council of Churches) speaks for all Christians historically, or even for all members of the Seven Sisters today, simply does not hold up to scrutiny. Roman Catholics, for example, were not a part of the organization because they were largely not welcome due to Protestant anti-Catholicism in its early years. Furthermore, many of these institutions simply lack the power or authority they did a century ago. This marginalization is part and parcel with the decline thesis, but it illustrates a disjunct, or rift, between denominational and institutional bureaucracies and many in the pews, as well as the growth of both pluralism and secularism in wider American society.

Rather than clinging to this past, as many within the Seven Sisters do, it is useful to begin to conceptualize a new Mainline. More than those outside the majority and even more than the decline thesis, looking for and at the majority can tell us a great deal about American religion. What we will find in making such a journey is that the Mainline has always been a part of the American experience. It has reflected in very real ways not only historic events, but the very face of the nation. Its history, its story, is a rich treasure just waiting to be found and appreciated.

If the past is to be our guide in discovering who the Mainline is today, then we must be prepared to embrace not only the flow of history, which shows a decided continuity within the Mainline in America, but the complex nature of Mainline Christianity in both the past and the present. In some ways, there has been more than one Mainline. In the colonial period, it was comprised of churches tied to their colonies and then states. After the Revolution, these denominations were joined by more evangelical denominations to form the Seven Sisters. By the mid- to late-twentieth century, this incarnation of the Mainline began to decline, forcing our discussion of a possible third reconfiguration of the group of churches that best reflects American Christianity.

As a collection of denominations, the Mainline has always been reflective of the America of their time and place. The story is full of saints and sinners, shortsighted pronouncements and visionary statements, not to mention doctrinal debates, theological discussions, and political shenanigans, all played out by those clinging to the cross of Christ. If not a uniquely American story, as an important part of the nation's history, it is no longer one that either can or should be ignored.

1

The Genesis of the Mainline

In 2007, to celebrate the 400th anniversary of the founding of Jamestown in Virginia, Queen Elizabeth II of the United Kingdom journeyed to the United States.[1] As the visiting monarch toured the re-created settlement, few commentators noted that the Britain's head of state was also the head of the Church of England, and so that the visit also marked a commemoration of the arrival of that branch of Protestant Christianity to the New World. Indeed, in some ways, Jamestown represents not just the first permanent English settlement in North America but the origin of the Mainline itself, a time during which people belonged to official churches, and those denominations shaped not only their members but also their communities and nations.

In American religious history, the story of the Mainline begins with the Church crisis that culminated in the Protestant Reformation. In looking back at the Reformation era and how it affected the discovery of the Americas and founding of the United States, the origins of the Mainline are in evidence. It is out of this period that the Mainline emerged, not quite into the power and glory of the Seven Sisters but surely with the promise of much to come. Still, the Mainline's creation took centuries to accomplish. Like Rome, it was not built in a day. And it is with Rome, or at least Roman Catholicism, that the story begins.

Colonial Origins

In some respects, Western Europe on the verge of the Reformation was basking in the glow of a golden age of Christendom. True, this Christendom was already not united, having witnessed a much earlier splintering between Western (Catholic) and Eastern (Orthodox) rites in 1054, as well as the more recent Avignon Schism (1309–78), which had found the papal seat of power transferred from Rome to France and then back again. True as well that it still faced a dangerous religious, political, economic, and military foe in the form of Islam. The Muslim conquest of Constantinople and the last vestiges of the Byzantine Empire was completed in 1453, and the threat of a Muslim invasion and occupation of Western Europe would not end until the 1570s.[2] But on the surface, the church was as strong and influential in faith and politics as it had been since the fall of the Roman Empire. It provided stability to much of Europe in the wake of imperial collapse, and these other factors seemed to matter very little to most of the faithful. This was the age of grand cathedral construction and of ever-expanding papal authority, which included appointing monarchs. The church seemed poised to grow on this secure foundation and to bring with it a new age of prosperity and piety.[3]

But that was the surface. In reality, this Catholic Christendom was on the verge of fragmentation, and that fragmentation helped to prompt the discovery and colonization of the Americas. There were two causes of the Reformation that are germane to the origins of the Mainline. The first is the theological and doctrinal debate within the Roman Catholic Church that culminated in the Protestant Reformation. The other was the growth, or strengthening, of nationalism within Europe. These two causes fed upon one another and were further inflamed by the printing revolution, which allowed the rapid dissemination of treatises, tracts, and books, and thus the diffusion of ideas and knowledge to an increasing number of people. Brought together, these factors helped create the modern world.

The mixture of faith and nationalistic influences can be clearly seen in two of the most significant men of the period: Christopher Columbus and Martin Luther. Both men and their achievements benefited from the state of flux in which Europe found itself, including the emerging debate over the proper role of church and state in the lives of both the nations and people of Europe. And, while neither man seemed destined for greatness at birth, both altered the course of history.

As an Italian, or perhaps more accurately a Genoan, Columbus grew up in the shadow of the papacy, which by the mid-1400s was as much a political as it was a religious institution. Since the fall of the Roman Empire, the papacy and the Catholic Church had filled much of the leadership void left by the vanished imperial bureaucracy, in addition to administering to the spiritual needs of millions of Europeans. Far from a dark period, these Middle Ages saw the church protect much of what is now Western Civilization. It did this by preserving ancient texts in libraries, founding colleges and universities, and sending out missionaries to spread the faith to "barbarians" across Europe.[4] Additionally, various popes ordered armies into the field, most notably during the Crusades, in an attempt to defend, enlarge, and recapture areas that had once been part of Christendom.[5]

This is the world that nurtured and shaped Christopher Columbus. It is because of the knowledge the church protected that he first started to believe it possible, from both a geographic and a historic sense, to sail west into the Atlantic Ocean to arrive in the Far East. And too, the church had been so active in "foreign affairs" that he believed his plan carried much spiritual (as well as economic) potential. Indeed, he saw these forces as intertwined—the money to be made from a more direct route to the markets and goods of Asia would produce European wealth to launch a new Crusade to free the Holy Land from Muslim control once and for all.[6]

Ironically enough, this goal is the reason the Italian Christopher Columbus ended up sailing for Spain. The Italian merchants and sailors, his peers, largely ignored his ideas because they were already part of the dominant trade route (along with corresponding product price markup) that brought Asian goods overland through Muslim occupied lands to Mediterranean ports dominated by Italian city-states for their transport into Europe. They had no intention of disrupting the arrangements they knew for something untried. The Portuguese, to whom Columbus also pitched his idea, dismissed it for other reasons. While not supporters of the Mediterranean trade route, they refused to finance Columbus because they had already done something about it. Portugal had circumnavigated Africa in order to reach Asia. While primarily done as a means to cut out the middle man, the Portuguese African venture had helped spark a naval/sailing revolution in Western Europe and created some of the first modern European overseas colonies. It was all done under the banner of the Portuguese monarchy's devotion to reestablishing contact with older Christian kingdoms, in this case, that of the mythic Prester John.[7]

These rejections eventually brought Columbus to the Spanish Court. For all the eventual problems he had with the Spanish government, at the time it was a match made in heaven. Newly united (via the marriage of Ferdinand and Isabella) and freed (the last of the Muslim Moors having been pushed out in 1492, after nearly eight hundred years presence on the Iberian Peninsula), the Spanish were receptive to Columbus's presentation that promised them wealth from a faster trade route to Asia, power within Europe because of it, and the possibility that both could then be harnessed to free the Holy Land. It was for these reasons that Columbus got to sail the ocean blue in 1492.[8]

Of course, Columbus did not land in Asia proper or off the coast of India as he first supposed. Instead, he "discovered" the Americas and pioneered the possibilities of what this New World could offer the Old, and vice versa.

Part of the eventual Columbian exchange was religion, with Catholic missionaries very much a part of the Spanish effort to colonize the New World, and the faith being given (along with gold and glory) as reason for the effort. We need not debate the sincerity of that religious belief, juxtaposed with brutal warfare, enslavement, and decimation by disease of Native Americans when considering its significance for colonization and the conquest of what the Catholic Spaniards deemed a pagan native population. That it was given as a reason is important enough when it comes to appreciating the origins of the Mainline.[9]

For his part, Columbus demonstrated both tendencies and worldviews. A devout Catholic, he believed that his faith was the one true way of knowing God. On one hand, this meant it was something to be shared and spread to unbelievers. On the other, if the cross of Christ was rejected, any resulting conflict or decimation by disease was not the fault of Europeans but rather of the "pagans" they had encountered who had spurned the true faith and the resulting outcome was the judgment of God. No matter how he looked at it, and no matter what we make of it, religious belief played a key role in the motivation of Columbus and of the long-term results of his transatlantic voyage.

If Columbus opened the door to religion playing a role in the European movement to the New World, then Martin Luther's actions both broadened and exploited this breach. While the German monk and professor of New Testament was neither the first (he was proceeded by John Wycliff and John Huss) nor the only one to seek reform of the church's administration (Erasmus was his contemporary) and uses of theology to justify some of its projects (the sale of indulgences, for example, was funding construction of St. Peter's Basilica at the Vatican in Rome), he is often credited with being the Father of the Reformation because his actions in 1517 were a tipping point in moving the reform debate from discussion to action. His success depended on the aid and support of local German nobility (most notably Frederic the Wise) and was copied, replicated, and transferred all across Western and portions of Central Europe.[10]

The Protestants (so called because of their protests about some of the Roman Church's practices) who broke with Catholicism over issues of reform and theology were a diverse bunch from their emergence, in terms of their own theology and their nationalities. Some of these newly minted dissenters objected to the Italian domination of the papacy and the Vatican as institutions, others sought to use the vernacular language in the publication of the Bible (making the Holy Scriptures more accessible to the common people of

Europe), while still others protested a wide variety of doctrinal innovations, traditions, and decisions advocated by the papacy (seeing them as nonessential to the faith). The two most important Protestant traditions for the future of the American Mainline were Luther's Lutheranism, which took hold in many of the German states and principalities as well as in Scandinavia (the forebearer of the Seven Sisters' Evangelical Lutheran Church), and John Calvin's Reformed (or Calvinism) Protestantism, which took root in portions of Switzerland, France (where it was particularly strong within the nobility), Holland, and eventually to portions of England and Scotland as well.[11]

While these two types of Protestantism differed in their stress on many points of doctrine (Calvinism came to emphasize the predestination of souls and the fear of the Lord, while Lutheranism emphasized the priesthood of all believers and justification by faith, and both held divergent views on the Eucharist), they shared a common belief in church influence on the state, but not the other way around. Luther believed the local ruler to be the supreme religious and political authority, while Calvin asserted the state should not interfere in the affairs of the church as well as concern that the papacy was a danger to the souls of those who worshiped in Catholic parishes and cathedrals.[12] Both men were also heavily reliant on the emerging print culture to spread their ideas and win converts to their cause. Indeed, Luther's revolt was predicated on the idea that people could read the Bible (and his tracts) for themselves and had no need for priests, bishops, or popes to interpose themselves between the individual and God.[13]

The conflict between Protestants and Catholics was not confined to debates or books. Indeed, Luther's Ninety-five Theses were more debate points posted on the cathedral door of a college town than they were detailed indictments of the church.[14] The moment Luther took his stand on faith alone, there was no hope of reconciliation between him and Rome. Thanks in large part to linkage between church and state (which had saved Luther's life when German princes' offered him protection after his excommunication), warfare and bloodshed were very much a part of the Reformation and the eventual Catholic Counter-Reformation. Both sides waged holy war against the other to take and retake spiritual and physical territory for much of the rest of the 1500s.[15] These wars of religion took a toll on the populations of many Western European countries and prompted new ways of thinking about the role of faith in the lives of both individuals and nations by the time the conflicts subsided.

As it happened, the merging of religion and nationalism furthered the cause of European colonization in the New World by helping spur intense competition in a variety of ways between nation states. Europeans, even as they fought over the Reformation, were in competition for economic resources and trade. Nations were attempting to become the most dominant power in Europe and saw colonies as the best means to achieve that goal quickly. And they were also in competition over propagating their brand of Christianity. The leading imperial powers in what was to become the United States all wrestled with faith and nationalism in different ways.

For the Spanish, there was little doubt that they were *the* Catholic power in the wake of Columbus's discovery and Luther's Reformation. Benefiting from finding and conquering the two richest and strongest Native American tribal empires (the Aztecs of Mexico and the Incas of Peru), the Spanish were overnight awash in a sea of wealth. Rather than funding a crusade to liberate the Holy Land, however, the Spanish opted to use their riches to build up the Roman Church and their own power. This often meant fighting Protestant (and at times other Catholic) nations in both the Old and New Worlds.[16] It also meant actively seeking to convert Native Americans by Catholic missionaries and by the sword. The empire the Spanish constructed heavily meshed the church with the state, and vice versa, with the church hierarchy handpicked by the Spanish Crown, and the institutional church used to help administer the far-flung colonial holdings.[17]

But the Spanish were not alone as a colonial power for very long, nor was their model the only one crafted by European Christians in the New World. The Portuguese quickly recognized their mistake in not backing Columbus and soon landed in Brazil with the full blessing of the papacy, which arbitrated and divided the Americas between Spain and Portugal in order to avert a conflict between the two powers. By the mid-1500s, the French joined them in the Americas as well. France, however, had been delayed by the Reformation. Like Germany, the French countryside was literally a battleground during the wars of religion that occurred after Luther's stand against the Roman hierarchy. With perhaps a third or more of the population becoming Protestant, it is little wonder that unlike Spain and Portugal (which Protestantism barely touched) and Germany (where, because of the fragmented nature of Germanic society, the faith of an area or principality largely depended upon where the local nobility opted to worship), in France a form of religious toleration, or at least coexistence, developed ahead of colonization.[18]

Codified as the Edict of Nantes in 1598, the concept of religious toleration had important and lasting affects in America, even as it proved to be short lived in France itself. The doctrine was crafted as a means to end the religious violence in the nation, the highpoint of which had been the massacre of Protestants on St. Bartholomew's Day in 1572, which had much to do with royal marriages and alliances. To bring peace to his country, the Protestant nobleman Henri of Navarre (soon to be Henry IV) agreed to convert to Catholicism in order to be crowned king (reportedly saying that Paris was worth attending Mass), and the edict was a means to allow Protestants to worship freely. Henri was eventually slain by a zealous Catholic who, perhaps correctly, doubted the conversion. But his death did not reopen the religious conflict. Rather, France came to embrace colonization as a means to rid itself of Protestant Christians.[19]

The French colonial agenda soon ran into problems. Many of the first voyages landed French Protestant colonists in the midst of Spanish territorial claims in the Caribbean and Florida, which the Spanish dealt with by massacring men, women, and children. When the French government moved its focus farther north, to what is today Canada, it escaped Spanish retaliation but found no easy path to wealth and dwindling numbers of willing colonists. In part this was because of past debacles and in part because of new conditions in France. The Catholic-controlled government initiated a new program of banishing Protestant ministers, thus cutting off the spiritual heads of Protestant congregations, and sending the remaining devout either into exile, back into the Roman Church, or opting out of organized religion altogether. With good economic conditions at home, there was also a lack of interest in leaving France. As a result, French colonies became small in size, Catholic in their religion, and based on good relations with Native American tribes. This development allowed the French to tap into the abundant fish and fur resources of North America, creating a transatlantic trade that brought them wealth in Europe without putting too much pressure on the Native Americans for land.[20]

So, where were the Protestant nations in this colonial scramble? While both Holland and Sweden established colonies in what became the United States, both stakeholds were small and eventually consumed by the nation that became *the* Protestant colonial power, Great Britain. And while the British were late in establishing colonies (Jamestown in Virginia was not founded until 1607), not only was it Britain's thirteen colonies that became the United States but the British experience with the Reformation that best explains its late entry into the Americas and the creation of the Mainline in the United States.[21]

The Reformation and the battle over it in England can be discerned from simply looking at the travails of the ruling Tudor family. Henry VIII had become king in 1509 upon the death of his older brother (and after Henry had spent time contemplating joining the priesthood). The crown came complete with a wife, his brother's widow, Catherine of Aragon (the daughter of Ferdinand and Isabella of Spain). When Luther and the Reformation burst onto the scene, Henry wrote a defense of the Catholic Church that won praise from Pope Leo X. But Henry's determination to produce a male heir to the throne, convinced as he was that his daughter Mary would be controlled by a foreign prince and thus make England a vassal state to a foreign power, eventually prompted him to use the Protestant crisis to achieve a divorce. This was the final blow to Rome's supremacy in the British Isles (which had come under increasing attack since the late 1300s, when the Oxford theologian John Wycliffe had worked on behalf of King Edward III to determine the proper relationship between church and state). Wycliffe went on to challenge the growth of wealth within the institutional church as well as the growth of shrines. In 1382, he translated the Vulgate Bible from Latin into English, helping unleash the Lollard movement of itinerant preachers as well as a firestorm of controversy before his death in 1384; Henry and his advisers established in 1534, by the Act of Supremacy, the Church of England.[22]

Henry's decision, expedited by the pregnancy of his mistress, officially removed the church in England from the See of Rome, placing it under the Crown's control. The king himself vacillated between what he knew (Catholicism), what he needed (a church that would allow a divorce or an annulment, making his daughter Mary a bastard and the soon-to-arrive Elizabeth legitimate), and what many of his advisors strove for—a Protestant church similar to those in Lutheran Germany.[23] His children truly dealt with the legacy of his decision. Edward, the eventual male heir, was a devout Protestant who died young and before his Protestant reforms had much chance to take root. Mary, not surprisingly, was an equally devout Catholic who, upon assuming the throne after Edward's death, attempted to eradicate the Protestantism she blamed for the disruption of her happy family life. While finding success in arresting, imprisoning, and even executing many leading Protestants, Mary had no children and so was followed on the throne by her sister, Elizabeth. The new queen, a Protestant, sought to defuse the religious struggle, vowing not to make "windows into the souls of men," while also crafting a Protestant national church as an arm of the state. Moving forward, England would be the Protestant power.[24]

Elizabeth I also launched England into colonization in the Americas. Combined with the new church, the nation was now set to leave its mark on the development of the American Mainline. The Anglican Church, as the

Church of England was eventually called globally, became the official church in many colonies, especially in Virginia where it was *the* religious establishment, with local taxes paid to support its existence. The denomination quickly became a bastion of the elite and the backbone of the eventual Southern planter aristocracy in the Americas. The church sought conformity, as dissenters from the Anglican fold not only had to contribute to it financially, but they could also face persecution. If there was a problem for the Church of England in colonial America, it was that it never developed an institutional hierarchy or framework provided by bishops and the bureaucracy of the episcopate that would allow it to adapt quickly to local challenges. It was, in other words, a shallow sort of establishment (even if the faith of those in the churches was often strong), with no bishop in America, and most of its clergy with more ties to England than the colonies and municipalities in which they resided.[25]

Despite the Anglican Church's official status, there was room for dissent within Christian England, which allowed for a good deal of diversity to exist on both sides of the British Atlantic. Perhaps the best known, and the ones with the largest impact on the future United States, were the Puritans. So named because they felt the Church of England remained too attached to the form and function of Roman Catholicism, the Puritans sought to purify the church on more Reformed Protestant lines.[26] Their failure to convince Elizabeth of this need and their disappointment in King James (formerly the king of Scotland, who took the throne of England upon Elizabeth's death), who despite being raised as a Presbyterian (the Scottish variant of Calvinism), quickly warmed to the notion of running his own church, led many Puritans to go to America. Others remained, eventually helping spur the English Civil War, in which Charles I (James's ill-fated son and successor) was killed, and a republic, headed by the Puritan Oliver Cromwell, was proclaimed.[27]

The Puritans who left for the New World (which differentiated them already from those who remained in England) came in two main varieties, each showcasing the complexity of their theology. The first were what might be called "orthodox" Puritans. This group believed they were creating a righteous example (through their own adherence to proper doctrine) for England, Protestant Europe, and all Christendom to follow. John Winthrop, who helped found Massachusetts, called what they were doing establishing a "city on a hill" when talking about the Puritan mission to the New World, where they could put their theories freely into practice. Their experiment was not a theocracy but a holy republic, a place where church and state functioned together toward a common end on shared principles, but not with a common leadership. Ministers were barred from holding public office, though church membership was initially a requirement to vote. So powerful was this vision that entire Puritan congregations uprooted themselves to come to America to help establish what became "New England."[28] The second group, the Separatists (whom most Americans know as the Pilgrims) did not share the optimism of the larger orthodox strain of Puritanism. They believed that Europe, England, and the church (whether the Church of England or the Church of Rome) were corrupt and beyond redemption. This feeling was reinforced by many of the Separatists' sojourn in Protestant Holland, which, while officially Reformed, was too tolerant for the dissenting Englishmen and women's religious tastes and social sensibilities.[29]

While these two groups of Puritans were different, they shared a sincere belief in sin and its consequences, and the assurance that Christ and his church were the only means of salvation and grace in the world. While their sincerity would later give rise to the stereotype of being "kill joys," they were, as a group, far from joyless. Rather, they worried about things that might lead to sin because of the eternal consequences attached to it. As such, they put their church, what became the Congregational denomination in America, at the center of life. Indeed, the church was often literally the center of Puritan towns, and served as a moral guide for its members and the wider community. The Puritan system was replicated throughout England's northernmost colonies, in places such as New Hampshire and Connecticut.[30]

All Puritans believed they had entered into a covenant with God. Like ancient Israel, they were to be God's people, and he was to be their God. This relationship strongly personalized God for the Puritans, but it also meant that there were many conditions that the Puritans had to meet to keep the covenant in place. Their church and colonies were crafted to try both to meet those goals and to mirror the covenant itself.[31] They expected God's blessing if they lived up to the covenant and God's punishment if they failed.

Covenant theology and the congregational way met with mixed results. Acceptance of it by the Puritans required adherence to both the ecclesiastical and temporal leadership, with membership being predicated on a conversion experience and public testimony to God's saving power. But Puritans also wrestled with whether they could, in fact, be sure of their salvation. Was their conversion real, or had they been tricked by Satan? For the first generation of Puritans, there was as much angst as there was joy in conversion, prompting in part what the historian Edmund Morgan has labeled the "Puritan dilemma," as they wrestled with being saints living in an ungodly world. Conceived as it was in the midst of a vibrant intellectual Calvinism, covenant theology when applied to colonization shows how complex Puritan thought was. While the Great Migration in the 1630s had been a bonding event, as the founding generation passed from the scene there was a good deal of worry over the fate of the holy experiment in New England.[32]

Hence, the second and third generations of Puritans in America devoted time and energy into crafting, debating, defending, and expanding the so-called Half-Way Covenant, which allowed those whose parents had been confirmed as church members to become partial members as well, without having had to have a conversion experience of their own. This compromise, though not accepted by everyone, was thought to be crucial to the survival of the New England experiment, even as it caused much debate within the church (including between such heavyweights as the Mather family and Solomon Stoddard) and opened the door to the eventual ending of Congregationalism as the founding Puritans had known it.[33] After all, wrestling with the concept of salvation was seemingly a hallmark of Puritanism, and thus of church membership and the privileges that went with it both in this world and the next. Under the Half-Way Covenant this struggle was removed from the equation.[34]

As dissenters, the Puritans might be expected to be upholders of religious toleration. This, however, was not the case. The sincerity of their beliefs led them to insist that those who objected to their views were not only wrong but probable agents of Satan. Protestantism in general, with Luther's argument of the priesthood of all believers and the notion that Christians could read and interpret scripture for themselves, contributed to this stance. But so too did Puritanism in particular, because it attempted to create a holy republic in both the New and Old Worlds. These factors led to dissent and splintering of this branch of Protestantism in America rather quickly.[35]

Probably the best-known story in this vein is that of Anne Hutchinson, who began instructing fellow Puritans in her home following church services. Often her teachings pointed out mistakes Hutchinson believed the minister was making in interpreting scripture. Eventually brought before authorities, Hutchinson largely held her own with her critics. While it is popular today to hold her up as a feminist icon, Hutchinson posed a threat to Puritan theology not because she was a woman but rather because she was attacking the basis of how Puritans believed God instructed his people. In her view, one needed to just wait upon the Holy Spirit to talk to one directly; there was no need for adherence to institutional forms per se. The Puritans believed that by banishing her, as they did in 1638, they were protecting God's holy experiment and defending the church as an institution. When she was later killed by Native Americans, the Puritans of Massachusetts ascribed it to divine justice.[36]

More importantly, the hard line the Puritans took led to the founding of more colonies. Dissenters fleeing from Massachusetts helped bring about the Baptist denomination, as well as craft a colony that allowed for true religious toleration. Of course it was not just any dissenter but rather one of the most devout of the Puritan faithful, Roger Williams, who helped nurture the Baptists and who gave birth to Rhode Island. Indeed, Williams was the ultimate dissenter in some regards. As one who believed firmly in the concept of congregational independence, he could not accept the mingling of church and state in Massachusetts, seeing no role for the state in enforcing congregational conformity nor in church attendance. He worried that his fellow Puritans had not made a clean enough break with their Anglican roots, and he could not he see how the Crown had some sort of divine right to the lands of the Native Americans. As he could not keep his views to himself, it is little wonder that he was eventually expelled from Massachusetts (though unlike Hutchinson, he maintained friendships with those who disagreed with him, most notably with John Winthrop).[37]

Rhode Island's example was utilized by other new colonies created in the wake of the Restoration of the monarchy in England, following Oliver Cromwell's death in 1658. Looking to pay off debts, King Charles II (the son of the executed Charles I) granted William Penn the right to found the Province (later the state of) Pennsylvania. A devout member of the Society of Friends (Quakers), and like many converts of whatever faith quite assertive, Penn quickly made his proprietary holding a safe haven for all manner of religious dissenters, a practice that was followed in nearby New Jersey and Delaware.[38] In doing so, Charles II was merely following in the footsteps of his grandfather and father. In 1625 George Calvert was made the First Lord Baltimore by James I (as compensation for years of devoted service upon his resignation from a royal post because of his Catholicism). In the early 1630s, Calvert presented a plan to Charles I for a new colony north of Virginia. In 1632 Charles I approved the colony, giving it to Cecil, the Second Lord Baltimore. As Catholics, the Calvert family made their colony Maryland a place of religious toleration, in large part because they could not find enough of their co-religionists to settle there.[39] To his brother James, the Duke of York (who would eventually be revealed as a secret Catholic), Charles II granted New York, which also followed a policy of religious toleration (perhaps out of immediate necessity, as it incorporated New Holland and New Sweden into itself). All three of these colonial benefactors practiced toleration, in part because it helped attract more colonists, making their holdings more profitable, and also because of their own religious backgrounds.[40]

Looking back at this colonial period, several popular narratives are shown to be based only in part on actual history. The first is the notion that religious toleration was an overriding goal for the English colonies. It was not. Most English Christians limited themselves to tolerating other Christians (in a broad sense), without neglecting doctrinal differences, most often limiting themselves only to tolerating other Protestants. Furthermore, tolerance, even of a grudging kind, is not the same thing as acceptance. While other variants of the faith might have been allowed, this did not stop most colonies from having an official, established church.

The other popular notion is to see the future United States as simply a "Puritan nation." When discussion turns to colonial religion, especially when it focuses on the Salem witchcraft trials (a common enough practice among Christians on both sides of the Reformation divide and on both sides of the Atlantic), not only are the Puritans blasted for their moralism but also for their intolerance, both of which are oversimplifications dealing more with stereotypes than with the Puritans themselves.[41] But this also masks a larger problem, assuming that one denomination defined the United States. Without taking anything away from the important role of the Puritans, it is more useful for our purposes to focus on the immense religious diversity of the colonies and what that came to mean for future generations of Americans.

Of Awakenings and Revolution

Where is the colonial Mainline, if there was such a thing? By far the largest and most dominant Protestant denominations in Britain's thirteen colonies were the Anglicans and the Puritans (the modern Episcopal and Congregational/United Church of Christ denominations). However, there were dissenters to this establishment. And it was the emerging evangelical movement that would help forge the Seven Sisters and which provides a core to the wide variety of theological and doctrinal differences, shaping them into a more coherent whole.[42]

These evangelicals, who sought to balance the Protestant intellectual tradition with emotional outreach designed to win converts, emerged in large part as a reaction to events emanating from Europe. The Enlightenment quickly swept across the Continent, moving the focus from faith to reason. This challenged the underpinnings of old European thinking, much as the

Reformation had taken issue with the religious and political foundations a generation before. But the Enlightenment movement, with its focus on reason, was multifaceted. While in France it took an antiestablishment bent, helping create both social contract theory in politics and fostering anticlericalism, it was not inherently anti-religious. Calvinists were very important in the coming and shaping of the Enlightenment in the British Empire.[43] In Scotland, they helped produce Common Sense Philosophy, which was applied to areas such as politics and religion. In England, the Enlightenment helped clarify the notion of natural laws, giving the world Sir Isaac Newton in science and mathematics, John Locke in politics—both of whom wrote extensively on matters of faith, and Deism in religion.[44]

Deism made inroads in Christianity during the Enlightenment because of the philosophical attractiveness of natural law and belief in human knowledge: That God had given humans reason, that God had created laws to govern human affairs, and that in deducing these laws, mankind would make the world a better place were assumptions that seemed to blend new and old ways of thinking in a compatible manner. But Deism took these starting points one step farther. Deists said that God was like a clockmaker, who created the world with laws, and then walked away from human history, only to return when the clock stopped at the end of time. The Bible was full of stories and myths to guide mankind, but talk of miracles and divine intervention were allegorical (or perhaps even errors) not historical. Christianity was the epitome of religion because it allowed humans to recognize God's plan (or Providence) via the teachings of Jesus—not Christ's death or resurrection, which was to Deists allegorical and spiritual, not something that actually happened—and appreciation for God's natural laws. In following their version of the faith, Deists strove for a rational understanding of religion's role in the world as history progressed.[45]

This variant of Christianity found a ready home in the Church of England, partly because the denomination required its clergy to be college educated, and thus exposed to new knowledge and teaching. But it also came at a time when Puritanism was well on the decline on both sides of the Atlantic. Indeed, some of America's leading Deists were Puritan converts to Anglicanism. Deism filled an intellectual void, quickly spread throughout the Church of England, and was soon filtering its way into the American colonies as well.[46]

Deism was not orthodox Christianity by any stretch of the imagination. In England, much of the counterattack against Deism centered on the Methodist movement, spawned by John and Charles Wesley and their friend George

Whitfield in the 1730s. Rejecting Deism in terms of its theology and its ramifications (which tended to reinforce the status quo), this band of preachers-in-training took their cue from the New Testament, spending much time studying scripture, singing and writing hymns, and preaching. In evangelizing to the great mass of society about their need to be saved from their sins, these revivalists went beyond the reach of the Anglican Church's hierarchy, into the streets and fields and directly to the people. Their revivals were not without opposition. Some recoiled at hearing their pastimes (heavy drinking, card-playing) being labeled as sins. Anglican bishops, worried about activities beyond their control, often condemned the revivals as well. Despite these opponents, the revivals were exceedingly popular and successful, and marked the onset of the evangelical movement. They were the heart of what became known as the Great Awakening.[47]

The Awakening's revivals were not confined to England, Wales, Scotland, or even portions of Ireland. They quickly spread across the Atlantic, bringing people back into churches.[48] Georgia, the final colony England established in North America, was founded on evangelical lines, although they were eventually abandoned as a basis of governance. The Wesleys and Whitfield spent time in Georgia, with Whitfield launching a revival that carried him up and down the Atlantic coastline. Indeed, he almost single-handedly changed the way people viewed what the church could be, in large part because of the connections he was able to make with his audiences.[49] His work inspired many, from the future Founding Father Benjamin Franklin (a Deist of Puritan stock who, if not converted, was compelled by what he heard and witnessed to become more active in philanthropy in Philadelphia) to Jonathan Edwards. This descendant of Puritan ministers on both sides of his family tree, including his maternal grandfather, Solomon Stoddard, Edwards was the greatest colonial divine of his generation. A powerful preacher in his own right, Edwards delivered one of the best-known sermons in American History: "Sinners in the Hands of an Angry God." In it, Edwards called to his congregation to repent of their sins, or face hell, noting that it was not only God's grace that could save them but also that grace keeping them from immediate damnation, a stark repudiation of Deism's worldview.[50]

Edwards, in many respects, showcases how New England and most of British North America reacted to both the Enlightenment and the changes that were overtaking the empire. As the region had expanded in the late 1600s, it had also been transformed from Winthrop's city on a hill into a major economic and business center. The resulting societal stress of this transition made it open to the Great Awakening's revivals, because people now were more aware of the problems that needed confronting. And since many Puritans and their descendants believed New England to have been in decline since the deaths of the founders, their jeremiads (calls to the people to come back to God's covenant), neatly culminated in the revivals of the Great Awakening and in the person of Edwards.[51]

When it came to theology, the Great Awakening marked a meeting of traditions. Arminianism, which embraced the idea that sinners were damned because they refused salvation, and Calvinism, which held to the belief in predestination of the saved, were both present.[52] But the real demarcation was over the ways individuals understood the revivals that became the hallmark of the time. Some (often referred to as Old Lights) decried the revivals because they upset the status quo, often happened outside the established churches and their structures, seemed to be based more on emotion than on intellect, and could not be controlled. At the other end of the spectrum were the New Lights who embraced revivalism as a gift from God and the rebirth of faith in the face of the Enlightenment. The New Lights, however, were split as the revivals ran their course in the 1730s and 1740s between those who accepted revivals for what they were (a momentary opportunity to reach the unsaved and unchurched) and those who believed the revivals were the new norm and the basis to transform society.[53]

Despite this debate, the Great Awakening not only saved orthodox Christianity from the clutches of Deism in the English-speaking world but also became a cultural touchstone for the generation who grew up in its wake. For many in England, it became an inspiration for launching reforms. In America, it was something virtually all the colonies were a part of, a common event that unified them.[54] And there were other events at work, which would unify the original colonies even more.

By the 1760s the English Atlantic world had taken part in the Great Awakening, but England was reaching the apex of its first empire. Its holdings were global in scope. It was surpassing the Spanish and had finally defeated the French, pushing their ancient foes out of North America altogether. But within this newfound strength there were also the seeds of the empire's destruction. Its supremacy meant external threats were now gone (at least for the moment), causing some in America to wonder why the colonies should be junior members of an empire that was seemingly sustained by American resources. In attempting to accommodate new citizens of the empire (the former French colonists in Canada primarily), England began making concessions, ranging from halting further westward expansion so to keep the Native American fur trade going to agreeing to allow a Catholic bishop to administer to the spiritual needs of colonists in Quebec. Neither decision was popular among the Protestant English majority living in the colonies. And then there were the taxes Britain needed to fund the acquisition and administration of the empire, taxes that were then passed on to the colonists, prompting resistance in defense of the notion of "no taxation without representation." A revolution was soon in the works.[55]

To be clear, religion was not the main force in the coming of the American Revolution. While there was worry about institutional Catholicism, most American pastors were struggling to get or keep their membership numbers up as the enthusiasm of the Great Awakening receded.[56] If there was a religious worry, it may have been more focused on the creation of an official Anglican establishment via the work of the Society for the Propagation of the Gospel (SPG), which sought to foster the state church in all the colonies, than it was about Roman Catholics.[57] While there is no direct link between evangelicals and patriot thought, the evangelical movement did add to the mix of ideas, and many evangelicals became Revolutionaries—but of course, so to did many Puritans and Anglicans.[58] And yet, religious faith, "provided essential moral and political principles to the revolutionaries" according to the historian Thomas Kidd.[59]

Perhaps the evangelical patriotism is best illustrated by John Witherspoon. A Scottish Presbyterian who came to New Jersey to take the presidency of the College of New Jersey (now Princeton University), Witherspoon mixed Enlightenment views with Calvinistic theology. His influence was vast, including nearly convincing a young James Madison to enter the ministry, and his politics were revolutionary. A signer of the Declaration of Independence, Witherspoon both preached and lectured on the patriot cause. After the war he helped create the Presbyterian Church's denominational structure in the United States, opting for this duty rather than attending the Constitutional Convention.[60]

Just as the Revolutionary War proved to be the inception of the United States, it also showcased future religious trends. The British strategy in many ways reflected not only colonial sectionalism but also religious beliefs. It was thought that Anglicans would not break with England; even the Methodists proved to be somewhat ambiguous on the topic of independence, with John Wesley opposing it. Massachusetts, it was believed by many in London, was the real problem. This bastion of Puritanism had never really been loyal to the Crown, and if it could be isolated, an example could be made of it. Indeed, Reformed theology in general was seen as a problem, with King George III supposedly calling the conflict "the Presbyterian war." On the

American side of things, the war was seen by the patriots as a moral imperative, with God being on the side of the new nation, but not discussed in such overtly denominational terms.[61]

The duration of the conflict, with fighting lasting from 1775 until 1783, was a test of faith for many Americans. Some who were sure in 1775 that God had called them to revolt began to wonder as the war continued if they were enacting God's plan or not. If the war tested their faith, it also gave the nation an appreciation for the religious diversity in the colonies-turned-states and the ramifications it might have on politics. The Declaration of Independence made implicit, if somewhat vague, calls to a higher authority when it came to rights. Just as important was the movement toward the disestablishment of churches from state government, unleashing the power of democratic competition between denominations that became the bedrock of American religious experience and was critical for the ultimate creation of the Mainline.

Nowhere was the disestablished future either highlighted or more of a struggle than in Virginia. Home to many of the leading Revolutionaries, the state was also the centerpiece of Anglicanism, both of the devout and deistic varieties, in the new United States. It was also home to a growing number of evangelicals, who had for years run afoul of the Anglican establishment. It was Thomas Jefferson who proposed disestablishment, with the support of Witherspoon's old student James Madison. What they ran up against was the widely held belief that Christianity should be honored as an institution by the state. But after the failure of Patrick Henry's general establishment plan (a compromise that would have allowed taxpayers to direct which church received their taxes), the Jefferson-Madison argument that Christianity in its diversity could stand on its own, carried the day.[62]

The religious diversity and tension created by and over the Great Awakening and Revolutionary War were exhibited in the Founding Fathers. Despite coming from a Puritan heritage, Benjamin Franklin was most likely a Deist. Likewise, the primary author of the Declaration of Independence, Thomas Jefferson, though raised an Anglican, also embraced Deism. But Jefferson also worked for disestablishment in Virginia (hardly the purview of Deists alone) and was far from being a "strict separationist" when it came to matters of church and state. Though often counted among the Deists, it is perhaps safer to say that George Washington was a disinterested Anglican who sought to have religion play a wider role in the life of the nation. Similarly, James Madison was an Anglican (his cousin (also a James) was one of the founders of the Episcopal Church) who flirted with Presbyterianism in college while becoming a friend to Virginia's Baptists when he supported Jefferson's disestablishment plan.[63]

Other Founders brought different religious views to the table. John Adams was a Yankee Puritan who married a minister's daughter. While he likely slipped into Unitarianism later in life, his cousin Samuel never lost the Puritan zeal of the founders of Massachusetts. Both branches of the Adams family utilized religion to push for and justify the War of Independence.[64] Likewise, the Virginians Patrick Henry and John Marshall along with John Jay of New York were evangelically influenced Anglicans.[65] New Jersey's John Witherspoon also fell into the evangelical camp,[66] while Alexander Hamilton (a devout Anglican who found a home in New York) hoped to see the new nation become a Christian republic.[67]

Though it is difficult to know for certain how profound were these Founding Fathers' piety, and that like today, religious beliefs or affiliations can change over the years, it is equally clear that this founding generation respected religious belief and believed that faith had an important role to play in the life of the new United States. While some sought to construct a "wall of separation" between church and state, it was also their thought that such a wall would allow both institutions to flourish on their own without overt control or support of the other. What the Founders achieved was the creation of a new nation and a new dynamic in the history of Christianity: toleration that promoted diversity.[68] And this is the concept enshrined in the Constitution.[69] Its formula put in place the key ingredients for making the Mainline of the Seven Sisters. All that remained was for a second revival to give the Mainline life.

2

Building the New Jerusalem

The High Tide of the Seven Sisters

"Late in the afternoon of a chilly day in February . . ." With these words Harriet Beecher Stowe began one of the most popular, controversial, and important works in American literature: *Uncle Tom's Cabin*. Written in response to the Fugitive Slave Law of 1850 and published in book form in 1852, Stowe's work is generally credited with helping to shift Northern public opinion from apathy to generally antislavery in nature, and thus adding to the other forces that brought on the Civil War.[1] But the book is much more than just a piece of abolitionist propaganda, for it marks the ascent of evangelical Protestantism in the United States and the corresponding arrival of the Seven Sisters as a virtual establishment in the young nation.[2]

The European roots and colonial founding gave American Christians all the necessary ingredients to create the Mainline of the Seven Sisters. The established denominations, the Episcopal and Congregational churches, with their cultural impact, were in place. The ending of state-sponsored churches (even if the states themselves retained a largely religious-based interest in the legal promotion of morality) over the first half of the nineteenth century not only unleashed the competitive nature of American denominationalism but corresponded to the rise of the democratic impulse, which saw the creation of new denominations and the reorganization of old ones. The Seven Sisters emerged out of this milieu, overcoming war and dramatic societal changes, and creating a virtual establishment that lasted well into the twentieth century.

Awakening and War

Even as the nation was recovering from the Revolution, it was pushing forward, or more precisely, westward. Between 1790 and 1860 the United States moved from thirteen states clinging to the Atlantic coastline to controlling

| 27

what modern Americans would view as the "lower 48." This westward expansion was met with a good deal of excitement as well as fear over the future, not only on behalf of the prosperity of the country but also for the nation's soul. As pioneers moved from the East, would God go with them—as westward expansion was couched in the religious notion of manifest destiny—or would they become cut off from organized religion and civilization, descending into some sort of lawless (and pagan) state of nature? The Episcopalians and Congregationalists were unready to deal with this potential problem, or at least they were unsure of how to act. The pillars of colonial Christendom were struggling to find their place in the new America as disestablishment hit them the hardest. The Episcopal Church was tainted by its English roots despite its new, official name as the Protestant Episcopal Church in the United States of America, and the Congregational Church was mired in a divisive doctrinal debate related to a proposed merger with the Presbyterian Church. For these reasons, many people believed the religious faith of the nation was at low ebb in the years after the Revolution.[3]

The nation now faced some real problems. The diversification of the American economy, which comprised commercial agriculture in the Midwest, cash crops in the South, and industrialization in the Northeast—corresponding to regionalism—and the South's reliance on slave labor, were all soon causing a political crisis that ended in civil war. While slavery was hardly the only issue discussed, it soon became the most important. Religious debate over it and calls for other reforms only exacerbated tensions in the nation.[4]

Likewise, the nation's Protestant Christians faced another challenge as well, which also affected the future Mainline. During the mid-1800s, the nation welcomed the first wave of large-scale immigration from Europe since the Revolution. Prompted by war, famine, and political disruption, and tied to both cheap land in the West and a growing industrial capability in the Northeast, these immigrants, primarily from Ireland and Germany, were largely Roman Catholic. To many native-born Americans, such an influx brought with it societal strain and challenge, and also religious tension. The Reformation divide between Protestants and Catholics was still very much alive, and the early nineteenth century witnessed a wave of anti-Catholicism, which included riots and bloodshed.[5] These events helped bolster both Catholic and Protestant identity, each largely independent of the other.

Not surprisingly, America's churches unleashed another wave of revivals along with reforms in response to these tensions. While not quite as transatlantic as the first, the Second Great Awakening was in many respects even more impressive in its scope and religious accomplishments for the country. Here was the emergence of evangelical Protestantism as a force, not just a movement. This was the time of the Baptists, Methodists, and Presbyterians, a period of evangelical dominance that would last for more than a century. Together with the Congregationalists and Episcopalians, with whom they shared a related Reformation Era heritage, these denominations created the Mainline.[6]

But that was in the long term. In the short term, the Second Great Awakening met a fundamental need for many Americans. People were yearning for a revival in the years after the Revolution. The pioneers wanted churches, welcomed preachers, and feared national religious decline, just like their fellow citizens back East. If the fear of decline was commonplace that does not mean it was not based in reality. The evangelical denominations were in the best position to address these fears, both real and imagined.[7]

Because they were not part of the old establishment, the evangelical denominations had the most to gain from disestablishment after the Revolution. They had few overt ties to old ways or old governments, and appeared as fresh and new as the country itself. In many ways Baptists, Methodists, and Presbyterians were in the best position to capitalize on the dislocations of westward expansion and industrialization, which included urbanization and immigration as well. For one, the evangelical denominations respected the mobility of the American population, whether native-born or immigrant. They went where the people were, rather than relying on "cradle to grave" membership or denominational loyalty. Additionally, the evangelical denominations were willing to act to deal with the problems of their time without much theological angst. Indeed, the evangelicals brought a "can do" spirit to facing down problems while also interjecting a good deal of optimism into how American Christians saw the United States.[8]

But exactly who were these evangelical denominations that were willing to take part in both rural and urban revivals to advance their belief that establishing God's kingdom on earth was possible? The Baptists, for example, were truly "of the people" and had helped make the case for disestablishment in places like Virginia. They made few demands on ministers establishing new churches, save that they felt called by God to the pulpit; this calling included being able to preach from the Bible, and being of good moral character, plus the ability to support themselves. The denomination was loosely organized and could offer very little in the way of financial support and so, was poised to grow rapidly.[9] The Methodists, led more by Francis Asbury, who had been appointed in 1771 to help guide the American wing of the movement, than by the Wesleys themselves, adapted to the frontier's spread-out communities by creating the circuit rider system: one minister administered to the spiritual needs of several "stations" on a rotating basis, connecting them together by riding from one pioneer community to another on horseback in between Sundays. This arrangement gave local lay leadership considerable control and responsibility, and promoted a collective sense of denominational identity and purpose.[10] The Presbyterians, after considering a merger with the Congregational Church (despite their shared Reformed heritage, the differences over church polity and oversight were to great to overcome), instead pressed ahead with plans to win the West by planting colleges and producing ministers to launch and lead new congregations as quickly as they could be formed.[11] All three denominations emphasized the power of preaching and creating an environment that attracted people to their congregations. These attributes quickly became hallmarks of American evangelical Protestantism.[12]

Revivals were soon sweeping over the nation again. Often centered on pioneer marshalling areas, such as Cane Ridge in Kentucky, the resulting enthusiasm and new church plants quickly put to rest worries that the pioneers would go unchurched.[13] But the revivals were not confined to the frontier. In places like upstate New York, industrialization and related population dislocation soon created what was known as the "burned-over district" because of the number of revivals and revivalists. The famed Charles Finney, a lawyer-turned-Presbyterian-evangelist whose tactics grew church membership but also downplayed the need to know much about theology or doctrine, won great numbers of souls for Christ and propelled lax Christians to action.[14] As membership rolls began to soar, the evangelical denominations became the largest in America. In the South the results were spectacular. There, "evangelical pietism" took hold to such a degree that it checked the growth of Unitarianism, theological liberalism, and even the perception that reforms were needed; at the same time this fervor helped bring Christianity to enslaved African Americans for the first time in large numbers.[15]

Not everything went smoothly within the growing evangelical movement, particularly in the area of race. In Philadelphia in 1787 officials at St. George Methodist Church stopped blacks from praying at the front of the church alongside whites. Upset by such overt racism in the house of God, Richard Allen and others created the African Methodist Episcopal Church in 1794. The new denomination had to fight to maintain its independence, and its struggles highlighted the factors of racism and paternalism that came with Christianity in a majority-white nation where slavery was legal. Interracial worship became a rare exception within evangelical churches, and helped exclude most African American Christians from being active in the Mainline. They were, instead, segregated into their own denominations.[16]

Despite the problems associated with race, the Second Great Awakening legitimized the evangelical movement within American Protestantism and solidified the place of Baptists, Methodists, and Presbyterians in the Mainline. It also created new denominations. While groups like the Millerites (now Seventh Day Adventists)[17] and the Church of Jesus Christ of Latter-day Saints (Mormons)[18] went on to carve their own niche in the American religious landscape, one new denomination, the Disciples of Christ, actually became part of the Mainline. The Disciples, or Christians, as they were also called, were founded by the 1832 merger of evangelical movements under the direction of Barton Stone and Alexander Campbell. They sought at first to use the revivals to forge not a new denomination but rather to unify American Protestantism under a single banner. When this did not happen, their new evangelical denomination emerged. The Disciples growth on the frontier made it a welcome member of the Mainline, adding more strength to the dominant evangelical bloc.[19]

Too, the Second Great Awakening was not just a revival of religion; it was also a launching pad for reforms. In many ways, reformist zeal contributed to the success of the Mainline's evangelical denominations. Evangelicals not only talked about sin, they sought to identify and eliminate specific sins that affected both individuals and all of society. America's churches thus became places where the rights of women were discussed, where efforts were launched to reform prisons and asylums, where initiatives were started to create a system of free, public schools, where alcohol was openly condemned, and where slavery (at least in the North) was openly blasted as an abomination against both God and man. In order to combat societal evils, men and women were called forth to do battle on the side of the Lord.[20]

One family that showcased the Second Great Awakening in all its facets was the Beecher family. Lyman Beecher was a Congregational/Presbyterian minister who strove to protect orthodox Christianity against a new threat, that of Unitarianism, in his native New England. Convinced that the future of the nation lay in a religious revival much like the one he experienced in college, Lyman dedicated his life, and his children, to the cause of the Second Great Awakening. The Beecher children were all well educated and expected to get involved in the reformation of American society. The Beecher boys were tasked with becoming ministers in newly opened congregations, and the girls were expected to be at the forefront of reforms as well. The children did not disappoint, even if they carved their own niches to their father's vision and some slipped from his orthodox faith. The younger Beechers were involved in nearly every type of reform, usually as its leaders and often from the pulpit. Among them was Catherine, the eldest of Lyman's children, who was a pioneer in female education among other pursuits. Edward served as minister in both urbane Boston and frontier Illinois, while also becoming a college president and vocal abolitionist. Thomas was not only a minister but also an advocate for prohibition. Baby daughter Isabella was a leader in the suffrage movement of the late nineteenth century; Henry Ward Beecher became the most famous preacher in the country, and Harriet Beecher Stowe, who wrote one of the most consequential books of the nineteenth century, *Uncle Tom's Cabin*. In much of the Midwest and New England, the Second Great Awakening mixture of personal salvation and societal reform, which the Beechers seemed to embody, took hold.[21]

The Beechers and their reforms, especially their antislavery efforts, were unwelcome in the nation's Southern states. While the Second Great Awakening led to a general revival of religious sentiment and church membership across the South, the notion of reform did not take root in the region. Indeed, even as evangelical churches became the norm in the South, they tended to tone down and eventually cease to discuss the long list of societal ills that their Northern brethren returned to with frequency, in order to reach upper-class whites and achieve respectability. Many of the reforms, it was alleged, were more Northern ills than they were Southern problems. Southern evangelicals believed that all people were sinners and that while faith in Christ could save an individual, nothing could be done to redeem society until the Second Coming. Attempting to do so was seen as futile. And when it came to slavery, Southerners, even those without a vested interest in it, were loath to change an institution that had biblical precedents (though not, it should be pointed out, the chattel variety of slavery that developed in the South). Indeed, as the 1800s moved on Southern ministers of virtually all denominations increasingly came to defend, not condemn the institution of slavery.[22]

And yet, antislavery sentiment was nothing new in American religious history especially if one considers the Society of Friends,[23] including within the emerging Mainline. There were Puritan voices who took a stand against the institution in the colonial period. Northern states had put slavery on the path to extinction, starting with Pennsylvania after the Revolution, and emancipation was even debated in some Southern states as well. Additionally there had been a good deal of antislavery agitation within the Baptist and

Methodist denominations in the South even before the advent of the Second Great Awakening. But the allure of respectability and acceptance was too great, and trumped the reform impulse.[24]

The issue of slavery, so important and contentious in the new United States, was the issue that nearly destroyed both the Mainline and the nation itself. As the Second Great Awakening began to run its course in the 1830s, the evangelical denominations started to feel the strain of one half of their members calling slavery a sin with the other half calling it a blessing from God. Between the late 1830s and early 1840s, the Baptists, Methodists, and Presbyterians all split into Northern and Southern branches, fracturing one of the most important institutional bonds holding the Union together. The Methodists could not even pretend to get along after the division. Indeed, it was James Andrew's elevation to the episcopate in 1832, and his ownership of slaves, (in what was a glaring disregard of the denomination's official doctrine) that precipitated the Methodist breakup.[25] As the sectional crisis spilled over into politics, leading to both secession and Civil War in the wake of Abraham Lincoln's election in 1860, both sides came to see the conflict in biblical terms. As Lincoln himself put it in his second inaugural address, the war was fought by people who "read the same Bible and pray to the same God, and each invokes His aid against the other."[26]

Not unlike the Revolution, the Civil War's cost in human terms took a toll on the nation's faith. Many Americans in both the North and South came to see the conflict as divine judgment on the nation for the sin of slavery. This knowledge led some to put their faith in God and even helped spur revivals within the armies of both sides. But the death toll of over 600,000 was staggering and led some to doubt the possibility of progress and of the optimism of prewar evangelicals.[27]

And yet, the war barely slowed the evangelical wing of the Mainline, which moved from one righteous cause to the next once the guns fell silent. The postwar Reconstruction period also had the unmistakable mark of the nation's churches upon it. Northern denominations were a part of the effort to remake the South, including aiding former slaves as well as rebuilding schools, businesses, and churches. Eventual denominational reunion was helped along by the commonality that America's evangelicals found in reforms beyond those associated with helping freed blacks. As general Northern interest in Reconstruction waned, white churches slowly ended support for blacks. This allowed white America to begin the process of national reconciliation, one result of which was the continued segregation of the nation's churches, with Sunday morning being perhaps the clearest example of the existence of the "color line." The new establishment crafted by American evangelicals after the war became based in embracing rather than challenging this and other aspects of American culture in part because evangelical Protestants believed they were the nation's cultural trendsetters and moral guardians.[28]

Such a conclusion included less emphasis by some leaders, including Henry Ward Beecher, on the importance of doctrine and theology, and a focus rather on some vague notion of God's love. Not all within the Mainline were willing to make such accommodations, though. For every Beecher there was also a Charles Spurgeon, the famed British Baptist who was still willing to stand by the Calvinism that Beecher had largely discarded, and who had a wide following in the United States. This emerging theological rift (and even the hint of transnationalism) was to have important implications for the Mainline in the coming twentieth century and beyond.[29]

To be fair, America's churches also became focused on issues other than doctrinal debates. The Mainline denominations, especially its evangelical wing, were known in the late nineteenth and early twentieth centuries for their overseas missionary efforts. There was a common belief that theirs would be the generation that would take the Gospel to the ends of the earth and save humanity for Christ's kingdom. This belief and the fruit it produced was destined to have a major impact in the late twentieth and early twenty-first centuries.[30]

New America, New Challenges

The Civil War's conclusion did not end the challenges before America's churches. Soon after the guns fell silent, they were facing not only the task of Reconstruction and Reunion, but also the transformation of society and culture in the United States. The new America that emerged in the late 1800s was defined in terms that many in the Northeast had known for most of the century: immigration, urbanization, and industrialization. These forces helped make the nation a global economic and military power, highlighted in part by America's victory in the Spanish-American War—a conflict that President William McKinley assured Methodist ministers he had committed the nation to only after heartfelt prayer.[31] To meet these challenges, America's churches formally established institutions and hierarchies, which taken together produced the Mainline.

In order to do this, the informal networks around and between the Seven Sisters needed to be more codified. To that end, the Mainline gathered in

Philadelphia in 1908 to create the Federal Council of Churches of Christ in America (or FCC). Their goal was to promote unified action in the face of the mounting problems facing the nation and its churches.[32] The process began in 1903, when a "letter missive" was "sent to the leading ecclesiastical bodies" by the National Federation of Churches and Christian Workers, arguing that "the time was ripe" to consider a formal federation. In New York in November 1905, thirty Protestant denominations gathered for the Interchurch Conference on Federation. This meeting produced a plan for organization, which was to "promote the spirit of fellowship, service, and cooperation." The plan was then sent to the various denominations for their approval, with a follow-up meeting to be held in Philadelphia in 1908. It was here that the Federal Council of the Churches of Christ in America was born.[33]

It is important to point out that the FCC did not supersede its constituent members. The goal was to work together, not end denominations by creating a single church. It was believed by those who gathered in Philadelphia that "the Christian bodies are nearer together than they were a decade ago and they are seeing things more nearly eye to eye than they were at that time." As such, its organizational meetings were filled with discussion and a good deal of harmony.[34] Still, there was tension within the FCC between those who were advocating social action and those who believed evangelism should be the cornerstone of church unity.[35]

Of course, creating such an institution went beyond mere coordination of activities. The FCC and its members were attempting to send a message that theirs was the authoritative, even official, voice of Christians in the United States. But by taking such a step, by having members, they were also excluding other denominations as well. Most notably, the Roman Catholic Church and the Southern Baptist Convention either did not or were not asked to join. The FCC then was largely the province of northern, native-born Protestants and, it should be pointed out, largely composed of whites. These facets of the Mainline were to prove equally important in the future as the Kingdom of God theology was developed.[36]

Of the trio of domestic forces shaping the nation's future, immigration posed the most immediate challenge. Most immigrants came from southern and eastern Europe, meaning that in religion they were Catholic, Jewish, and Orthodox Christians, and some were atheists. The nation's churches recognized that they needed to reach out to these new Americans. Some Protestants took direct action, opening mission houses to aid immigrants and help in their Americanization.[37] When it came to immigration, the FCC took a measured approach. On the one hand, the Committee on the Church and the Immigrant Problem believed that the pervading opinion of immigrants by most Americans (one of "disparagement") "ill consists with the spirit and teaching of Jesus concerning human brotherhood." On the other hand, the FCC also believed that it was imperative that nation's churches look after the "religious care" of the immigrants, which implied bringing them into the Protestant fold.[38]

To further extend a hand to immigrants, the emerging Mainline brought Evangelical Lutherans into the mix, completing the lineup of the Seven Sisters. While this action showed the ability of ethnic groups to Americanize (even if at times reluctantly), the Lutherans were also a very interesting choice for such a role. Having been a part of the American religious landscape since the colonial period, their inclusion seemed more a nod to the forces besetting the emerging America of the twentieth century than risking the Protestant establishment. It was, in other words, far from an attempt to include these new Americans or their denominations. With a wide variety of national/ethnic variation, the addition of the Lutherans was a means for the other Sisters to appear to reach out to immigrants without actually doing so. For in the Lutherans, native-born Protestant Americans found the people they wished more immigrants were: people not that dissimilar to themselves.[39]

Urbanization, on the other hand, while a major change, was not as disruptive to American religious life, or at least not as disruptive as some American Christians liked to pretend. While there were difficulties with vice in places like Chicago and New York, which eventually helped spur a new round of revivals and reforms, it is not that Americans became less religious as they moved into the cities. Dwight Moody, a Unitarian-turned-evangelical-Protestant, pioneered urban evangelism in Chicago by utilizing hymns, preaching, and a revival atmosphere. With thriving churches in Boston (Tremont Temple and Park Street), and with famed evangelist, innovator, and showman Aimee Semple McPherson in Los Angeles, there was as much ground gained in the cities as there were souls lost. Christians were more than willing to make their case for faith in the city, often convincingly so. Moody believed that if the cities could be saved, the nation and the world would then follow. Evangelicals were sure they could do just that, even as they wrestled with the many changes spawned by modern America.[40]

In the long term, however, it was industry that transformed the nation and posed the greatest challenge to the Mainline. The rise of big business meant that people in the late nineteenth and early twentieth centuries could amass huge fortunes by luck, intelligence, hard work, and ruthlessness—not always in that order. And it caused a very difficult question to be asked, as the disparity between rich and poor became increasingly clear: Could these "captains of industry" or "robber barons" be counted as good Christians? Should churches support the rise of labor unions to counter the power of such people? And on a larger note, should Christians become involved in reform movements to deal with the problems associated with immigration, urbanization, and industrialization?

Looking at the likes of people as Cornelius Vanderbilt, Andrew Carnegie, John D. Rockefeller, and J. P. Morgan can be a useful way to view how the Mainline attempted to deal with these questions. Most of these men had humble origins, which included membership in Mainline churches. Rockefeller was Baptist, Vanderbilt and Morgan were Episcopalians. Most felt a duty to support religion in some way, even if they might be seen as largely keeping their faith out of their boardroom practices. All were noted for their philanthropy, which included giving money to churches and religious organizations. Indeed, Andrew Carnegie even authored a book, *The Gospel of Wealth*, based on the notion that the rich should give away all their money. That this philanthropy tended to be for the direct benefit of people like them, middle and upper class and culturally Protestant, created as many problems for the Mainline as it solved.[41] It did little to either help their workers or, in the minds of many, wash away the sins committed in accumulating the wealth to begin with.

But because a virtual religious establishment was crafted around the Mainline denominations, it was up to the Seven Sisters, not the Carnegies or Rockefellers, to find an answer to the questions facing the new America, and their theological response was to attempt to craft the Kingdom of God on Earth. Not only was this construct, soon named the Social Gospel, paired with Progressive politics, seen as a reform engine, but it was also a means to solidify the cultural establishment of the Mainline in the face of both external and internal pressures.[42] Part of this process was the transformation of the millennial belief that once the church had achieved a certain level of progress, Christ would return to establish his kingdom into a belief that the church itself could create the kingdom through a continual effort at improving the world with God's help.[43]

With four of the Sisters being evangelical denominations, much of the impetus to fashion the Kingdom of God theology was on the Baptists, Methodists, Presbyterians, and Disciples of Christ. However, one of the hallmarks of theological innovation in American evangelical Protestantism had been the desire for "practical ends." This tendency was more moderate than liberal but was often somewhat shallow. In other words, many American evangeli-cals had largely abandoned theological discussion because they were busy doing other things, like launching reforms. As a result, and because of the competitive denominationalism, they never really developed a coherent theory about how the church was to operate other than to "do." As their cooperative reform work helped soften the doctrinal distinctions between them, and denominational labels became less important, a "nebulous doctrinal identity" began to take hold in the Mainline. As a result, the leading denominations of the Seven Sisters had virtually no means to protect them from emerging cultural trends, leaving them unprepared for either where their foray into theological construction would take them, or challenges to their faith and position in American society.[44]

These problems were further exacerbated by the cultural dominance the Mainline's members found themselves in. Being the establishment had many privileges but also many temptations. Rather than worrying about *growing* members, denominations started to focus on *making* members. As early as the 1840s denominational hierarchies and leading figures such as the Congregationalists Horace Bushnell and Washington Gladden had started to contend that there was no longer a need for revivals or conversions. Christians could be raised and nurtured, no one needed to be "saved." This dovetailed nicely with notions of "respectability" and being part of the status quo, rather than critiquing it.[45]

American evangelicals of the late nineteenth and early twentieth centuries believed that Christianity was the only real basis for civilization. Nonetheless, there was also concern about intellectual trends emanating from Europe since the 1870s, especially the "higher" textual criticism of the Bible that seemed to breed skepticism in faith, which had long been considered one of the bedrocks of Western Civilization. This led some, such as Moody, to argue that the world was getting worse and to begin to doubt whether American society could serve as a beacon to the rest of the world.[46] And so, even as they were fashioning the Kingdom of God theology, the Mainline was facing intense internal debate about the future. As no consensus developed either within or among the Seven Sisters on these issues, the debate was destined to be divisive and long lived.[47]

Not surprisingly, the Mainline attempted to patch these rifts by focusing on reforms. Indeed, the Kingdom of God theology was based on reforming America and then the world. In some respects, it was a merger of the Puritan "city on hill" message with the ethos of the Second Great Awakening. Despite Moody's concern, the theology was steeped in the belief in the notion of progress.[48] The underlying theological movement behind the Kingdom of God was the Social Gospel. Adherents included both politically liberal and conservative Christians who believed that each sinner needed to find salvation but that laws could redeem all society from sin. It proved to be a reform engine, driving a host of movements.[49] The reforms that grew out of that effort and the political involvement that these reforms required exacerbated debate over the proper role of the church in American life, set the stage for the culture wars of the late twentieth and early twenty-first century, and in some ways marked the beginning of the Seven Sisters' decline.[50]

Yet, such active Christianity appealed to many of America's denominations and their members. These believers argued that the Social Gospel would produce a "Christian state" that would bring peace to the world and end poverty and hunger, as well as promote morality. Through the Social Gospel, the church would thus not only "win men to Christ" but also "create a force that combats every evil militating against the Kingdom of Christ," especially things that "preoccupy the thoughts and distract the attention from sacred themes and associations."[51] The Social Gospel provided America's Christians with the needed theological focus to combat these evils; since in the years after the Civil War, Christians tended to be so distracted by the number of reforms that they were unable to effectively organize to deal with any of them.[52]

The theological focus that grew out of the FCC's creation also helped spawn state and local church federations and ministerial associations to give Protestants a united voice in the affairs of American society. In urban areas, church federations attempted to work with politicians to curb "wine rooms, saloons, hotels of prostitution, houses of prostitution, dance halls, and picture shows" as well as promote "child welfare, Sunday observance, and public health." Social Gospel Christians believed "The Church stands for everything that is good and practical and wholesome in our community life," and they urged lawmakers to use their power to destroy "evil influences." Adherents were organized to vote by issue and to deal with political resistance at the ballot box.[53] Ministers were encouraged to condemn evil from the pulpits, mobilize their congregations to combat it, and dismiss members who would not endorse the reform cause.[54]

The Dry Crusade

The trend to organize to affect change also trickled down to the specific reforms themselves.[55] One such movement was the push to outlaw alcohol, the last hurrah of united Protestantism in America.[56] Formed in the 1890s, the Anti-Saloon League (also known as the ASL or just the League) soon surpassed other dry organizations by harnessing evangelical Protestantism from within. Founded by a group of midwestern ministers who were steeped in the Republican-oriented business ethos of the time, the ASL sought to bring various groups together by promoting incremental prohibition. The League's founders believed that Christians had to be involved in the wider, societal culture, and that the saloon and the culture attached to it posed the gravest threat imaginable to Christian America.[57] The ASL worked for stronger laws and supported more centralized, state-level, law enforcement agencies.[58] Baptists, Methodists, Presbyterians, and Disciples of Christ felt a special attachment to the ASL. They believed in its bipartisan activism, and its message that came to blend moral rhetoric with economic incentives.[59] As such, the League is a near perfect example of the Mainline's cohesion and the utilization of its Social Gospel–driven Kingdom of God theology.

The dry worldview was shaped by the dangers and vices they associated with alcohol. They never expressed doubts that calling on churches, especially their own denomination, to push for prohibition was a dangerous Church/State issue.[60] Religion was part of the public square, and such participation was expected by the vast majority of Americans. Utilizing the League, drys were able to enact local and state laws during the early twentieth century and then the Eighteenth Amendment and the Volstead Act, making all America dry by the dawn of 1920. Most drys, while pleased with their success, did not think in terms of symbolic justification, for while laws were important, enforcement and acceptance of laws was even more imperative to them.[61] Drys seemed to understand that it would take time and effort to achieve complete victory, perhaps as long as a generation,[62] and by the mid-1920s, they had seemingly triumphed. National prohibition was popularly enacted and supported by a diverse coalition of people who saw it as "the greatest moral, educational, and economical triumph ever won by any nation in all time."[63] The years ahead, however, severely tested dry optimism.[64]

In order to maintain Prohibition, Protestant drys needed to reach out to America's growing Roman Catholic community. And while there were dry Catholics, on the whole, anti-liquor Protestants failed in their effort to use Prohibition to overcome the Reformation rift. This was due in large part because the two portions of Christendom organized themselves differently in attempting to achieve reform goals but also because of the Protestants' own anti-Catholicism, witnessed by the exclusion of Catholics from the FCC.[65] For their part, Protestant drys, despite their hopes, had a difficult time understanding Catholicism. Their unease with Catholics tended to be centered on immigrant culture and the church hierarchy that sustained it, rather than the theology of their co-religionists.[66] Furthermore, Catholic drys had a difficult time combating the overwhelmingly Catholic ghetto's neighborhood saloon and drinking's popularity among immigrant groups.[67] As a result, drys abandoned the hope of making Prohibition a force for Christian solidarity.[68]

As the 1920s progressed, drys increasingly focused on law enforcement. This brought them into conflict not only with wets but also with those who had to actually enforce the laws. Drys found that victory was more difficult to maintain than it was to achieve, because reality was different than rhetoric. Law enforcement needs differed across the country, and police activity rarely lived up to dry hopes. Still, enforcement was good enough that it caused those engaged in the illegal trade to be creative and on their guard.[69]

The dry good times came to an end with the onset of the Great Depression. Drys had long contended that Prohibition was behind the nation's economic prosperity, but when that ended the noble experiment was in jeopardy. Wets aimed straight at people's pocketbooks. Beer might not be soup, but it could mean jobs, and if it also meant money in the wallets of workers and owners, and tax revenue for local, state, and national governments, so much the better. Morality and anti-vice were now secondary considerations. With the full weight of Franklin Roosevelt's New Deal against it, Prohibition collapsed.[70]

The dry defeat was devastating.[71] They now faced an America that believed their reform was both a failure and wrong, despite the prevalence of their evangelical Protestant culture. Although many drys remained unrepentant and even held out hope that they could reorganize and make a victorious comeback, as time passed, dry voices became less and less noticeable on the national and even local scene.[72] The dry base receded from the Seven Sisters of Mainline Protestantism toward smaller, less influential denominations.[73] With most dry leaders dead, old, or too disillusioned to keep going,[74] rank-and-file drys adapted to the reality of repeal.[75]

Though it has been seen as a "burden" for Protestants, Prohibition's repeal was vigorously fought.[76] The failure to keep the dry reform intact was not from either a lack of effort or because the majority of Americans rejected the concept of moral order. Rather, a new breed of wet politician was able to offer a different version of that order to many Americans both within and outside of the Mainline. Furthermore, drys had eliminated the saloon without preparing for victory. Many assumed their work was done, so educating the next generation about the danger of drink was not prioritized until the threat of repeal became real, nor did drys fashion a coherent, integrated, national enforcement plan; with new immigration laws in place, the fear of a foreign, wet, culture submerging a dry, American culture lost its power as an argument. Without these conditions, and because modern America now had the technology to negate the dangers of the saloon (via home refrigeration) and needed jobs because of the Great Depression, alcohol returned.[77] In doing so, the Twenty-first Amendment can be seen as the first chink in the Mainline's armor, proof that in a pluralistic society the FCC could not speak for all Christians nor all Americans.

Of Modernists, Fundamentalists, Moderates, and Darwin

Reforms like Prohibition, whatever their short- or long-term success, could not hold the Mainline together on a theological basis.[78] Broadly speaking, there were three groups within the Seven Sisters who debated the merits of the Social Gospel and its reforms: The modernists, fundamentalists, and moderates. Each group was, at the outset of the Mainline's ascendancy and development of Kingdom of God theology, devoted to their denominations and the advancement of Christianity. Their breaking point was over how these ideas were to be applied and what was to become of them.

First were the modernists. This group pushed for theological changes based on new trends in biblical scholarship that so worried others in their denominations. More often than not, modernists believed that change was equal to progress in making the Gospel more accessible and relevant to the citizens of modern America, without always considering the implications to the faith they sought to enhance. For example, modernists undercut supernatural claims made by the Bible, and even argued that Jesus was more a moral teacher than a Savior or Messiah in the traditional Christian sense. They took special aim at the apostle Paul; the chief author of the books of the New Testament, for what they claimed was the "altering" of Christ's message and intent. This path led some of their number toward secularization and a liberal theology, which at times agreed to a retreat of the church from the public sphere—a move made all the easier by the defeat of Prohibition.[79]

And it was for these very reasons that the modernists were opposed by fundamentalists, those who sought to protect their faith from a transformation that would embrace the world at the expense of the Word. As the historian George Marsden has argued, fundamentalism was the part of American evangelical Protestantism that was most shocked that American culture seemed to be turning away from God in the early twentieth century.

Fundamentalists were torn between those wanting to attack errors, such as A. C. Dixon, a North Carolina–born Baptist and an associate of Moody's, and thus engaging in intellectual debate witnessed by the publication of *The Fundamentals: A Testimony to the Truth*, an eventual collection of ninety essays gathered in twelve volumes between 1910 and 1915. Proposed to defend "basic Christianity," these writings ignored the trends and worked instead for a revival of religion within their respective denominations. The essays were edited by Dixon and a Congregational minister and fellow Moody associate Reuben A. Torrey, and financed by oilman and philanthropist Lyman Stewart to be given away free to evangelical ministers. Others became convinced that separation was the only recourse they had to the rise of modernists within the Mainline. If not always a cohesive opposition, the fundamentalists were a legitimate theological effort to counter modernism. It seemed clear to them that "a secularized church could not halt the apostasy of the culture." The Presbyterian J. Gresham Machen, a conservative scholar who defended the traditional Westminster Confession during debates at Princeton Theological Seminary over this Presbyterian creed, went so far as to say that if the church abandoned its historic teachings, Christianity as an organized religion would vanish.[80]

Moderates, the third group, were those Christians within Mainline denominations who attempted to navigate the conflict between fundamentalists and modernists. From a theological perspective, moderates might politically come from either camp but who held that denominational unity was more important than scoring theological points, either for defense of tradition or in support of innovation. Often condemned by both sides for going too far (or not far enough) in either direction, and despite constituting a majority on any given point under debate amongst the laity, their voice was often drowned out as they strove to find consensus.

The tensions among the three groups came to a head not over reforms like Prohibition but rather over the theological implications of a scientific theory: that of evolution. While modern science arose "in a culture dominated by a belief in a conscious, rational, all-powerful Creator," the rift between science and religion had more to do with theological developments than it did any long-running feud between the two.[81] Charles Darwin's theories about the origins of life helped make science a faith itself and challenged the Christian worldview.[82] And though Darwin's work had been around and debated since the late nineteenth century, it really only became an issue for the American Mainline in the 1920s, when evolution made its way into school textbooks and more American children were in public schools. Prior to this time, there had been willingness, even among many fundamentalists, for reconciliation between the new scientific theory and faith. But as the 1920s dawned, Christian scientists were not as able to step in and "soften" or reconcile Darwinian science with Christianity as they had been able to do with other scientific theories and discoveries before. Coming at the same time as the demise of the Prohibition consensus, the debate over evolution became another example of the cultural disengagement of some members of the Mainline.[83]

Which group controlled the denominational leadership soon became central to how a given church was going to react to Darwin's theory. For some, the coming debate was not even so much about the scientific theory of evolution, which was already splintering off from Darwinian evolution, but rather about Social Darwinism and eugenics.[84] Notions of "natural selection" based on "the survival of the fittest" when coupled with ideas about racial and genetic superiority struck many Christians as unbiblical. Among them was the lay Presbyterian, former secretary of state, and three-time Democratic presidential nominee William Jennings Bryan. Bryan believed that this variant of Darwinism preached hate and left no room for God in the world. He was also a majoritarian who believed that parents should have control over the public schools they paid for so that their children could get an education. Bryan had no problem with evolution being taught as a theory, but did not want it to be put forward as a fact. By the early 1920s, he had become one of the most prominent spokesmen in the anti-evolution movement, devoting increasing time to it on the public speaking circuit than to other favorite topics like Prohibition and women's suffrage. He also began organizing fundamentalists in an effort to take control of the leadership of the Presbyterian Church.[85]

Bryan was not alone in entering the debate. On 21 May 1922, Harry Emerson Fosdick, a renowned Baptist preacher, gave a guest sermon at the First Presbyterian Church of New York City. His topic was "Shall the Fundamentalists Win?" Written in the aftermath of an attempted fundamentalist surge within the Northern Baptist Convention (and ahead of a similar one within the Presbyterian denomination), Fosdick argued that liberals and modernists were accommodating the church to the modern world by accepting evolution, while conservatives and fundamentalists were intolerant and trying to oust those who refused to accept their doctrines. He believed that liberals and conservatives needed to get beyond doctrinal disagreements such as the virgin birth (which he said modern man could only take to mean Jesus' birth was special in some unknowable way), and Christ's Second Coming (which he believed could be the progress of the church instead of an actual physical return), and focus on what united them, not the theological debates that were dividing them.[86] Fosdick's address was blasted by Clarence Macartney of the Arch Street Presbyterian Church in Philadelphia in a widely distributed sermon titled "Shall Unbelief Win?" Macartney, who had worked to reinvigorate his congregation and who had had a feud with Fosdick dating back to the First World War, believed that scripture, not man-made theories, was the ultimate authority when it came to theology and that evolution was largely incompatible with the Bible.[87] The fight was now on.

The coming of this debate all but destroyed the Kingdom of God theology that had held the Seven Sisters together. Fundamentalists soured on the Social Gospel, believing it had become a tool of secularism, and perhaps they were not that far off. Some liberal Social Gospelers had come to the conclusion that Christ was important only as a moral example, while most conservatives still believed that faith and action had to be taken together. J. Gresham Machen's *Christianity and Liberalism* (published in 1923) argued that the liberal faith being advanced by his modernist opponents could no longer be considered as Christianity. There was open discussion of denominational division, which was soon covered in the secular press. The battle lines were drawn, and the emerging majority within the Mainline seemed to place most moderates in alliance with fundamentalists in supporting "no compromise" with modernists.[88]

Within the Presbyterian Church, for example, this debate was exemplified by many of the denomination's leading pastors. "Liberal evangelicals," such as Henry Sloane Coffin, believed that creeds were best attempts, not timeless statements of the faith. The conservative Charles R. Erdman, on the other hand, argued that the church needed to be united around a common theme, Christ, and that evangelism was more important than defending or advancing any one segment of the faith. He wanted peace and, like Coffin, did not want to see the Presbyterian Church split. Indeed, conservative moderates wanted to "preach Christ" much more than defend doctrine. Neo-orthodoxy arose as many former liberals, including Coffin, later became less optimistic about humanity and grew concerned about secularism. The point was that both men were evangelicals, and for a time, the debate remained largely confined within denominational leadership circles.[89]

At this time, however, neither modernists nor fundamentalists could afford to back down, and that hurt the vast middle in between the two sides.[90] Fundamentalists were reacting to perceived threats to the Christian faith. Perhaps if the emergence of modern America and ideas such as Darwinism had come at a more gradual pace, the result might have been different. Had

America been a less evangelical place, things might have been different as well. But neither of those things occurred, and the eyes of the nation soon fell on Dayton, Tennessee.

The legal battle in Dayton was a test case, and in some ways, a publicity stunt. After the state of Tennessee, with the full support of Bryan and other fundamentalists, passed a law similar to ones in Florida and Kentucky making it a crime to teach the theory of evolution in the public schools, citizens in the town of Dayton saw an opportunity to generate some publicity for their community in order to stimulate the local economy. They initiated a court case against the science teacher John Scopes, with his knowledge and participation. In terms of a trial and media attention, with William Jennings Bryan assisting the prosecution and famed attorney Clarence Darrow and the ACLU taking over the defense, they got more than they asked for. The town's fathers, unfortunately, did not get the sustained economic boom they had hoped. In the end, despite long remembered (and at times misremembered) closing arguments and theatrics, Scopes was convicted of violating the law. As for the ideological participants, the case did not end the fight at all.[91]

While technically the anti-evolution side had won the case, "liberal commentators of the day typically viewed fundamentalists as servile rubes immune to shame," and thus the Scopes trial had far-reaching negative public relations ramifications for fundamentalism.[92] To be clear, the trial was not a crushing defeat for the fundamentalist side. Even if northern states did not enact anti-evolution laws, many southern and western states did, which in turn, influenced textbook writers. Most of those in the Seven Sisters, including many conservatives, were more than willing to reconcile faith with science, as they saw science as not disproving or approving their faith but rather illuminating it.[93] But more than its outcome, the trial and its coverage allowed "elite American society" including many modernists to stop "taking fundamentalists and their ideas seriously." And it was this public relations verdict that soured many moderates from continuing to ally themselves with fundamentalists, not the result of the Scopes trial per se. The moderates had come to value their place in American society and the way others saw them as more than a continued adherence to traditional doctrine. Thus, the conservative-fundamentalist alliance was fractured, a crucial development, which hastened a fundamentalist withdrawal from public engagement of their foes, and led many fundamentalists to create their own subculture and by doing so distance themselves from mainstream American culture.[94]

How the fracturing of the alliance played out depended on the denomination. While most conservative moderates remained in their denominations, many fundamentalists took refuge in specific congregations or left the Mainline outright. Southern-based denominations, such as the region's wings of the Baptists and Presbyterians, tended to not tolerate dissent and remained in the hands of conservative moderates and fundamentalists. Among Northern Baptists, on the other hand, the majority were moderate conservatives, whose alliance with fundamentalists eventually splintered in the years after Dayton. In the northern Presbyterian case, conservative moderates opted to compromise with modernists to save the denomination. But the price was increasingly inclusivist doctrine, which embraced the values of the moment. In both the Congregational and Disciples of Christ denominations, the principle of congregational freedom was advanced, turning the debate into a local issue. In the Methodist Church, fundamentalists did not have a tradition of strict doctrine to rally around and so were increasingly marginalized in the years to come despite large numbers of conservative moderates in the membership. As for the Episcopal Church, while there were conservatives, moderates, liberals, and modernists, there were virtually no fundamentalists, and so long as Darwin was not seen as attacking the denomination's traditions, there was very little debate.[95]

The Mainline of the Seven Sisters, despite the failure of Prohibition and the war between modernists and fundamentalists, seemingly had survived even with some fractures and looked toward the mid-twentieth century as a time of rebirth. But for this incarnation of the Mainline, their struggles had only begun. The division within American Protestantism over modernity weakened its hegemonic grip on America.[96] The future held both prosperity and decline even if the Seven Sisters did not yet realize it; that eventual decline, the result of neither failed reform nor internal debate over evolution, was largely self-inflicted.

3

A Mighty Fortress in Decline

In 1929, one of the most prominent Methodist congregations in New York City announced plans for a new church home. The Madison Avenue Methodist Episcopal Church purchased property on Park Avenue for a larger building. By the fall, on the eve of the stock market crash, details were finalized for the construction of one of the most stunning churches in the nation. Though it took nearly two decades to complete, due to depression and war, eventually the congregation had a new building, one that allowed them to be active in the city, meet the needs of its members, and transport those who visited to a new level of worship, via the exquisite Byzantium inspired mosaic tile work, the icons from the private collection of Tsar Nicholas II, and artwork taken from European Orthodox churches. The newly named Christ Church Methodist Church was ready to be God's witness to New York City.[1]

As the twentieth century progressed, the Seven Sisters were able to continue their dominance of American Christianity, despite the infighting that characterized the century's early decades. Thus, culture wars and political disputes went hand in hand with growth and affluence, despite two world wars and the Great Depression, just as Christ Church Methodist was eventually able to build and furbish their new church home in a manner that befitted their location. By the 1940s, a period of tranquility and near consensus began to emerge within the Mainline—for with liberals' ascendant both politically and judicially, and growing in their control of the Seven Sisters' hierarchies, it seemed just fine to ignore conservatives and fundamentalists (and the associated controversies) altogether.[2] The Mainline's position seemed secure.

But strain began to show by the 1960s and 1970s, and the façade of Mainline Protestantism eventually cracked beyond repair; even outside observers were talking of "Mainline decline." And decline was happening even among the evangelical denominations.[3] As liberals and conservatives within the Seven Sisters entered this time of trial and debate, perhaps nowhere were the stresses and strains, internal and external, more explicit than in the Episcopal Church.

It is to the American branch of the Anglican Communion that we now turn for a specific example of what happened to the Mainline in these years.[4]

Like the other Seven Sister denominations, the Episcopal Church enjoyed growth following World War II. Indeed, the war and the earlier Depression had been a trying and yet exciting time for the churches, serving as a catalyst for resurgent church membership and a decline in the battles between modernists and fundamentalists. Even as congregations became more partisan, determining their reaction to the New Deal, for example, was based largely on the politics of their members not their theology. The Federal Council of Churches expanded their role nationally, even as it became obvious that they lacked the zeal to lead the church in winning souls for Christ, facing challenges from both liberal and conservative evangelicals. Episcopalians, however, were confident, as were most members of the Seven Sisters, that growth and prosperity would continue to occur naturally.[5]

Indeed, America after World War II was in the midst of forging a national consensus based on the importance of religious expansion. This civil religion, endorsed by President Dwight Eisenhower, was largely an expression of the dominant role the Seven Sisters had in the life of the nation (culturally Protestant, even if more inclusive of Catholics and Jews), including in the newly popular suburbs that began popping up as a sign of postwar prosperity. And that dominant role began to breed complacency within the Mainline of its place within American culture.[6]

These feelings of consensus, if not conformity, were reflected in theological trends that sought to leave the modernist–fundamentalist debates behind the Mainline, even if the theologians themselves did not always agree. After the war, many Protestants subscribed to the theological notions put forward by Norman Vincent Peale, a Methodist-turned-Dutch Reformed minister; those concepts centered on applying the principles of Christianity to everyday life and the "power of positive thinking." For much of the 1950s there seemed to be much to be positive about. Churches were growing, the nation was prospering, and civil religion was firmly a part of America's Cold War culture.[7] Indeed, the '50s were a flourishing period for theologians. The decade saw the rise in prominence of men such as Paul Tillich (who sought to make sure that the Christian message was applicable to each new generation), H. Richard Niebuhr (who critiqued both conservative and liberal Protestantism), and Reinhold Niebuhr (whose work on Christian ethics rivaled that of his brother Richard).[8]

During the 1960s and 1970s, however, shouts of euphoria gave way to anguish as a variety of issues threatened to rip the Mainline apart. As modernists rose to dominate denominational hierarchies, the moderates and fundamentalists felt increasingly ill at ease, despite the consensus-era theological writings of Peale, Tillich, and the Niebuhrs.[9] The external challenges of the civil rights movement and the Vietnam War left the Episcopal Church and many of the other Seven Sisters divided and wondering exactly how Christians were to be active in the world, as well as what the role of the church should be in such divisive times. Internal ruptures over female ordination and Prayer Book revision were specific theological challenges—echoed in other denominations—to the ways Episcopalians understood their denomination and worshiped God on Sundays. To the surprise of many, laity and clergy often found themselves at odds over these issues. Taken together, they raised serious questions about the composition of the Episcopal Church, American Mainline Protestantism as composed by the Seven Sisters, as well as whether Christians could maintain a middle ground in an increasingly politically polarized society.

External Stress

Civil rights was the first issue the Mainline confronted head on that shook the postwar consensus. The Episcopal Church's leaders and bureaucracy had started to dismantle its own segregationist polices during the 1940s and 1950s, justifying its decisions on traditional Anglican theology that called for unity in Christ, which they now applied to race relations.[10] Lay Episcopalians largely supported the National Association for the Advancement of Colored People (NAACP) and the concept of integration, and the denomination even created the Episcopal Society for Cultural and Racial Unity (ESCRU) for those who wanted to do more to combat prejudice in American society.[11] The ESCRU organization was committed to achieving the "total participation in the church for all persons without regard to race, class, or national origin."[12] In this, they echoed pronouncements made by the National Council of Churches—the new name for the older Federal Council of Churches—and thus the official voice of Mainline Protestantism.[13]

There was a tension built into American Christianity's grappling with civil rights because of the history of race relations in the country. The antebellum South, as we have seen, was a place where Christianity was both a means of salvation for black slaves as well as the "master's religion," which in those days included Episcopal masters who allowed their slaves to become evangelicals. The North, although it gave to the country abolitionism, also was filled with a good deal of racism and acquiesced to the creation of a "separate but equal" nation following the Civil War. Indeed, white racial reconciliation was in some ways driven by the Episcopal Church, which unlike its evangelical counterparts in the Seven Sisters, had not splintered over the issue of slavery. That African American ministers, such as the Reverend Martin Luther King Jr., could not depend on the support of their white co-religionists and fellow pastors in striving for even basic civil rights was an apparent part of the movement almost from its launch in the post–World War II period.[14] While groups like ESCRU were reflective of where some in the Mainline were on the issue of race, northern and southern whites generally liked not having blacks in their churches, and certainly African Americans generally enjoyed running their own churches. Although some were willing to challenge the color line, most whites were at ease with segregation.[15]

Episcopalians became more involved in civil rights as the 1960s progressed. While many saw the issue as a clear-cut case of right and wrong, as events unfolded from sit-ins and freedom rides to marches and demonstrations, these emotional issues carried the denominational hierarchy in one direction and many in the pews in another. More clergy than laity felt compelled to speak out in favor of civil rights, and while the vast majority (79 percent) of Episcopalians supported ending segregation, fewer were willing to support such a "radical" notion as whites and blacks living in the same neighborhood (29 percent).[16]

This divide only produced problems for the denomination. Clergy and those in the church bureaucracy were often in a better position to be active in the movement, but laity with children and jobs found it difficult to go to the South to march. Since being involved in events such as the Freedom Rides tended to transform participants into activists, this became an important differentiating factor. So many ministers headed south that the National Church began receiving complaints from parishioners, via their bishops, that people could not find their pastors.[17] Furthermore, liberal clergy and those who worked in the denominational bureaucracy tended to be more active in civil rights, creating not only a potent political divide but also a split between the parish level and the church hierarchy.[18] If activist ministers were assigned to a conservative parish, there was potential for confrontation between clergy and laity.[19]

A new source for dispute emerged from civil rights as the movement slowed in the mid-1960s. Black Power advocates, who believed that "religion secures people to the system and does it in the name of God," began to gain popularity in the wake of political victories such as the Civil Rights Act of 1964 and the Voting Rights Act of 1965, which ended legal segregation but could do little to immediately end racism. As Black Power leaders called into question the motives of whites who supported the civil rights movement, many whites were both confused and caught off guard by charges that despite their marching, they were part of the problem. The general civil rights consensus was beginning to fragment.[20]

The resulting confusion exacerbated the tensions within the Episcopal Church. Even as ESCRU began advocating teaching "empowerment" to blacks who sought the help of the denomination, many lay Episcopalians argued that while all were equal before God, not everyone was equally talented.[21] Rather, people needed to use to the utmost the gifts that God had given to them. As northern whites were not "social crusaders," they did not want their churches "to be used, or become identified exclusively with any movement or goal, however worthy its purpose."[22]

In 1967, the denomination took dramatic action that showcased the various divides. With race riots raging across the nation, the presiding bishop John Hines, the leader of the Episcopal Church, challenged his fellow Episcopalians at the Seattle General Convention to allow "self determination" for groups. He said "we in the church are part of the problem" and that "the winning of the Negro has been slow and entirely unspectacular." Hines called upon the denomination to give $3 million to help "empower" blacks. This figure included funding for groups that were not affiliated with the denomination; ESCRU endorsed the idea, and a larger sum was passed by the convention. Though it was seen as a way to find "liberation" from racism, the end result created more problems for the Episcopal Church.[23]

Discontent with the Seattle Convention was soon made known to the hierarchy.[24] One Hoosier Episcopal minister wrote the presiding bishop to say:

> In these most perplexing times there are some of us who do not have time for marches and demonstrations because we are trying, with the help of God, to be faithful where we are with what we have. . . . I came home from Seattle much disturbed. While others saw in your eloquent opening sermon a stirring call to service, I heard that to be poor is somehow sinful, therefore we shall sacrifice truth and dignity for reckless irresponsibility.[25]

But, overall, most Episcopalians, especially the clergy, believed the denomination needed to be doing more for the cause of civil rights, though there was also concern that the demands for Black Power could ruin everything that the Episcopal Church was working for.[26]

These fears were soon justified, at both the local and national levels. James Forman, who was the international affairs director of the Student Nonviolent Coordinating Committee (SNCC), had come to believe that African Americans were a "colonized people inside the United States." Forman went to the National Black Economic Development Conference (BEDC) in Detroit in April 1969 and announced a plan. Since Christians had organized the conference, Forman believed that Christians needed to pay for their part in America's racist past. Demanding reparations from the nation's churches seemed like the proper course of action, and with that, Forman crafted the Black Manifesto.[27]

The manifesto was a marriage of Marxist thought and Black Power rhetoric. The preamble stated: "To win our demands we will declare war on the white Christian churches and synagogues and this means we may have to fight the total government structure of this country." Forman believed the United States was run by a "racist, imperialist government that is choking the life of all the people around the world" and claimed that the United States was "the most barbaric country in the world." He contended that the manifesto would "bring this government down" by "armed struggle" if need be. Forman's organization initially demanded $500 million in "reparations" from the nation's churches and synagogues, but the figure was later revised up to $3 billion.[28]

The concentration of national church offices in New York City allowed for rapid and dramatic presentations to all of Mainline Protestantism, with varying results. Forman demanded $60 million from the American (Northern) Baptist Convention, which was denied. The General Board of the Disciples of Christ also rejected his demands for money but did launch a $2 million racial "reconciliation campaign." The Evangelical Lutheran Church was requested to pay $50 million. Forman ordered the Presbyterian Church to pay him $80 million and grant blacks 60 percent of their future profits. The denomination instead voted to raise $50 million for minority related projects. The United Methodist Church agreed, in part because of the manifesto, to spend $4 million on minority community efforts. Only with the descendants of the Puritans did Forman find success. The United Church of Christ had Forman speak at its General Synod, after which they pledged to raise $10 million for him.[29]

On 1 May 1969, Forman presented the manifesto to the Episcopal Church for its consideration. On 13 May, he wrote to Presiding Bishop Hines and demanded $60 million, plus 60 percent of all future income. Though Hines called the manifesto "calculatedly revolutionary, Marxist, inflammatory, anti-Semitic and anti-Christian," he did not reject the document out of hand. Instead, he called a special convention of the denomination to address Forman's requests.[30]

In the months before the meeting, local congregations were faced with addressing the manifesto themselves, as Forman's adherents spread out across the nation and took the manifesto directly to the nation's congregations. Many devised strategies to deal with being "visited" by representatives of the movement, which usually occurred during Sunday services. Congregations limited who could speak from the pulpit and put ushers on high alert. Clergy tended to be more sympathetic to the goals if not the tactics of the Black Manifesto group than were the laity. However, denouncements of the manifesto were heard from the pulpit on occasion as well.[31]

The Episcopal Church's special convention was held in South Bend, Indiana, from 30 August to 5 September 1969. There, the Reverend Paul Washington of Philadelphia introduced Muhammad Kenyatta, one of Forman's lieutenants, to the convention so that he could officially present the manifesto to the governing body of the denomination. Kenyatta told the delegates that their denomination was "part of the present racist struggle," and that Forman's BEDC was declaring war on racism, capitalism, and imperialism. In waging their war, they did not rule out the use of violence to achieve their goals.[32]

After the address, the Episcopal Church, like other members of the Seven Sisters, voted to reject the BEDC's rhetoric but agreed to give $200,000 to black Episcopalians, many of whom supported the BEDC. Hines ordered the money to be spent by the General Convention Special Program (GCSP), whose board believed black causes should be supported. Despite what the convention said, ESCRU argued that the money should be given directly to the BEDC. National black church groups, such as the National Committee for Black Churchmen, supported the manifesto and the money its demands brought to them.[33] Forman might have been able to achieve more success had he been more astute in dealing with the bureaucracies and organizations within the largely white Mainline denominations and if he had built more support for the manifesto with the Mainline's black members. As it happened, blacks were generally willing to accept less money from their denominations for their own projects rather than support his demands.[34]

Lay white opinion was largely against the manifesto and the actions of the special convention from the start. Many Episcopalians preferred quiet, long-term action to flashy programs that were "here today and gone tomorrow."[35] As their denomination expanded its support to include not only black empowerment groups but also Native American and Hispanic organizations, members warned of a pocketbook boycott if spending was not curtailed. These calls intensified and became a reality when it was learned that some of the groups the Episcopal Church had supported financially were involved in incidents of violence. By 1972, the church had paid out $6.5 million to minority improvement projects through GCSP, but such was the drop-off in giving that Hines was forced to resign. He was replaced in 1973 by the more conservative John M. Allin, who ended the GCSP soon after taking office. By the time he did, however, that body had spent $7 million, and the cessation of donations continued by many members for other reasons.[36]

The laity of Mainline churches saw activism as a good thing in principle. However, they did not like specific initiatives that hit close to home, or "binding statements" that were made on behalf of the "whole church." "Radical social activism" repelled members. Nationwide, 72 percent of all Episcopal laity did not think that clergy should walk a picket line, an opinion that helped cause ESCRU to dissolve in 1970. Conservative believers tended to not want government intervention on behalf of minorities. When court-ordered busing reached the white suburbs in the early 1970s, another backlash started. Desegregated, but more importantly, forcibly integrated schools, were still another issue on which many of the laity and denominational leaders disagreed.[37] In the end, the debate over civil rights opened the door for other conflicts to enter and assail the Episcopal Church from within.[38]

In fact, the war in Vietnam was more divisive to the Episcopal Church than were civil rights, clearly showing the divide between the denomination's hierarchy and many of its priests on the one hand and the majority of the laity on the other. It struck at the heart of the denomination, which as the "Church of Presidents," had so often been called upon to bless the nation's wars. Like most American denominations at that time, the Episcopal Church believed that communism was a real threat to the country and needed to be dealt with. The question was if it had to be dealt with in Vietnam. The conflict half a world away sparked a confrontation between very different interpretations over what being a Christian in America meant within both the Episcopal Church and the rest of Mainline Protestantism during a time of war.[39]

While the majority of Americans stood against communism during the Cold War, evangelicals and fundamentalists were among the most vocal religious "Cold Warriors." Many in the Mainline, on the other hand, sometimes came under attack as conservatives asserted that both political and theological liberalism were gateways to communism.[40] In the case of Vietnam, the Episcopal Church never took an official stand on the conflict, and because of this it allowed local clergy to make pronouncements that seemed to speak for the entire denomination, often against the wishes of parishioners.[41] While only a small percentage of the denomination's clergy actually took part in the antiwar movement, the Episcopal Church did have a number of priests who became quite vocal on the subject. As with the civil rights movement, the majority of those who did speak out came from the ranks of the denomination's hierarchy "where they were not subject to direct pressure from the laity and did not risk losing their jobs." This number included such notables as Paul Moore (a decorated World War II veteran, an Episcopal priest, and bishop of the diocese of New York) and the author and "celebrity priest" Malcolm Boyd.[42] Such actions were echoed in the other Mainline denominations and from such sources as the National Council of Churches.[43]

Most congregations did not suffer an extreme confrontation over Vietnam. Many tried to park political matters "at the door," and members, whether for or against the war, found other outlets to express their opinion about Vietnam.[44] While conservatives hoped that "ministers who presume to preach should deal with basic problems of philosophy, religion and ethics, leaving their congregations to make specific applications in the daily conduct of their lives,"[45] many believed that "good" Christians had to take a stand against the war. This meant not being in the armed forces, not paying "war" taxes, not working for "war" industries, not supporting the draft, and even picketing military bases. The Reverend Malcolm Boyd, for example, called for a new "hippie morality," and said that America was exhibiting "genocidal tendencies" in its "immoral war" in Vietnam.[46]

The longer the war went on, the more the Episcopal Church as a whole followed Boyd's lead. At the 1969 Special Convention in South Bend, where the Black Manifesto was discussed, Vietnam was also an issue. Some clergy held an antiwar rally during the proceedings. Both the manifesto and the antiwar rumblings angered conservatives within the denomination. And while they could do little nationally, they did start to make their voices known at the parish level.[47] Conservative-led congregations passed resolutions condemning draft dodging and openly supported members deployed to Vietnam. Some even expressed a wish that the country's leaders would fully commit the nation to winning the war. This conservative sentiment was reflected nationally, where anti-communist ideology remained high, and war protesters, even at the height of their strength, were always outnumbered by people who supported the war.[48]

The antiwar faction was clearly in control of both the Episcopal Church and Mainline Protestant bureaucracies. During the early 1970s, the Episcopal Church passed or considered a host of resolutions calling for an end of American involvement in South Vietnam and critiquing the conduct of the government both at home and abroad, including calling for "peace education" in the nation's schools.[49] Likewise, the Evangelical Lutheran Church went on record in 1966 as having "reservations" about escalating the war. In 1967, the Presbyterian Church noted their concern over America's involvement in Vietnam. That same year, the United Church of Christ (formerly the Congregational Church) expressed doubts about whether continued escalation would profit anything. By 1972 the UCC was openly supporting war dissenters. The American Baptist Convention called on President Richard Nixon to pull all U.S. forces out of Vietnam by 1971. President Lyndon Johnson, a member of the Disciples of Christ, was angered that his church never took an official stand on the war. When they finally did, it was in 1973 and the denomination endorsed amnesty for draft dodgers.[50]

The war produced changes within the Episcopal Church. Prayers for the armed forces were omitted from one of the "Trial Use" prayer books but were restored in the official revision of the 1979 Book of Common Prayer, and the national and denominational flags were no longer presented to the congregation prior to each service. Furthermore, the war helped unleash social changes and reform movements that would follow the denomination long after the fall of Saigon.[51]

Internal Pressure

It was with theology, not national issues, that the biggest rifts within the Episcopal Church developed. On a very basic level, the denomination, as a part of the Anglican Communion, rests upon the "heritage of faith" resulting from the historic English episcopate and a worship style based upon the Book of Common Prayer. It is not a denomination that demands or expects uniformity of belief, only adherence to these two principles. Yet the challenges of female ordination and a new Prayer Book, because of the theological and doctrinal reorientation inherent to both, jeopardized the very soul of the denomination and were more traumatic than either civil rights or Vietnam.[52]

These reforms came at a time when theological conflict and doctrinal change were sweeping Mainline Protestantism. The divide between many of the laity and their ministers caused by external issues was now being exacerbated by changes to worship led by what some people in the pews considered to be pastors who were better able to organize a protest than they were to deliver a sermon.[53] Within the Episcopal Church, many of the laity concluded that their denomination was abandoning its core beliefs. And it was in this environment that the denomination announced it was going to begin ordaining women and revise (yet again) its Prayer Book.[54]

No one in the denomination was taken by surprise by either of the developments. Since the emergence of the civil rights movement, the Episcopal Church had suffered with tensions between laity, clergy, and the denomination's bureaucracy. And once again, it was the latter that was pushing for the reforms. But the ordination of women was to be more disruptive to the Episcopal Church than external issues, in large part because it was such a visible change. Women had a long history of being involved in social activism within the denomination, and by the 1960s some wanted to become ministers of the Gospel. Once women won the right to be seated at the conventions in 1970, the days of the all-male episcopate were numbered, and the denomination itself was called upon to repent for its delay in advancing pulpit equality.[55]

The battle lines were quickly drawn; despite the fact the denomination had no history of women behind the pulpit. Opponents of female ordination argued that the change was too drastic and would endanger ecumenism, one of the principle goals of the denomination, which they saw as more important than pulpit gender equality. In particular, they expressed worries that an endorsement for women priests would lead to problems with the Roman Catholic Church. Supporters of female ordination, on the other hand, were concerned about things other than Christian unity.[56] At the 1973 General Convention in Louisville, Kentucky, advocates argued that men and women were equal in the sight of God and thus both sexes could become priests. They also charged their opponents with being sexists and not up to date with secular society. Despite these arguments, ordination was narrowly voted down.[57]

As this back-and forth-debate continued, some women decided to take matters into their own hands. They first turned to the bishop of the diocese of New York, Paul Moore, whose liberal views included support for ordaining women, which issue he came very close to doing so in 1974 but did not. Because of Moore's reluctance, a group of eleven women convinced three retired bishops to illegally ordain them in Philadelphia later that year. John Allin, the presiding bishop, refused to recognize the ordinations as valid, and the House of Bishops was called upon to decide the matter. In a vote of 129 to 9, the body ruled that the ordinations were invalid. Seven bishops abstained from the vote, arguing that while the ordinations were irregular, they were not wrong. Sixty-seven bishops then co-sponsored legislation needed to allow female ordination.[58]

Perhaps surprising some, it was the Midwest diocese of Indianapolis (not one on the East or West coasts) that now leapt into the forefront of the issue. Bishop John Craine, a man respected by both liberals and conservatives within his denomination and diocese, was a supporter of female ordination. However, he also believed that such a change needed to be done gradually and by the book, and he skillfully began preparing two women for ordination in that way.[59]

As the 1976 General Convention in Minneapolis approached, it became obvious that momentum was building for officially endorsing female ordination.[60] Wasting little time after the convention voted in favor of women priests, the diocese of Indianapolis announced that Jacqueline Means was to become the first female priest in the nation, with her ordination set for 2 January 1977 at All Saints Episcopal Church in Indianapolis. The event turned into a "media circus," with a "standing room only crowd" of onlookers, who sat not only in the pews of the cathedral-size sanctuary but also on three tiers of bleachers erected for that service. Means knew that she was both making history and, in the minds of those who opposed her ordination, destroying tradition; she told reporters that she was "troubled" by the discord within the denomination caused by female ordination. Indeed, some members of the diocese, foreshadowing what was to come nationally, left the Episcopal Church in protest.[61] But by and large, Hoosier Episcopalians were proud of the fact that the first "legal" ordination took place in Indianapolis, even if they were unsure about the decision to allow women behind the pulpit.[62]

Through the late 1960s and early 1970s, as the issue was debated, some Episcopalians tried to find a middle ground. The Conscience Clause was passed by the 1976 General Convention, which allowed individual bishops to decide whether to ordain women in their diocese, but this proved to be a short-lived compromise. People on both sides argued that either female ordination was right or it was not. Those who believed strongly that it was improper left the denomination. Many of those who stayed did so because they accepted the change, even if they initially disagreed with it.[63]

The Episcopal Church's decision to embrace feminist demands and ordain women changed the denomination by making pastoral oversight more therapeutic in nature and less austere, as well as opening the door for discussions of inclusive language in scripture and liturgy.[64] It also avoided a long, drawn-out conflict within the denomination: female ministers were not new in American history, but worries in the late nineteenth and early twentieth centuries that women had come to dominate American Protestantism led to calls for a "muscular Christianity," which helped bury this tradition within the Seven Sisters.[65] To have the Episcopal Church embrace female ordination helped give the movement instant respectability, spurring other denominations to follow their example. By the late twentieth century, with the formation of conservative evangelical groups such as Promise Keepers, a new round of working to get men back "right with God" had begun, but largely outside the old Mainline. And while there were denominations without female ministers, there were also no organized outcry to remove women who were already ordained or stop others from following in their footsteps.[66]

Female ordination fed directly into the battle over Prayer Book revision. The Episcopal Church, like other Anglican bodies, liked to say it was diverse theologically but united in worship. The Book of Common Prayer allowed evangelicals, Anglo-Catholics, and liberals to be part of the same denomination by making theology secondary to a singular worship experience. As demands for pluralism and modernism mounted within the denomination, Episcopalians placed an even greater emphasis on the unity created by the Prayer Book. Any change to it was a threat to the theology of worship that bound the denomination together.[67] When amplified by female ordination, calls for a new hymnal, and the changing role of baptism (from a part of a rite of confirmation to one administered to infants), the theological crisis produced by Prayer Book revision constituted not only a change in liturgy but a threat to the way many envisioned their denomination should function.[68]

Prayer Book revision, this time focused in part on modernizing language, was discussed and begun in the 1960s. By the early 1970s, the Episcopal Church was starting to get feedback from its members on the various trial liturgies. Not surprisingly, the older a person was the more they disliked the proposed changes, although some young adults also resisted the change because they "had grown pretty comfortable with the old ritual." In the main though, older members tended to like the proposed Rite I, which was closer in language to the Elizabethan wording of the 1928 Prayer Book, while younger people supported the modern sounding Rite II.[69] Despite some reservations, the majority of the church came to embrace the concept of a new Prayer Book.[70]

The proposed changes came at a time when the centuries-old conflict between Low Church (those who wanted the denomination to be more Protestant) and High Church (those who wanted it to be more Roman).[71] Episcopalians were also focused on grappling with the external pressures of civil rights and Vietnam. While conservatives in both camps were trying to hold on to what they knew, the trial liturgies were designed to pit them against one another. The eventual Rite II incorporated many of the liturgical features that High Church Episcopalians approved of, so as to be difficult for Low Church Episcopalians to stomach. Likewise, Rite I was too Low Church for those in the High camp to accept.[72] Despite creating the Society for the Preservation of the Book of Common Prayer, whose mission was to save the 1928 Book of Common Prayer from "poor revision," and gaining the support of Presiding Bishop Allin, who was against "unnecessary" changes, conservatives could not halt the momentum the forces in favor of revision had already accumulated.[73]

As it became obvious that a new Prayer Book would be adopted, people began to leave the denomination. But not everyone who supported the 1928 version left or embraced the forces behind the liturgical change. For some who remained in the Episcopal Church, the changes in the Prayer Book did not make them angry, only sad.[74]

The wide acceptance, or at least acquiescence, to the new Prayer Book unleashed dramatic change for the denomination. The new Prayer Book, formally adopted in 1979, gave a High Church feel to services while using modern language. It was the Low Church group that was forced to adapt to changes such as receiving communion every Sunday, referring to the minister as "Father" rather than "Mister," crossing oneself, using incense in services— all things that many had been raised to regard as "papist" and the antithesis of Anglicanism. In addition to losing much of the Elizabethan language of the 1928 Prayer Book, the Low Church group lost, through attrition and lack of regular use, their much beloved Morning Prayer as the primary worship service. The unity that the book once provided became very "murky."[75] While some Episcopalians recognize there is richness in the current Prayer Book, and that the current trend of using only Rite II limits their "exposure to new images and piety," most have adapted accordingly.[76]

The spirit of revision that swept the Episcopal Church was part of a much wider liturgical movement that overtook many branches of Christendom during the mid-twentieth century. Included in this, of course, were the massive changes that the Second Vatican Council brought to the Roman Catholic Church.[77] For supporters, these modifications to worship practices helped unify these denominations via a new liturgy, promoting a sense of real community. The divide between the priest and the laity lessened, and a collective sense of what "we are experiencing" replaced it.[78] Yet many congregations had problems with the transition, some losing members as result. And even though the Episcopal Church did not shatter because of the 1960s and 1970s, it did splinter.[79] The memory of what happened has prompted concern about what more liturgical changes might do in the future, spurring a move toward small, gradual "updates" rather than wholesale alterations.[80]

The Onset of Decline

While the Episcopal Church managed to survive the trials of the 1960s and 1970s, the question facing it, and indeed all the members of the Seven Sisters, became whether they would continue to decline in the twenty-first century.[81] For the first time since perhaps the Second Great Awakening, people began to question the formulation of America's Mainline. One of the chief reasons, it seems, has to do with the rift between many of the clergy and laity and the denominational hierarchies. The Seven Sisters have either lost or managed to keep roughly the same level of membership numbers since the 1970s, but they have not grown as a percentage of the population or at the same rate as other denominations. As a result, while they still hold a place of influence in American society, it is increasingly a historic influence, and that has opened the door to the question of whether a new Mainline has emerged.[82]

In 1972, the sociologist Dean Kelley offered some possible explanations in his book *Why Conservative Churches are Growing*, in which he argued that most Mainline denominational leaders expected successful churches to "preserve a good image in the world" by embracing modernity, be "democratic and gentle in their internal affairs," "responsive to the needs of men" by being active in social reform, and "not let dogmatism, judgmental moralism, or obsessions with . . . purity stand in the way of . . . cooperation and service." The only problem, according to Kelley, was that these assumptions about success were wrong. It was not the Mainline that was attracting members but rather denominations and congregations that tended to be more "strict" in their adherence to doctrine and expected high levels of commitment from both their actual and potential members. As it turned out, strictness tended to be found most readily in congregations and denominations that were openly conservative in their political views, orthodox in their theology, and willing to be involved in local (rather than national) reform projects once the needs of its own parishioners were met.[83]

If one needed an example of Kelley's thesis in action, the Episcopal Church during the 1960s and 1970s provides it. The denomination reshaped "their ministries to fit the pattern of a new social order." Community service centers were organized, schools built, civil rights and Vietnam War were debated, and both the priesthood and the very liturgy of the denomination were altered and accommodated to a changing world. The result was not a growing, thriving denomination nationwide but rather a rift between the national and local manifestations of the denomination, as well as a membership and financial crisis.[84] With little clear understanding as to what it means to be an Episcopalian in denominationally plentiful America, the Episcopal Church has found little success in being viewed as largely politically liberal. No matter the local diversity of thought on issues, neither goal of the 1960s leadership has proven to be that great of an asset.[85]

To the further detriment of the Seven Sisters, and especially to the Episcopal Church, attempts at attracting new members via these changes has not made up for a lack of evangelization.[86] The Mainline has tried appealing to youth, women, singles, and minorities through new programs and policy changes, but not actually evangelizing them, has met with little success nationwide. Conservatives are quick to point to changes made in the name of "relevancy" as evidence of "mainline decline," while liberals say that the problem is not the changes per se but that there have not been enough of them. Indeed, the former presiding bishop John Hines believed that people left the Episcopal Church because it was not active enough in social issues.[87] In some respects, this polarization, at least on the denominational level, is simply a reflection of wider American society since the 1960s, and so, while painful for many Christians, should not be all that surprising. While the decade saw some commentators ready to say that the future of Christianity lay in remaking its basis along some sort of ethical guidelines and divesting itself of the supernatural, it was those denominations that did not follow this path that have flourished in the years since. Liberal churches, it seems, were left disorganized when their theories did not work in the ways expected and were thus unable to accept the reality of decline.[88]

The Episcopal Church and the other Seven Sisters endured much during the 1960s and 1970s. They still hold a great amount of promise and importance, even if they no longer have the membership or influence they once did.[89] And, as we will see, while it may be appropriate to reconsider their role as the "Mainline," they also offer an intriguing look at what denominations can do during times of strife in order to maintain their membership and influence. But the future of American Christianity, by the late twentieth century, belonged to those outside the Episcopal Church and the old Mainline.[90]

4

The Politics of Decline

Founded in 1695, Christ Church Episcopal in Philadelphia boasts a rich history. Home to patriots (including a signer of the Declaration of Independence, Francis Hopkinson) and loyalists (Hopkinson's brother-in-law, the Reverend Jacob Duche, who was for a time the chaplain of the Continental Congress before emerging as a Tory) during the Revolution, a spiritual home to many of the Founding Fathers (George Washington worshiped there), the congregation has deep roots in the community and personifies the establishment of the Seven Sisters. It sits just a few blocks away from Independence Hall, the Liberty Bell, the National Constitution Center, and a variety of federal buildings, including the district courthouse.[1] As an Episcopal church and thus part of the Seven Sisters, Christ Church is a good example of the establishment the Mainline had become. Its location also serves as a reminder of how politics and law affected decline as well.

Looking back, the decline of the Seven Sisters seems quite obvious. But to those who were in the midst of it, the gradual slide and rapid fall came and, in some ways, remains quite shocking. While decline changed the relationship of the old Mainline to American life and culture, it did not usher in the demise of any denominations or the creation of any new ones. Institutionally, the Sisters remained intact and congregations remained plentiful. But wider currents were afoot that would lead to a re-evaluation and a reconfiguration of the Mainline itself. Interestingly enough, these changes came not from the pulpit but from the realm of politics.[2]

A discussion of the connections between politics and religion is both necessary and necessarily complex. For all the talk about separation of church and state in the United States, American politicians spend a lot of time discussing religion, especially American Christianity. Since the Founding Fathers achieved religious liberty for all by *not* creating a national church, thereby unleashing religious consumerism, the nation has debated the role faith should play in the life of the country, including if religious voices should be pushed entirely from the public square.[3] At the same time, political commentators talk of red states (Republican) and blue states (Democrats), and the supposed underlying political values that these terms then hold. The religious divide between these poles creates much confusion within American Christendom over how faith should (and does) impact politics and politicians. After all, despite labels, politics cuts across denominational lines. And ones' denomination does not necessarily correlate to ones' political position on a given issue. For examples, the United Methodist Church is the spiritual home to both former president George W. Bush (Republican) and the secretary of state Hillary R. Clinton (Democrat). Roman Catholic politicians, such as former New York City mayor Rudolph Giuliani (Republican) and the senior senator from Massachusetts John Kerry (Democrat), must contend with the ramifications of being pro-choice on the issue of abortion while also being members of a church that is just as staunchly pro-life. In short, denominationalism is no predictor of political affiliation.

This political insight is another way to gauge the decline of the Seven Sisters, while at the same time problematizing Dean Kelley's now classic Mainline decline thesis. How did the culture wars influence decline? What political alternatives emerged in the wake of Mainline decline? Is there a continued role for the Seven Sisters to play in postdecline America? These are important questions for a nation that talks of a wall of separation but whose politics is infused by Christian morality.

Of Culture Wars and Walls

Though Americans have, since the time of the Founders, lived with a wall of separation between church and state at least at the federal level, the doctrine has been somewhat nebulous in its application. In some respects, it is more an idea, a value that is cherished, than it is a reality. While the notion that in the United States there will be no state-sponsored church, the belief that religion, or specifically Christianity, has no place in the public square is a much more recent development.

Indeed, the rise of secularization in this sense happened at the same time as the onset of decline within the Seven Sisters during the 1960s and 1970s. In that way, decline can be seen as part of the culture wars that emerged in the nation's political life in the 1970s and 1980s. Despite some soul searching on the part of politicians and political pundits, these wars continue to the present. From prayer and Bible reading in public schools to public displays of religious belief to hot-button issues such as abortion and homosexual rights, there has been very little in the way of restraining clashes over what the proper relationship of church and state should be.[4]

The center of much of this debate has been the Constitution's establishment clause of the First Amendment—"Congress shall make no law respecting an establishment of religion, or prohibiting the free exercise thereof"— and what exactly was and is meant by "establishment" and how that might affect the "free exercise" of religion.[5] Not surprisingly, the federal courts have become involved in the discussion over the years. But tellingly for the Seven Sisters and their decline, the Mainline showed a good deal of complacency in the outcomes of the cases that were litigated. Indeed, when it came to school prayer (the landmark case being *Engel v. Vitale*, a case from New York decided by the U.S. Supreme Court in 1962) conservative Christians were divided. Some hailed the rulings striking down prayer in the schools because Roman Catholics had supported nonsectarian prayers. But as it opened the door for other cases, conservatives began to rally against liberal "judicial activism." Then came *Schempp v. Abington School District*.[6]

In 1957 Ellery (born Ellory) Schempp, a student in the Abington School District in eastern Pennsylvania, wrote a letter to the American Civil Liberties Union (ACLU) stating that as a Unitarian, he felt uncomfortable reciting the Lord's Prayer and the required biblical passages each day in school because they conflicted with his church's doctrinal interpretations and political belief in the separation of church and state. Like many states, Pennsylvania had statutes authorizing such recitations officially for the purposes of moral, ethical, and civic (in the midst of the Cold War against communism) purposes. The Philadelphia ACLU chapter believed that the prayer and Bible readings posed real constitutional issues. Their board, however, was divided as to what action to take but eventually decided to press ahead with a lawsuit. They also asked Henry Sawyer, a prominent Philadelphia attorney, to get involved, rather than using one of their own staff attorneys, so that the case would not instantly be branded in the public eye as the "ACLU vs. prayer." Sawyer quickly opted to focus on the Bible reading alone, believing that it was both an establishment (by the state requiring religious practice) and an infringement of the free exercise of religion (by forcing people who may not believe in the same way to be part of the same captive congregation).[7] Sawyer made it clear in his argument before the federal court that the reading of scripture was an establishment of religion, even if the passages were selected at random.[8]

By the time he took part in *Schempp*, Sawyer was an experienced trial lawyer with the law firm of Drinker Biddle and Reath, and whose career was on track to define church–state relations in the United States. Born in 1918, Sawyer served in the navy during World War II and Korea as well as with the U.S. State Department. He joined the Drinker firm in 1948, and soon found himself involved in various communist-related free speech and freedom of association cases. Still, the *Schempp* case was "low profile" within the firm, despite Sawyer's prominence, so as not to disturb conservative clients.[9]

Of course there was more to the case than just Sawyer's decision to focus on Bible reading. Edward Schempp, Ellery's father, was a member of the ACLU and a leading Unitarian.[10] And the family was not just challenging a local school board but also the state of Pennsylvania, which had passed the law requiring Bible reading at the start of the school day in order to help instill morality in the state's youth. The legislature eventually included an exemption clause for just such the reasons the Schempps were claiming, allowing students to not take part in either the prayer or Bible reading, and as the school pointed out, the only complaints it got were from the Schempps.[11]

A federal three-judge panel heard the case because of the constitutional questions involved.[12] The judges ruled that even with an exemption clause in the law, the Bible readings violated the First Amendment—including the establishment clause—as applied to the states via the Fourteenth Amendment's citizenship provisions. Furthermore, as Judge William Kirkpatrick noted during the trial, if the Bible reading was not scholarly or devotional and there was no instruction attached to it, the panel was left to wonder what exactly the point of doing it was.[13] The case was soon appealed to the U. S. Supreme Court, where the school district eventually centered its defense on the existence of the exemption clause.[14]

The creation of that clause caused the Supreme Court, which heard arguments after the panel had initially sided with the Schempps but before the creation of the exemption clause itself, to order the panel to reconsider the case based upon the new version of the law. In these proceedings, Edward Schempp asserted that taking the exemption would make his children pariahs, as well as have them labeled as "atheists," "odd balls," and possibly as communists.[15] The school district then argued that Schempp no longer had standing to sue, since his children were no longer in the schools.[16]

The chief circuit judge John Biggs authored the eventual decision, holding that the statute requiring Bible reading violated the establishment clause, "notwithstanding provision in the statute for excusing a child from the reading," in part because it included mass recitation of the Lord's Prayer.[17] The Pennsylvania General Assembly, the judge asserted, was placing a Christian ritual in the schools, "seeing fit to breach the wall between church and state" to further a religious, not secular, educational goal.[18] Sawyer's argument had carried the day.

The Supreme Court then considered the three-judge panel's decision for a second time in 1963, coupled with soon-to-be-famous atheist Madalyn Murray's case in Maryland against reciting the Lord's Prayer.[19] In some respects, the *Schempp* case need not have been heard at all, as the Supreme Court had recently ruled that school prayer was unconstitutional. Nonetheless, the case was selected to drive the point home.[20] Justice Tom Clark delivered the opinion of the high court, stressing both the history of religion in America and of religious freedom. To the majority of the justices, the establishment clause was not just about privileging one faith over another; it was a means to avoid officially sanctioned sectarianism. Schools are to be for "secular" education and government is to be neutral toward religion and not a body where the two become interdependent. The justices feared that some form of establishment might emerge from such a union. While religion and education had a long history together, the "statutory provision for daily religious exercises" was more recent. The Court asserted that "no one denies that they [religious principles] should be taught to the youth of the State," rather that the public schools should not be the place to do it.[21]

Of course, the *Schempp*-era cases were not the final words on the matter. Despite the initial outrage and lingering discussion of the courts "taking God out of the classroom," the Seven Sisters did not organize in a real way to do anything about it. Instead, they largely acquiesced, sure of their own cultural standing, at a time in which the nation still adhered to a civil religion of sorts. When the matter has come up in the years since the 1970s, it has more often than not been done by conservative politicians and by members of other denominations, who have pointed out that some of the parties to suits like the Schempps had motives beyond constitutional principles. In *Schempp*, the plaintiffs' Unitarian faith played a role. A liberal offshoot of the old Congregational Church, and the bane of orthodox Christians since Lyman Beecher's time during the Second Great Awakening, by the twentieth century Unitarians and Universalists were crafting a secular church that had little in common with most Christian denominations. That the Mainline took virtually no stand on this point speaks volumes to where the Seven Sisters were headed within American culture, since many denominational leaders even agreed with the demise of prayer in schools. But there was also a good deal of dissent, and it was finding a voice in high-profile evangelists like Billy Graham.[22]

The non-action on the part of the Seven Sisters is also evident from another case coming out of the Keystone State. When the Pennsylvania legislature enacted a series of measures to advance secular education, all of them were tested in the federal courts under the establishment clause. In 1969, a federal three-judge panel from the Eastern District of Pennsylvania heard the first of the so-called *Lemon* cases.[23] This litigation focused on an act that authorized the state to purchase "secular educational services from nonpublic schools" including teachers, textbooks, and classroom materials. Not surprisingly, Henry Sawyer led the plaintiffs' legal team, which argued that the state was funding religion-based (largely Catholic) schools (where a quarter of the state's student population was enrolled) via the law. Two members of the judicial panel ruled that those seeking to enjoin the act lacked standing to do so, and that the law was not a violation of the establishment clause. While most of the schools that contracted to provide services were sectarian schools, what they were provided was secular in nature. The act was passed to avoid with a "crisis in education." The other panel member dissented, saying that the door was opening to First Amendment issues by entangling church and state, because where money goes, so too does oversight.[24] In other words, the fear was that any state tax money might be used for religious ends, which would require the state to have financial oversight of a religious organization.

The case was directly appealed to the U.S. Supreme Court, where it was consolidated with a case from Rhode Island in 1971 of a similar nature. The high court, led by Chief Justice Warren Burger, echoed the dissent's concerns in pronouncing the Pennsylvania law unconstitutional, since it allowed the state to audit a school's books in order to make sure that they spent money on secular subject-area teachers, textbooks, and materials. This fostered "excessive entanglement" because to make sure that nothing religious took place, the state would need to monitor both the schools and teachers involved. The justices crafted a three-prong "*Lemon* test" to guide them: first, laws needed to have a secular legislative purpose; second, the principle and primary effect must neither advance nor inhibit religion; and third, laws must not create excessive entanglement between church and state.[25]

However, issues and new legal challenges quickly arose under the *Lemon* test: Did the Supreme Court's decision mean that schools that had purchased services could not now be reimbursed for them? The same federal three-judge panel said that the schools could be paid, despite the law being declared unconstitutional, because they had acted in the good-faith belief that the law was constitutional when entering into the purchase of service agreements with the state. To make *Lemon I* retroactive and deny schools the funding for what amounted to one academic year would unfairly burden them.[26] When the case went to the Supreme Court, the justices agreed with the decision, finding it to be "practical."[27]

But the federal courts were not yet done with *Lemon* cases. Another one, this time arising out of a new statute allowing for the "reimbursement of tuition paid by parents who send their children to nonpublic schools," was presented to another federal three-judge panel in 1972, which found the law unconstitutional. The judges based their decision on the fact that the funds could be used for religious purposes, and any state oversight of the funds would be entanglement, in particular, because parents could use the money to send their children to religious schools, thus using state funds to advance religion.[28] The United States Supreme Court agreed with the three judge panel, noting that the problem for those who now wanted the state to aid religious education was not with the courts, but with the establishment clause.[29]

The establishment clause had now come to be defined by secular forces outside of the Mainline. In 1974 this point was driven home when the three-pronged *Lemon* test was utilized in yet another Pennsylvania case. In *Meek v. Pittinger*, the federal district court for Eastern Pennsylvania was asked to rule on a state law, this one allowing public schools to loan or make available speech and hearing services, textbooks, instructional material, and equipment to private schools. Again a federal panel heard the case. The majority of the (2 to 3) panel found that the state was simply trying to help all students within the state, in both public and private schools, to have the same services and opportunities available to them. While not all of the provisions passed constitutional muster (the loaning of equipment, such as movie projectors, the panel ruled could to easily be diverted to religious purposes), most of the statute was fine.[30]

In his dissent, Judge A. Leon Higginbotham noted that the state's intent was a good one, but that the possibility of unintended consequences, or a sort of entanglement by degree, could very easily result. He also noted

> Tragically, some persons, before the ink here is hardly dry, will claim that the dissent is anti-religious or fails to appreciate the importance of religion and religious education in our society. Such distortions would be far from the truth. Each of my children, as a matter of parental choice, has attended nonpublic schools which have a religious focus and are sponsored by a religious body. But it was a private choice; the taxpayers under the constitution are not permitted to pay the price for my religious preferences.[31]

Once again the U.S. Supreme Court heard the case on appeal. The majority, brought together around Justice Potter Stewart's opinion, followed Higginbotham's lead in upholding only the textbook loan provision, and declaring the rest unconstitutional.[32]

The *Lemon* cases once again raise the question of where the Mainline was at this crucial time. Those adherents were generally not the ones building schools to meet parental demand for other educational venues, nor were they the ones advocating for the laws that eventually became challenged under the *Lemon* test. One might assume that this lack of involvement had to do with the demographic or religious makeup of Pennsylvania, or even that their lack of participation was because of Mainline decline. But the reason these cases originated in Pennsylvania was not because the Seven Sisters were "weak" in the Keystone State, but because the judicial and legal makeup and tradition of the federal district court for Eastern Pennsylvania offered a favorable climate to bring such legal actions. The cases, and thus the state, were symbolic of what was happening across the nation.[33]

The *Lemon* cases were not the only ones involving the establishment clause before the federal courts in Pennsylvania during the 1970s. Since the late 1940s, the Department of Defense had donated closed military facilities to the Department of Health and Human Services, which could then "gift" the property to a state or interested third party. The theory behind this process was to advance governmental goals (the use of the property) at no cost to the taxpayer (because of the bureaucratic red tape involved in actually selling government property), despite the fact that there was no revenue generated from a sale. When that third party was a religious organization, some taxpayers cried foul, believing a violation of the establishment clause was the result. The Warren Supreme Court allowed federal taxpayers to challenge such sales if the transfer of property fell under such scrutiny.[34]

In 1975, when the Valley Forge Army Hospital in Pennsylvania closed, the Department of Health, Education, and Welfare gifted it to the Northeast Bible Institute, which then renamed itself Valley Forge Christian College. In 1981 Americans United for the Separation of Church and State (AU) filed suit in the federal district court for Eastern Pennsylvania, contending that the college was a wholly religious institution and the transfer of more than seventy acres (complete with buildings) ran afoul of the establishment clause. From their perspective, the issue was the religious nature of the institution. From the college's perspective, there was a question as to whether AU had standing to sue to block the school from taking possession of the property.[35] At the federal district level, Judge J. William Ditter ruled in favor of the college's position. The Third Circuit reversed him, but the Supreme Court then upheld Ditter's original decision by a vote of 5 to 4. Interestingly, while the

Carter administration was reluctant to take the case to the Supreme Court (as it was officially a defendant), the Reagan administration reversed course and supported the college. That may have been key, as the Court, speaking through Justice William Rehnquist, put a halt to liberalizing trends in this area of law, requiring plaintiffs to show an actual "injury" (or proof of an establishment clause violation), not just the theoretical potential of one, with the decision.[36]

This brief look at these cultural issues and some of the related legal battles demonstrates that by the onset of decline, the Seven Sisters had either grown so complacent with their place in wider American society or were so consumed with internal debates as to miss out on wider currents in American culture. Liberals and modernists largely ruled their denominational hierarchies and saw a loosening of denominationalism because of mergers (the United Methodist Church and the United Church of Christ are but two examples),[37] and a growing divide among many in the laity over internal decisions. It is little wonder that many members of Mainline congregations desired an opportunity to somehow bring about a moral crusade over what they saw as a decline setting into wider American society, and they needed to find an outlet in the emerging conservative political movement rather than from their own churches.

That American Christians should seek to enact reforms should come as no surprise. "Reform" after all, is the response that American churches have had to crisis since the colonial period. Whether it was in reaction to Deism in the eighteenth century, societal strain in the nineteenth, or moral reforms in the twentieth, launching a crusade has been part of the (largely) evangelical makeup of the Mainline's churches. But the reaction in the late twentieth century was different: while churches were involved, it was not the Seven Sisters, and more often than not the evangelical laity who remained within the old Mainline sought to reform society via the ballot box much more than from the pulpit.

Of Moral Majorities

In order to better understand the interplay of religion and politics, one need only look at the presidents elected during the 1970s and 1980s, when decline was becoming an uncomfortable reality for the Seven Sisters. In doing so, special attention should be given to the political forces and how the three men who served in the Oval Office during this period understood American religious life and, by association, their relationships with the Mainline. In some respects, they did nothing out of the ordinary from their predecessors in office when it came to faith and politics. But in other ways they helped usher in a whole new understanding of the Mainline's relationship to American politicians.[38]

First elected in 1968, the Republican Richard Nixon resurrected his political career based on the wider culture war and tensions over Vietnam. His references to the "silent majority" of Americans who were not protesting the war nor civil rights, struck a chord with the majority of voters not once, but twice. Religiously, Nixon was not a part of the Mainline. He was raised a Quaker, and indeed to the extent that the Mainline was "the establishment" Nixon more often than not counted them as a potential enemy to his policies more than an ally. It was perhaps for this reason that Nixon made so much of his relationship with the evangelist Billy Graham, signaling the president's own break with the Mainline, more so than recognition of their denominational decline. But this no doubt helped his prospects with evangelicals that so many liberal Protestants had attacked the 1964 Republican nominee, Barry Goldwater. To them, Nixon, if not perfect, was at least someone who would take on both the liberal political and religious establishments.[39]

Nixon resigned and was replaced in office, following the Watergate scandal, by the Republican Gerald Ford in 1974. In some respects, Ford exemplified the Mainline. He was an Episcopalian and a well-liked and respected member of Congress. Unlike Nixon, who had tapped into populist anxiety in the midst of riots and marches, Ford attempted to reassert consensus-style politics. But he failed to appreciate and understand the growing political conservative movement and its looming religious counterpart. As the conservative movement turned toward social issues like abortion and the debate over the proposed Equal Rights Amendment, Ford ran into a problem, compounded by underestimation of the significance that conservatives placed on such issues. His greater political challenge came in the form of the Democratic governor of Georgia, James Earl Carter.[40]

Carter represents a clear break with the Mainline. Georgia's governor brought a very public light to his personal faith, that of being a Southern Baptist during his campaign for the presidency. While not the first member of the denomination to reside in the White House, Carter's public discussion about salvation, sin, and faith in general was a marked change from notions of a nondescript civil religion most of the Seven Sisters had supported since the 1940s. By proclaiming himself to be "born again," to be openly evangelical, Carter launched a "revolution" in the relationship between politics and religion.[41]

Carter, however, was on the wrong side of the coming conservative political swell, even if his personal faith found him in a denomination that was not a part of the Seven Sisters. He was evangelical but not conservative. And he was not ready to deal with evangelicals in opposition to him.[42] In 1980 he was defeated by the former California governor (and actor) Ronald Reagan. While Reagan was a member of the Mainline, having grown up in the Disciples of Christ denomination and later becoming a member of the Presbyterian Church, his political conservatism had led him into contact with many of those outside of the Seven Sisters' fold. Thus, he was perfectly at home with fundamentalists and conservative denominations, as well as with evangelicals who might still worship within the Mainline. Indeed, Reagan openly endorsed conservative evangelicals.[43]

Reagan's rise politically mirrored the rise of organizations that, in a broad way, came to embody the emergent Religious Right. One such organization was the Moral Majority. Founded in 1979 and led by Jerry Falwell, a Southern Baptist minister in Virginia, the group and others like it (such as Focus on the Family) were horrified at what they believed to be the moral decline of the nation, precipitated by liberals in government, on the nation's federal courts, and in the Mainline's pulpits. They were worried about abortion on demand, God being banished from public schools, and the demise of traditional "family values." But as shocked as they were, the important thing is that they organized to do something about it. Falwell's leadership in this movement is especially noteworthy. After all, he criticized portions of the civil rights movement, arguing that pastors should preach the Gospel and let God transform people and society, as there was no need to wage reform wars. And yet he founded the Moral Majority, after he himself had reached a breaking point of sorts, embracing the old evangelical reform ethos.[44]

While many commentators at the time were surprised by the emergence, or re-emergence, of both political and religious conservative voices, they should not have been. The Moral Majority was walking in the footsteps of other parachurch organizations that were more theologically conservative than the Seven Sisters' institutionalized bureaucracies, including Youth For Christ and Campus Crusade for Christ (both of which are campus outreach organizations, geared chiefly toward college aged young adults).[45] Likewise, the Moral Majority embraced the counterculture mentality not of the 1960s but that of many fundamentalists after the *Scopes* trial. These conservative Christians established their own organizations, schools, sponsored their own approved music and television shows, and created their own literature. They lived in the world claimed to be not of the world, and now these conservative evangelicals hoped to save the world, and especially the United States.

Where had they been? The answer actually moves away from the accepted notion of the post-*Scopes* retreat of fundamentalists (conservative Christians never retreated from the public square nor did they suddenly reappear at the end of the twentieth century), and more toward the reaction of the post-Prohibition Mainline. Many within the Seven Sisters came to see that there was no sure victory when entering into the political fray. Thus, after 1933 they proved increasingly reluctant to do so. Being part of the status quo was believed to be better than trying to change things. When the Mainline did offer a political opinion post-repeal, it was more often than not as part of the consensus. This complacency opened the door for liberal activism in the 1960s and 1970s, as generally moderate leaders of the 1930s and 1940s left the scene and were often replaced by theological liberals. For most politically conservative members of Mainline denominations to act, they had do so outside of their own denominational structure, as the modernists took control of the Seven Sisters.[46]

These conservative Christians did not find much comfort in the arms of their fellow denominational members. Theological and political liberals were also forming parachurch groups to further agendas that moderate members of their denominations would not support.[47] One such group we have already encountered was the Americans United for Separation of Church and State (AU). Founded in 1947 to oppose proposed government aid to religious (mainly Catholic) schools, the group became a champion for those on the Religious Left who sought to combat religious conservatives, including being involved in court struggles like the ones from Pennsylvania. In 2009, the organization was headed by a United Church of Christ minister, and thus has claims to respectability within the old Mainline and with non-Christians who share its program of attacking the Religious Right and political conservatives.[48]

Of Religious Right and Left

Already the terms "Religious Right" and "Religious Left" have been used without much explanation. In part, this is because the terms are largely self-explanatory: political believers who are conservatives are often labeled as members of the Religious Right, while their liberal counterparts within Christianity are part of the Religious Left. In some respects, what we have are simply new labels for the modernist/fundamentalist debates of the early twentieth century with a more politicized bent as opposed to theological reference. Although, as we will see, the moderates can complicate this divide and the resulting discussion to a great degree.[49]

There are of course problems with using broad terminology to define groups of people, let alone whole denominations since they can render an inaccurate picture of American Christianity. There are moral issues that transcend partisan labels and religious faith that runs deeper than politics.[50] The prime example of this mischaracterization is the more than 60 million evangelicals in America. Their very size makes them a more complex group than categorizing them as "Religious Right" or "Religious Left." Evangelicals have never been of the same mind on all political issues, but both historically and presently they do believe moral values influence political choices.[51] It is not surprising, then, to see them organize to impact, or attempt to impact, politics and culture. Indeed, the First and Second Great Awakenings are largely their story. Since the 1960s, evangelical-based organizations such as the Moral Majority and Christian Coalition have been formed for the specific purpose of focusing evangelicals on certain political issues or conservative candidates, though groups such as these usually do not last very long. Other organizations, such as the National Association of Evangelicals, have attempted to take a longer and perhaps less partisan view of the interaction of Christians with politics.[52] But all of them are merely tapping into a historic tradition of evangelical activism, even if forays into politics have led to as much frustration as victories.[53]

The evangelical experience of engagement is something we have encountered before, most notably in the case of Prohibition. And yet, one thing that has changed since the dry years when it comes to the voice of Christian organizations in the public discourse is that they do not dominate the way they did when drys helped craft the Eighteenth Amendment. It is clear that large parachurch organizations like the Anti-Saloon League, or even denominational or transdenominational bureaucratic bodies like the National Council of Churches, can issue pronouncements on behalf of their constituent members without necessarily speaking for them on topics as far ranging as the federal budget,[54] or involvement in the armed forces during times of war.[55]

Another difference is that there is more opposition to Christian voices being heard in the public square. America is a more secular place than it once was, with some people both in and outside the church working to make it even more so. Evangelicals and others must now make the case that they should help shape wider culture. Since they believe that the church has an obligation to "continually exert a strong ethical influence upon the state, supporting policies and programs deemed to be just and opposing policies and programs that are unjust," it is hard for them not to attempt to do so. Such notions were taken for granted during the age of Prohibition, and Christian involvement in taking part in political discourse, whether from the Right or Left, has a long history of working in public/private partnership with local governments without such work being detrimental to either.[56] In other words, secularists have the historic burden of proof as to why Christians should now *not* be part of the public square, not the other way around.

Despite this shared history, the Religious Right and Left are often at odds with one another over the proper relationship between church and state. In part, this tension has to do with the evangelical makeup of the Right, even as the formerly staunch evangelical denominations of the Seven Sisters are more aligned with the Left. This development is reflective of Mainline decline, but it also shows the power of the old evangelical model of reform and revival being a vital part of American Christianity.[57] Just because the Seven Sisters are less likely to act does not mean evangelicals are going to follow the same path.

Because the Religious Left has largely stayed within the Seven Sisters, it is smaller and less organized, and thus has a smaller potential voice than does the right wing of American Christianity.[58] Indeed, the Religious Left actually faces an uphill battle in terms of engaging the Right without hyperbole. Part of this dynamic has to do with who makes up the Religious Left. In the main, it finds its home in the denominations of the Seven Sisters, where alliances of modernists and moderates have largely held sway within denominational hierarchies since the 1930s. It was this alliance that allowed the attempted recasting of Christianity in the 1960s and 1970s, and it is this group of Christians who are most worried about conservative churches being engaged in politics.[59]

It is from the Religious Left that the most strident calls for Christians to refrain from being vocal about how their faith has led them to their particular political worldview. It is also the Religious Left that calls on Christians involved in politics to avoid issues that would be "divisive," at least on subjects on which they disagree with the majority. While the Religious Right is often associated with the Republican Party, the moderates within the denominations that the Religious Left holds sway over have made a compelling argument that it would be a good thing to see Christians really active in both political parties. After all, Protestants and Catholics already make up much of both parties' membership.[60] Even some conservatives have called for evangelicals to engage political issues without the need for compromise with political parties. In short, they are talking about the end of the Religious Right.[61] Though that is doubtful, the allure of the moderate call is powerful.

Thus, a figure such as William Jennings Bryan (the early twentieth-century Democratic leader who led the charge against Darwinian evolution) might seem a viable historical reference for the moderates to utilize in such an effort, there are problems. Bryan was very much influenced by the Social Gospel and was an advocate of all sorts of political programs that conservatives, both then and now, would find anathema. However, the very fact that he was orthodox in his Christian beliefs, and indeed was a champion of the fundamentalist cause, more than likely would mean he would not be welcome within the Democratic Party of today.[62] If Republicans are accused of using religion to win votes, Democrats, it can be said, often seem to misunderstand the role of faith at the ballot box.[63]

Yet despite the gulf between them, there are moderates within both the Religious Left and Right. Evangelicals are hardly monolithic, and there are some like Jim Wallis—a moderate evangelical pastor, whose politics are more liberal than conservative (he headed "Evangelicals for McGovern in 1972")—who have made a strong case that one can be a traditional Christian and not vote Republican. His organization, Sojourners, was founded to make sure that progressive evangelical voices were not missed. At the same time, he believes that the Right "distorts" evangelical faith and has attempted to critique the Religious Right.[64] Another moderate evangelical is Tony Campolo, who has argued that Jesus is neither a Republican nor a Democrat, calling on evangelicals to apply God's word on an issue by issue basis. Campolo, in particular, has argued that Christians should be wary of seeking power as a means to influence culture, proving to be a more-moderate moderate than Wallis in some respects.[65]

Hence, the more important revelation in looking at the Religious Left is the continued debate between moderates and modernists. For, at the same time moderates are reaching out, modernists continue their drive to offer alternative interpretations of traditional Christianity. This quest includes those who search for the "historical Jesus" (via the Jesus Seminar movement, a gathering of theologians, philosophers, and historians who seek to determine what Jesus "really said"[66]) as well as members of the clergy, such as the retired Episcopal bishop and best-selling author John Shelby Spong. While Spong oversaw his flock in the diocese of Newark, he became an articulate spokesman starting in the 1990s for a postmodern interpretation of Christianity that sought to transcend, when it did not repudiate, core Christian doctrines and beliefs. Spong argued that his alterations, if they were not revelations, were needed to keep Christianity current and thoroughly in step with the modern world. In this regard, Spong is the descendant of modernist theologians who advanced higher criticism and evolution in the late nineteenth and early twentieth centuries. Spong has produced a small cannon of books critiquing biblical interpretation and imagery (because he claims traditional readings of the Bible have been hateful toward women, children, and homosexuals), as well as a reinterpretation of the Gospels, ranging from disputing the virgin birth to calling Jesus' death on the cross a "resurrection experience" among his disciples as they thought about what Christ had taught them and how his work could transcend his death if they spread his message.[67]

If the moderates have been largely quiet about Spong's theories, the Religious Right has not. Spong has been critiqued by people both within and outside of the Anglican Communion for his alterations to Christianity. The Reverend Peter C. Moore, former dean of Trinity Seminary, has argued that the former bishop "has essentially placed himself outside the Christian tradition and had used his privileged position as a bishop to attack it." The Anglican bishop N. T. Wright has taken Spong and others like him to task for not doing serious historical work when discussing the "historical Jesus," as well as for the assumptions that flow from such a flawed creation in their hands. Spong, in their minds, is little more than a "celebrity heretic."[68]

But such attacks have not deterred the modernists and even some moderates within the Religious Left from assaulting the Religious Right. There is a plethora of books, some by noted scholars, that take aim at conservative Christians, offering varying interpretations and almost always issuing an ominous warning about what is going to happen to America if evangelical Christians (broadly and often widely defined by the authors) continue to be active in politics or the wider culture. Such worry, whether secular or from within the old Mainline, can border on the hysterical with visions of the United States becoming a theocratic, imperialistic, despotic nation in pursuit of the world's oil.[69]

If the modernists are guilty of having produced a straw man to attack, some within the Religious Right are also guilty of believing they have or deserve more influence than they indeed wield.[70] But there is little doubt that the emergence of the Religious Right as a group corresponded to the rise of the conservative movement within the nation's political life.[71] And because that movement was so tied to the resurgence of the Republican Party, their coexistence was bound to be conflated. That being said, while evangelicals tend to be the more orthodox (in terms of traditional Christian theology) that does not mean that all are members of either the Religious Right or the Republican Party. But being orthodox in the faith, regardless of ones' evangelical status, is a requirement for being part of the Religious Right.

Reports of the Religious Right's decline and demise are overexaggerated.[72] Indeed, while the Religious Right's constituency is made up of evangelicals and fundamentalists, it also includes many Roman Catholics. If the Religious Right has a major problem, it is that since the Scopes trial and its aftermath, its fundamentalist wing has lost the ability to define itself to the larger public, while its evangelical wing was for so long silent in the face of their common opponents. Not unlike the Puritans, the fundamentalists have been relegated to being known as narrow-minded as an automatic response whenever that term is invoked. Indeed, the very word "fundamentalist," has come to define theological conservatives, few, if any, of whom, have ever actually read Dixon's *The Fundamentals*. But if the journalist Colleen Carroll and others are correct that young adults are opting for denominations and congregations that are more traditional in their doctrine, then the collapse of the Sisters seems imminent.[73] If that is the case, then American Christianity currently may be witnessing the most dramatic demographic and denominational membership shift since the onset of the decline of the Seven Sisters in the 1960s and 1970s.

Prayers for the President

In the wake of Ronald Reagan's election, the concepts and organizations of the Religious Right and Left began to more clearly solidify. More importantly, they did so against a backdrop of interesting political developments. The Cold War came to a conclusion, and the nation wrestled with its status as the sole remaining military super power. Domestic politics kept the economy in focus while also leaving room for cultural issues to play, at times, a pivotal role. The men who followed Reagan in the White House reflected these trends and their religious overtones, as well as the continued decline in status of the Seven Sisters.

Reagan's vice president, George H. W. Bush, won the presidential election in 1988. An Episcopalian, Bush had a better understanding of Religious Right than had Ford, but was still at times uneasy with them. While he did utilize "family values" as an election issue, his break with the Mainline came in 1990–91 when he relied on Billy Graham to give moral sanction to the Gulf War following Iraq's invasion of Kuwait, after his own denominational leadership balked at the suggestion.[74] He was defeated for re-election by William Jefferson Clinton, the Democratic governor of Arkansas, in 1992. Clinton was a Southern Baptist but often attended United Methodist Church services with his wife, Hillary. A centrist Democrat with infidelity issues, Clinton often talked about his faith and his need for moral guidance. In many ways, while hardly a champion of the Religious Right, Clinton was a good example of a moderate evangelical within the Seven Sisters, who was attempting to practice what Jim Wallis would soon make famous with his Sojourners.[75]

The man who succeeded Clinton in office in 2000 was George W. Bush, the Republican governor of Texas and the son of President George H. W. Bush. Raised an Episcopalian, Bush became a Methodist following a conversion experience prompted in part by discussions with Billy Graham. More conservative than his father, the younger Bush became for some a poster child of the Religious Right, one who often talked about his faith and the role it played in his presidency. His re-election in 2004 was aided by the emergence of "values voters" who turned out in support of the president (largely over the terrorist attacks of September 11, 2001, and the issues against homosexual marriage.[76]

In 2008 the Illinois senator Barack Obama was elected president, returning the Democrats to the White House. While a historic event in and of itself—Obama became the first African American to win the presidency—his victory carried with it implications for the Seven Sisters as well. A member of the United Church of Christ, Obama's denomination is largely dominated by the modernist wing of the Religious Left, and many of his policy initiatives have long been supported by liberals in the pews and bureaucracies of the old Mainline.[77] Still, he was able to win many of the (largely swing) evangelical "values voters" from 2004, who allowed economic concerns in 2008 to trump any worries about Obama's potential political agenda.[78] While criticized for not doing it the "right way" (or perhaps, the Right's way), Obama follows in the footsteps of the nation's previous chief executives by using biblical/Christian imagery in his speeches and reaching out to people of faith.[79]

If the presidents since Reagan have brought about a sort of back and forth when it comes to the influence (whether real or imagined) of the Religious Right, many questions still remain about the future of the Seven Sisters in the modern political environment. Since the 1980s the influence of the old Mainline has declined along with the denominational size. Despite Obama's election, it seems unlikely that these trends will be reversed. But it also remains to be seen if that victory will translate into the decline of the Religious Right or not (despite the speculation of some on both sides of the political and religious divide). Furthermore, if the Sisters' can not raise their voices when one of their own is in the White House, will they ever be a political force again?

We have seen that religious belief has been a factor, though not the only one, when it comes to the nation's politics and electoral decisions. And that fact has important implications for the decline of the Seven Sisters. It appears that most Christians have more in common with one another than many realize and can still rally together to support a wide variety of causes and reforms, politics does matter. And in the American political climate of the past forty years, the Seven Sisters have largely failed to blossom.[80] While there are political reasons that decline has persisted, there is also more to the story of Mainline decline than can be contained in just a discussion of the separation of church and state.

5

In a State of Perpetual Decline

Meridian Street United Methodist Church is the mother church of Methodism in Indianapolis. Founded in 1821, on what would eventually be the site of the statehouse, the congregation has been home to prominent city leaders as well as a vice president of the United States, a U.S. senator, and the governor of the state, not to mention leaders within the denomination. Over the course of its history the congregation has built various church home along Meridian Street, from the famed circle at the heart of Indianapolis to a new location a bit farther north by the dawn of the twentieth century to even farther north as the city's population and limits grew. Although the congregation is part of the Seven Sisters, the ups and downs of its membership and the movement of its church plant since its founding also represent the wider issues facing denominations, both inside and outside of the old Mainline, as the twenty-first century began.[1]

There is more to the decline of the Seven Sisters than the types of theological and political reasons we have already discussed. In many respects, the onset of decline in the 1960s and 1970s was a perfect storm of sorts, with internal and external reasons coupled with a new political environment. But decline was also spurred and perpetuated by the rise of consumerism, the communications revolution, and the challenges of cultural engagement beyond politics. These factors continue to have implications for the Seven Sisters and for the emerging new Mainline of the twenty-first century.

Revisiting Classic Decline

When it comes to the decline of the Seven Sisters, theology and doctrine does matter.[2] If the Episcopal Church is not testimony enough, consider the Methodists. The denomination, which boasts such storied congregations as Meridian Street, had rapid membership gains from their founding until the 1860s, with additional spikes in the 1870s and the 1910s, and were part of the evangelical core of the Mainline. Despite having gone through doctrinal controversies in the late nineteenth and early twentieth centuries, the Methodists retained many members easily described as both conservative and orthodox, and successfully reunited as a single denomination after the Civil War; the church also merged with smaller denominations of Wesleyan heritage. Still, decline appeared on the denominational radar screen in the 1950s, and by the 1970s absolute membership numbers began to drop.[3]

ˋ   Why did this happen? The Methodists, it turns out, followed in the path of the Episcopal Church and other members of the Seven Sisters, such as the UCC, with many members growing complacent, others seeking "respectability" as part of the middle class (and thus less interested in disrupting the status quo),[4] and some open to reshaping their version of the Christian faith for the modern world. In other words, they became victims of the classic decline thesis put forward by Dean Kelley, which, as we saw in the case of the Episcopal Church, argued these very things.[5] And while there have been challenges to Kelley's thesis, most notably with the claim that demographics (i.e., conservatives have more children, rather than liberal theology are really to blame,[6] the fact is that these critiques can be seen as augmenting Kelley's work by considering such factors as consumerism.

Beyond Classic Decline: Consumerism

Consumerism is hardly a foreign concept to Americans. People shop for bargains all the time. But that they also shop for churches is a concept that many have found difficult to accept, perhaps because such an approach makes churches seem like goods or a commodity rather than the source of the Good, and because of fears that accepting consumerism is akin to making the church into a business, just another organization dedicated to the bottom line. Yet, ignoring the reality that since denominational decline set in, there has been a corresponding decline in denominational loyalty. For good or ill, the democratic tendency in American religious history has helped commodify where people worship and gives them a wide variety of options.[7] Since the 1970s, they have been exercising their choice to shop around with great regularity.[8]

Consumerism does not just affect denominations; it really is best seen at the local level. After all, a person might decide to leave church A for church B, but that person makes that choice, in part, based on specific congregational options that are available to him or her. It is a decision that might very well be reached on the basis of factors beyond the doctrinal ones showcased in Kelley's classic thesis. As it turns out, people leave or join churches for a variety of reasons, ranging from if it has a good youth group or a great choir to who the pastors are, the type of worship service (traditional vs. contemporary), whether it has a center aisle for use in a wedding, or an adequate kitchen for potluck dinners. All of these local factors have contributed to decline by helping shape the choice to leave or join a congregation.[9] Congregations work very hard, and spend a good deal of money, attempting to attract and retain members based on perceived trends both locally and nationally that have little to do with doctrine.

The Local Condition

The real consumer choice in America is picking from similar, not different, products. If people grow dissatisfied at one church, they will look for another that meets their needs. But they will often look for something similar to the one they are leaving, possibly even within the same denomination. The local congregation is what matters with this choice, because people worship close to where they live. And at this level, the Seven Sisters have more often than not lost out.

Where the "local" is matters to understanding broader decline trends. Urban churches can be massive, historic structures that have little relationship to their surrounding neighborhoods. Suburban churches can often be cut off from what is going on in their larger, local community. And rural churches can be as small and as isolated as any church located in the heart of a city. Likewise, congregations in all three areas can be places where people flock on Sunday.[10] All of these locations can impact the size of and desirability of joining among potential members. What matters is that by and large people have been opting not to join congregations affiliated with the Seven Sisters.[11]

Part of that consumer choice is driven by mobility. Once, the concept of neighborhood churches and parish boundaries meant something more than arbitrary lines on a map. Churches were made up of people who helped build a specific congregation; they lived nearby and their social intercourse was in the various church-group offerings. And then came cars, suburbs, and roads. People no longer had to live near where they worshiped (or worked or shopped for that matter). It was a radical change. Some churches moved with their congregations, even if they never recaptured all the old intimacy. But more importantly, many churches—with the blessings of their denominations—proved reluctant to build new neighborhood congregations. Since most people were members of the Seven Sisters before 1950, and the decline set in during the 1960s, it is likely that these factors were influenced by sub-urbanization. As many Mainline denominations failed to move, their place in suburbia was taken by other denominations and churches. People now had choices. Neither Protestants nor Catholics were truly ready for this event.[12]

With this change, classic decline set in. Many of the new suburban congregations were theologically conservative and tended to be closer knit than liberal ones. As numerous studies have noted, the Seven Sisters make fewer demands and have no "obvious recruitment mechanism," and have long been losing ground to those congregations that do.[13] People did not leave en mass, but rather trickled out, becoming an exodus over time. And they have ended up going to evangelical or nondenominational congregations located closer to their new homes.[14]

The important point for understanding decline is that those who found a spiritual home in the new conservative churches often did not start out there. Perhaps the largest factor in church membership is what a person knows or where they grow up attending. Terms such as "cradle Catholic"[15] and "cradle Presbyterian" are often used by commentators, as if people are predestined from birth to one branch of the Christian faith. Furthermore, terms such as "lapse" and "lax" are also used to describe members in part because both congregations and denominations are loath to lose members simply because of sparse attendance by individuals.[16] While this terminology further reinforces the skepticism that many have toward the reported membership numbers, it also highlights the importance denominations put on those numbers because, after all, that is what helps determine denominational status and even membership in the Mainline.

As we have seen, the strategy that most congregations of the Seven Sisters adopted in the late nineteenth and early twentieth century was to *raise* Christians rather than seek converts.[17] This was an important departure from their historic roots for many denominations. Once, such as during the Second Great Awakening, evangelicals like Charles Finney saw revivals as the normal way for the Protestant faith to function. After the Civil War, though, leading theologians, such as Horace Bushnell (a Congregationalist who rejected the basic tenants of Calvinism), began to argue that Christians could be nurtured or raised, and that there was no need to "save" people via dramatic conversion experiences. This thinking within evangelical denominations corresponded to a wider cultural trend to tone down popular religion. In later years, revivals became scheduled events, not spontaneous occurrences, and often tended to slowly fade from church calendars altogether.[18] Church membership became more about birth than rebirth, and revivalists such as Billy Sunday (the famed early twentieth-century revivalist and dry advocate) or later Billy Graham were often condemned by ministers of the Seven Sisters.

However, the shift from conversion to youthful confirmation did not pay the dividends that those advocates such as Bushnell had hoped in the long term. While it brought stability and respectability, it came at the cost of zeal and led to complacency. It helped hasten the rise of denominational bureaucracies that were more interested in maintaining the status quo than they were spreading the Good News. In short, it set the stage for Mainline decline.

Decline and the Dilemma of Denominationalism

If local conditions and consumerism played important roles in the decline of the Seven Sisters, what role has denominationalism itself played in the fate of the old Mainline? We have already discussed the importance of decisions made by denominational leaders, and the impact and divergence upon and among many of the laity at the local level. But there is more to denominations and decline than just that; denominations themselves, as organizations, contributed to decline.

In that sense, decline and denominationalism has little to do with the formation of new denominations. For even with the decline of the Seven Sisters, no new *major* denominations have been produced since the 1970s. Perhaps the reason is that it is very easy to start a congregation, of any stripe, in America. The tradition of religious freedom and pluralism make it so. One need only look at the history of Anglicanism in the United States to witness this dynamic in play. Here is a denomination that survived the Revolution, yet is consistently wracked by schism and defection. Yet none of the Anglican breakaways has surpassed the Episcopal Church, even though rumblings within it continue. For another example, take the United Methodist Church, which claimed to have grown by a million members in 2006. The problem is that this is a global figure, with the increase coming chiefly from the more theologically conservative Global South, and it is these international gains that offset the general trend of denominational decline in the United States. Rather than bucking the trend, the Methodist case tends to reinforce the notion of Mainline decline and shows how it corresponds to what some have called denominational "restructuring."[19]

Of course, denominations in general come with their own sets of baggage. Institutional bureaucracies of denominations can become unrepresentative of their membership and yet be made up of congregations that are very responsive and reflective of that very membership. Denominations that are in decline, and perhaps even those that are not, tend to have bureaucracies more interested in institutional survival than they are in concepts like doctrine. Still, even in-touch bureaucracies face weakening denominational authority and loyalty because members have found other ways to stay in touch with one another outside of the institution and congregation, chiefly through the Internet and email. Thus, it is not just the Seven Sisters who have cause to be worried about denominational decline; any denomination can fall victim to it.[20]

All denominations (on some level) have cause to be concerned with the rise of nondenominational churches. After all, if congregations can thrive without a denominational hierarchy, they can cause those who remain in those churches to begin to question the effectiveness of such institutional structures. While there had been a long history of "community churches" or "union chapels," which were often denominationally neutral, the rise of true nondenominationalism can be best seen as starting in the 1970s at about the same time as Mainline decline, with the emergence of the "Jesus Movement" and the associated creation of Calvary Chapel and the Vineyard churches associations. The birth of these bodies of believers was a direct critique of the Seven Sisters on both a theological and an organizational level.[21]

Hence, the rise of nondenominationalism, both as a concept and as a label, is significant. Because nondenominational congregations have been very good at attracting younger members, there is concern that the decline of the Seven Sisters is only the end of the beginning, not the beginning of the end of decline. Some Christians have made a conscious decision not to affiliate with churches that are part of a denomination, and some even avoid using words like "church" because of the cultural baggage many associate with it, including being under a denominational hierarchy as well as notions of formality and "stuffiness." Calling yourself a "fellowship" or a "mission" is a way to harken back to the days of the early Christians; it can also imply that the modern church (with its bureaucracies) is too little focused on Christ, almost akin to what Martin Luther was arguing during the Reformation.[22]

This is not to say that becoming or starting a nondenominational congregation is a guarantee either of a large or even youthful membership. In the hills outside of Irvine, Kentucky, for example, there is nestled the small Sand Hill Christian Church. The congregation describes itself in the following way: "Sand Hill Christian Church is a local church without any ecclesiastical ties or denominational headquarters. We remain simply an undenominational, nonsectarian body of believers in the Lord Jesus Christ."[23] It is solidly evangelical, though even its membership is graying, just like many Seven Sisters congregations.

And yet, nondenominational congregations seem to be here to stay, which perhaps helps to explain why, despite the decline of the Seven Sisters, no new denominations have been formed in recent decades. Many Christians simply were tired of denominational hierarchies. Nondenominational congregations gave safe haven to people leaving the Mainline, contributing to the creation of the Religious Right. Those nondenominational congregations thrived, in large part because of such figures as Billy Graham who helped forge new parachurch organizations, which in turn helped them be active beyond their congregational walls. As a result, they have made a denominational revival, especially by the Seven Sisters, less and less likely. American Christians, as consumers, have seemingly made their choice.[24]

Beyond Classic Decline
Communications Revolution and Virtual Congregations

While continued decline has both local and denominational rationale, there is more to it than just consumerism. It may be a stretch to say that portions of the Bible, such as St. Paul's letters or the later writings of the church fathers, crafted an early form of the print culture and thus communications media; however this phenomenon has long played an important role in helping spread and foster Christian identity. Understanding this helps explain modern denominational decline and offers additional insight to how decline happened and why it continues.

For Christians, the printed word was the first way the faith fostered community in a larger sense than the local. More recently, one need only look at its role in helping spread the Protestant Reformation and, to a degree, the Catholic Counter-Reformation in the 1500s. Print culture helped Christians find out what was going on in other parts of Christendom and to feel part of one another in the ups and downs of living in a turbulent time. It even aided, as newspapers became increasingly common, to create minor (and sometimes major) celebrities out of ministers who got their sermons published or syndicated. In the nineteenth century men such as Henry Ward Beecher and Thomas DeWitt Talmadge (a staunch evangelical and evangelist who was the pastor of Central Presbyterian Church's Brooklyn Tabernacle) are just two such examples. Print culture helped (and still helps) to foster an imagined community of believers in a very real sense. And this spirit is still seen within Christian literature today, proving to be a rather neutral playing field when it comes to decline.[25]

While Christians in America have long stressed the power of communication in the form of print,[26] the telecommunications revolution of the twentieth century proved largely detrimental to the Seven Sisters. It began with radio in the 1920s and 1930s: because radio stations for many years were required by law to provide community programming, they turned to Mainline churches to fill such time slots. But they were also willing to allow other denominations and congregations to buy airtime as well. Safe in their position, the Mainline tended to take the free slots to broadcast their services, despite the fact that the paid slots tended to be at better hours and ended up attracting larger audiences. By the time the Mainline in the form of the FCC realized what was happening, it was too late. The fundamentalist groups only grew once stations were allowed to count paid air time as public service time, further squeezing the Seven Sisters. Three of the top religious radio personalities of the period were Aimee Semple McPherson and Charles E. Fuller (both fundamentalists) and Father Charles Coughlin (a Roman Catholic). More radio ministries quickly developed, along with the growth of radio sales, also largely outside of the Mainline. Some churches launched their own stations, and in the case of the Moody Bible Institute (Dwight Moody's church and college in Chicago), their own national radio network.[27]

Radio broadcasts begat the first "virtual" congregations to Americans. Christian radio soon transcended merely (re)broadcasting sermons, becoming a ministry in and of itself. Radio allowed not only for ministerial outreach but also for an outlet for a "Christian perspective" on the news of the day and for music. As such, it was by radio that Christians, most often conservatives and fundamentalists, began crafting a Christian subculture in the United States. Because of this parallel Christian "pop" culture, it became easy for even "separatist" fundamentalists to be safely in the world without being of the world. Even as new mediums, such as television and the Internet, were developed, radio continued and continues even today in this function for many American Christians.[28]

Television soon followed both radio's wake and its pattern when it came to religious broadcasting. In many ways though, television became even more dominated by evangelical and eventually Pentecostal voices than did radio. Indeed, the rise of televangelism and of this being perceived as both a ministry and as an arm of churches was something few Mainline denominations or congregations embraced.[29] Their lack of participation opened the door for other Christian groups. Television is often credited with making Roman Catholicism more acceptable to Protestant Americans. And for that, Christians in America have Bishop Fulton Sheen and his television show to thank.

Sheen, who had hosted the popular *The Catholic Hour* radio program in the 1930s and '40s, made the switch to television in 1951, pioneering a nonsectarian style that helped pave the way for religious programming at times other than Sunday morning. His two shows, *Life is Worth Living* and *The Fulton Sheen Program*, ran throughout the 1950s and '60s, commanded an audience at their peak of 30 million viewers, and netted Sheen an Emmy.[30]

With television, viewers (or "partners") could not only hear a service but also see one, making them feel even more a part of the life of a church or congregation than radio's virtual congregationalism did. By the 1970s and '80s, just as it became obvious that the Seven Sisters were in decline, religious broadcasting stations began appearing both locally and nationally. Soon broadcasting increased across the Christian and religious spectrum with the advent of cable television, and Mainline ministers and ministries continued to fill timeslots in both the early hours and on Sunday mornings of regular broadcast stations. Then, suddenly, evangelical and Pentecostal ministers like Jim Bakker, Jimmy Swaggart, Oral Roberts, Jerry Falwell, Pat Robertson, D. James Kennedy, and Robert Schuller became household names, due to their larger budgets, flashier sermons and popular gospel music, and "folksy" demeanor of the preachers. The end result was the further marginalization of the Seven Sisters; televangelism was proven to be effective in reaching people, and there was a decided lack of the old Mainline in prominent markets and timeslots.[31]

Even the above list shows the potential religious diversity television brought to Americans. Bakker was an Assemblies of God minister who created (and lost) a televangelism empire. Swaggart is a minister of a Full Gospel congregation in Louisiana, one that he turned into a televangelism mainstay. Roberts, a Pentecostal evangelist, Falwell, a Southern Baptist, and Robertson, a Southern Baptist charismatic, created televangelism empires and founded colleges. Kennedy, a conservative Presbyterian, and Schuller, of the Reformed Church in America, both created megachurches (large congregations, often with thousands of members who continually strive for more members) geared around television ministries. Television also opened doors and promoted the pastoral careers of a growing number of African American ministers such as Creflo Dollar and T. D. Jakes, making them household names across the nation.[32]

As important as television was in the last half of the twentieth century, its impact pales in comparison to the power of spreading a message over the Internet or creating virtual congregations. Today a person can read, listen, and watch sermons anytime and anywhere. Thanks to email, churches and congregants can be in touch almost instantaneously. And unlike both radio and television, it is also easier for denominations, including the Seven Sisters, to have a greater presence on the Internet. It is more economical and practical for a local Methodist Church, for example, to have a website than it is for them to broadcast their sermons via radio or television every week. However, because nearly everyone can utilize the Internet, its effectiveness as a medium at either stemming or containing decline is rather diluted.

Indeed, while the Internet is much more of a level playing field, it is also the most specific form of virtual congregationalism. Someone channel surfing on radio or television probably is more apt to try something new or listen to a different perspective longer than those surfing the web. Virtual congregationalism in terms of membership is probably lowest in virtual reality. It is all too easy to click on another church's website and search for something else, and never visit the same website again. A person is more apt to listen or watch someone of a different denomination on radio or television, and come back again, than they are on line.

Still, the Internet does promote virtual congregations in multiple ways. As a means to inform members of goings on, the Anglican Communion provides a good example of this phenomenon. The Internet is a way for the laity in large and small geographic dioceses to feel a part of what is going on. For this purpose, WebPages are indispensable for diocesan work in the twenty-first century.[33] As the Anglican bishop Michael Hare Duke said of the Internet:

> [It] keeps open lines of communication so that we are aware of what the grass roots are thinking as well as the official pronouncements of the Church. It is a great way to stop fresh ideas becoming the prerogative of those who can afford to get into print at an official level. This is the engine of the revolution, even though there is an awful lot of chaff to sift from the wheat![34]

The Internet has affected the way people around the globe view the Anglican Communion. The discourse that takes place within the Communion's parts and within its constituent members is now a matter of public consumption, promoting an open (if at times painful) discussion of both day-to-day operations and larger theological debates. For dioceses, the Internet is a great benefit because it facilitates more interaction between members. This is true of dioceses that cover diverse geographic areas, such as in Europe, as well as within "monster" single dioceses in places like Texas. It speeds communication between those dioceses separated by miles of land and sea.[35]

Because the Internet brings people, dioceses, and provinces together, it has affected the ways Anglicans and Episcopalians view the Anglican Communion. The Internet allows people who might not otherwise meet to get to know one another; it helps to "form community" by giving people an opportunity to talk and discuss issues, and to help in times of need.[36] As the theological rift in the Episcopal Church has expanded to the Anglican Communion, some members have come to see the Internet as a means by which the Communion can be brought closer together, while others view it as a means by which it is being torn farther apart and polarized. The issues surrounding polarization are not new; the Internet is just the latest (and fastest) means to facilitate their discussion. As Bishop James Tengatenga has noted, "[the Internet] certainly has increased communication and as such has brought it [the Communion] closer. This does not mean closeness in thought or agreement but simply proximity and access. I do not think that it has polarized it but only brought into the public the polarities."[37]

In the twenty-first century these two trends, using technology to spread the Good News and to promote a counter or critique to prevailing cultural trends, can be seen in a wide variety of mediums beyond radio and television. This includes the Internet, movies coming out of Hollywood,[38] and in both fiction and nonfiction books.[39] Technology remains a tool in whatever form it takes for both those inside and outside the Mainline.

These tools of virtual congregationalism raise the important question of whether they can replace actual interaction among the faithful, and to what degree this development of virtual congregations has contributed to denominational decline. Do "members" feel "allegiance" only to that "virtual" church or not? In other words, is watching a televangelist the only "church" they have or is it a safety net, a backup, another service they "attend" on a regular basis? Is viewing a service or sermon on a website a form of entertainment, something that is very different, perhaps even amusing, from their normal church? Is their viewing of a virtual service background noise as they complete other tasks, or do they actively partake, Bibles in hand? Perhaps most importantly, do people vary whom they listen, watch, or view online? Do they stick to virtual congregations of the same denomination they are a part of or do they try something else? All these are important questions awaiting further study, but they are also questions that show how subversive virtual congregations can be to denominations.

Indeed, this latter point is the most important when contemplating the topic of American Mainline Christianity. In some respects, asking the above questions is the important thing, because answering them would be nearly impossible on a definitive scale and would vary with each individual believer involved. One can, however, make some headway simply by looking at the marketplace. In other words, if it is impossible to get at the *who* in any real way, it is much easier to discuss *what* they want, and go from there.

What American Christian consumers encounter most often and are thus most likely to choose in virtual congregations (whether in print, radio, or television) are evangelical and conservative theological Christian writers, broadcasters, and bloggers as the prime forces and influences. This means that evangelical and conservative messages, though hardly monolithic, are pervasive. While others might utilize virtual congregational methods, the main message that most people absorb is apt *not* to be from the liberal wing of the Seven Sisters.

Cultural Engagement

Although American Christians have exercised their consumer choice increasingly since the onset of decline, there are other cultural forces at work that have kept the Seven Sisters from maintaining their status as the Mainline. One of the factors at play is the way denominations and their institutions do or do not engage wider culture. Rather than a fundamentalist retreat or isolation from the mainstream, what is at stake instead is how religious Americans interact with the wider trends of secularization.

By and large, Americans have struck a balance in their culture between the sacred and the secular. Even though American culture, historically and constitutionally, is not "Christian" in nature, Christians deserve credit for helping to shape the national culture and what it means to be an American. What many Christians fear is being shut out by forces beyond their control, from continuing that tradition of influence. Their enemy is commonly referred to as "secularization," though how secularization impacts culture and indeed how Christianity engages culture also affects decline.

Historically, Christianity has been a notable cultural force in American history. The Great Awakenings, Progressive-era reforms, and the civil rights movement all provide examples of the interaction between Christianity and American social movements. At times this engagement has exhibited more intellectual force than at others, but always the church has played some role (and sometimes several) in the cultural discourse.[40] And while most Americans accept, to borrow Thomas Jefferson's phrase, a "wall of separation," the question that looms over that wall, when it comes to denominational decline, is what happens as areas once considered to be part of the sacred become increasingly secularized.

The process of something cultural either being or becoming secular is not new. Over the course of history, religion has always adapted to new cultural trends and developments. Secularization has spawned revivals within existing religious traditions as well as having prompted the creation of new ones. In that regard, it has been a catalyst for many of the events that have helped craft the Mainline. Religion is both more resilient and more dynamic than it is often credited with being in the face of secularization.[41] Thus, secularism is not, in and of itself, a bad thing. It is simply something not directly a part of religious life, and even then, it need not rule out Christian involvement. That being said, secularists can pose a problem for religion when they seek to preclude people of faith, as people of faith, from being involved in culture. Because many in the modernist camp have also been allies with secularists, the battles between modernists and fundamentalists have often affected the wider culture even as they have attempted to chart a course for the denominations in question.[42]

While fundamentalist and conservative Christians have long bemoaned the rise of secularism, there is good reason to question how much power secularism actually has in America. Considering the number of people who claim to believe in God, secular humanism, the most antireligious form of secularism, is probably less potent than either its supporters or detractors assume. Indeed, a resurgent Deism and even religious apathy are perhaps more influential.[43] At the same time, many Christians believe there are legitimate concerns about the possibility of secular humanism taking hold of the state's apparatus and beginning to push for a secular dogma via the power of the government. They fear that this could happen if secular humanists were abetted by liberal theology that disregards the tenets of orthodox Christianity and accepts the notion of cultural relativism. The theologian Bernard Meland argued in *The Secularization of Modern Cultures* that this kind of "rabid" secularization can destroy the moral base of society[44] and undermine Western Civilization.[45]

Where do American denominations, and their real and potential decline, fit in all this? Can evangelicals and fundamentalists realistically argue that secularism and modernism are major elements of the decline of the Seven Sisters, or is it only a "boogey man"—there more for the sake of argument than anything else? When modernists and their allies assert that secularization is a force happening outside of the church and is something that denominations must adjust to, are they being accurate or are they being naïve to secularism's real and potential consequences?[46] In some respects this debate is simply a new way to frame the old discussion of theological engagement that first emerged around Darwinian evolution, and eventually became a part of the decline of the Seven Sisters. And, as such, it is merely updating the terminology of the old debate.

However, the extent to which secularism affects the Mainline is another matter. While the Seven Sisters declined, in part as a result of such forces, secularizing trends within wider American culture did not harm American religious life in general. American Christianity has long been "characterized by a Protestant Christian consensus that is not defined in denominational terms."[47] While denominations may rise and decline, the faith remains. As a result, the Mainline as a concept is still very much alive even as the Seven Sisters weaken.

That being said, each denomination has had its own history of engaging wider American culture and dealing with the fallout of secularization. Perhaps nowhere are these dilemmas, debates, and tensions surrounding cultural engagement seen more clearly than in the topics of education and politics. In both areas, culture is important, and in these areas sacred and secular have a long and shared history in the United States. In considering anew the topic of education, a pattern of cultural disengagement emerges in the case of the Seven Sisters that has played into their decline, much like we saw earlier with politics.

In America, Christianity (along with other faiths such as Judaism) has a long history in promoting education. This educational focus came about, in part, because of a Protestant emphasis on believers being able to read the Bible and local (and to some degree state) governments allowing churches take the lead, most probably in order to keep taxes low. Indeed, churches often served as the first schoolhouses, via Sunday schools, in new communities; denominations founded colleges and universities to carry that faith into wider society as well as to train the next generation of ministers of the Gospel. By the dawn of the twentieth century, the Mainline was so entrenched within education that it became complacent, at least until the emergence of legal cases like *Schempp*.[48]

So pervasive was Protestantism in the realm of education that it caused Catholic immigrants to seek schools of their own in order to teach their children not just their version of the faith, but also reading, writing, and arithmetic. Perhaps the best example of anti-Protestantism that sprang from the immigrant ghetto in the late nineteenth and early twentieth centuries came in the area of education. As one Catholic paper noted, "Catholics do not want the public schools abolished or abandoned. They serve a most useful purpose for those who do not put religion before material things—the agnostic, the atheist, the socialist." Catholics were also opposed to Bible reading in public schools because "every one of the English Protestant versions [of the Bible] has been proven to be downright perversions of God's word," drafted as they were by "apostate priests."[49] While much has changed since then, the desire of American Christians to have their faith (often quite specifically) be a part of education remains quite strong, as witnessed by the growth of the home school movement.[50]

Interestingly, that desire contributed to the secularization component of decline. As Roman Catholics in the early twentieth century won legal cases over schools and school funding, some Protestants formed organizations to keep "papist" religion away from their children in the classroom. One such group, Protestants and Other Americans United for the Separation of Church and State, we have already encountered as Americans United for the Separation of Church and State.[51] Within a few decades AU would help push religion, in the form of Bible reading and prayers, largely out of the public schools altogether.

While in some Roman Catholic circles it is common to explain the formation of groups like AU as little more than a new vestige of Protestant anti-Catholicism, it is more of an emblem of secularization's contribution to the decline of the Seven Sisters. By saying that there was no longer room for *any* religion in education as a means to block Catholic influence and by aligning themselves with more secular groups, the Protestants who supported such endeavors were willing to halt cultural engagement in the area of education. With less reinforcement of religious, specifically Christian, ideas and a corresponding change in Sunday school curricula, which began to downplay theology and doctrine in favor of more "relevant" topics (including in the 1960s an emphasis on folk music and art), there was a decline in Protestant biblical knowledge and a general loosening of denominational allegiance.[52]

This cultural retreat in the realm of education by the Seven Sisters is clearly seen in higher education. Colleges and universities that were founded under the auspices of the Seven Sisters began, by the mid-twentieth century to either de-emphasize their religious past, spin off or generalize their seminaries, or to openly promote secularism. Harvard is a perfect example. Founded in 1636 to train Congregational clergy, its current website states that, while it was heavily influenced by the Puritans, it was never officially a Congregational school. Such modern claims might surprise Harvard's founders and even some historians. Its origins did not stop it from becoming a hotbed of Unitarianism, and thus a place of heated religious debate in the nineteenth century.[53] Princeton's Presbyterian heritage and Yale's Congregational roots are similarly downplayed.[54] When the College of William and Mary removed the cross from its chapel in 2007, intense controversy erupted. The college's president argued that the cross might offend non-Christians but could be put up for specific Christian worship services. Detractors pointed out both the history of the Wren Chapel building as well as the interesting intellectual leap to de-Christianize the chapel in case someone might be offended. A compromise was reached wherein the historic cross has been placed in a glass case toward the front of the chapel and could be placed on the altar on Sundays and during Christian worship services.[55]

Examples can easily be cited of Baptist, Lutheran, Methodist, or Disciples of Christ schools and colleges that have "loosened" their denominational ties, if not rejected them altogether.[56] But other denominations and their colleges have not had such a falling out: the Southern Baptists offer one such example. Baylor University in Texas was chartered in 1845 and continues to embrace its faith roots. Affiliated with the Baptist General Convention of Texas, it is the oldest continually operating institution of higher education in the state and the largest Baptist school in the world, even if the religious ties sometimes raise issues about its academic mission, and vice versa. It seems that the trend among schools with religious affiliation is that once they begin to lessen their ties to denominations, the more secular they become.[57]

Another excellent example of a school fighting to retain its religious identity is the University of Notre Dame. The Reverend John I. Jenkins, the current president of the university, believes that there is a difference between academic freedom and what a university, in his case a Catholic university, should officially sponsor. Jenkins confronted this issue shortly after ascending to his post over the question of whether Notre Dame should be affiliated with a "Queer Film Festival," a performance of *The Vagina Monologues* on campus, and a call for students to present papers on "sexual experience, abortion, contraception, theology of the body, and a number of other issues" in a potentially morally neutral way, under the title "Her Loyal Daughters" with the "her" being "Mary, the mother of Jesus, the patroness of the university." As Jenkins told the university faculty, "many people feel passionately about the issues under consideration," and he hoped the discussion would remain respectful of positions other than their own, keeping away from "polarizing and unyielding polemics" but that all should keep in mind "the distinctive character of this Catholic university," which meant there were some lines he would not allow to be crossed.[58]

Jenkins believes "the world needs a university that draws upon an ancient moral and spiritual tradition to address moral questions."[59] This commitment made the uproar over the 2009 commencement address all the more interesting. The university ignited a firestorm after inviting President Barack Obama to be its speaker. While there is nothing out of the ordinary in such an invitation, the president's stance on abortion was a lightening rod of controversy within a university and denomination that prides itself on its pro-life position. Boycotts were launched and several bishops refused to come to the ceremony. The struggle for what it means to be a Catholic university in the twenty-first century still remains to be discovered.[60]

The Roman Catholic nature of Notre Dame was something that Jenkins's predecessor in office, the Revered Edward A. "Monk" Malloy, was also concerned with; indeed, Malloy said that preserving the university's "Catholic mission and identity" was "first and foremost" on his agenda when he became president. "If I failed in that and succeeded in all the rest, I would not feel I had done a good job" he told the *Notre Dame Magazine* shortly before leaving office.[61]

Thus, while not every college and university has turned from its religious heritage, there are other factors at play beyond religious fervor on campus when it comes to a school's place in wider American society. For example, students pick Harvard not for its roots but for its status and academic excellence. And yet many students (and their parents) choose schools that are overtly religious in nature. Indeed, conservatives and fundamentalists founded their own colleges in the wake of the modernist takeover of denominations and of school administrations. Today there are more than one hundred evangelical colleges, such as Wheaton College, Bob Jones University, or Patrick Henry College, that require evangelical faculty but whose enrollment numbers are also growing by leaps and bounds.[62]

Of course, none of this is really new. Americans have been debating religion and education since at least the Scopes trial in the 1920s. What has changed has been the reintroduction, the re-engagement, of fundamentalist/evangelical intellectuals in the wider American culture in the wake of World War II, and the emphasis their arguments have placed on a continued Christian presence in public debates. This agenda contrasts with that of the Seven Sisters, and it should not come as a surprise. Calvinism, as the historian George Marsden has noted, was a vibrant intellectual movement that drove American Protestant thought, via the Presbyterian and Congregationalist denominations, during most of the nineteenth century.[63] The Dixon *Fundamentals* were designed as a defense of the faith, and were a major intellectual and theological undertaking. Many evangelicals wondered where their next Jonathan Edwards was, as opposed to Billy Sunday, even as they blasted theoretical trends that made them seem anti-intellectual.[64]

For this intellectual tradition to reassert itself, then, provides a clear distinction to the often watered-down theology offered by many in the Seven Sisters. However, most evangelical Christians and even most Protestants are not as intellectually engaged as these few well-known examples might suggest. As the historian Mark Noll pointed out in *The Scandal of the Evangelical Mind*, there has been a tendency among evangelicals and fundamentalists to focus on elements of the faith such as the end-times, rather than on theology or doctrine. This focus has produced a prophecy-interpretation cottage industry, with sales of books on the topic spiking every time there is a crisis in the Middle East, despite biblical reminders that no one knows the date of the end-time and attempts to predict it is both unfulfilling and a potential diversion of a Christian's appropriate tasks.[65] And yet, even if they are at times engaged in pursuits other than those Noll finds intellectually fulfilling, evangelicals and fundamentalists also tend to dominate Christian fiction and nonfiction literature, debating the morality of government policies (both foreign and domestic) and raising cultural questions (including the role of Darwinian evolution in America's schools), which foster debate and discussion.[66] The denominations of the old Mainline are more often than not silent, meaning that once again, the conservative wing of American Christianity pervades the debate over culture and faith.[67]

Culturally, since the end of World War II, the Seven Sisters have slowly declined and disengaged from wider American life, as we have seen. At the same time, a resurgent evangelicalism and fundamentalism has offered a critique of the culture to which the Sisters were acquiescing. Thanks to the reinvigorated (broad) evangelical movement following World War II, the battle between modernists and fundamentalists was renewed. Part of this resurgence had to do with the migration of southerners to other parts of the nation. Conservative evangelicals also began to address their lack of unity. Pentecostals and fundamentalists worked to find more common ground by focusing on their mutual dislike of modernists within the Seven Sisters and made more of an effort at allying themselves with evangelicals who remained in the old Mainline. As a result, these groups and churches overcame separatist tendencies and divisions within themselves and found new allies.

One example of this new focus on cooperation involved the historic Park Street Church in Boston. This bastion of Calvinistic Congregationalism had stood against Unitarianism and continued to fight against modernism, even as its denomination increasingly embraced it. After World War II, the congregation was headed by the Reverend Harold Ockenga. He was born into a Methodist family and schooled by conservative Presbyterians, who helped him secure one of the premier Congregational pulpits in the nation. Ockenga helped lead the National Association of Evangelicals (NAE) and was an early supporter of Billy Graham. Along with J. Elwin Wright (a leader of New England's evangelicals), he also helped found Fuller Theological Seminary in California in 1947 as a means to promote and protect conservative evangelical theology by raising up a new generation of pastors to combat the modernists, and what he viewed to be their increasingly secular agenda. In many respects, Ockenga and his fellow conservatives set the stage for seizing the initiative when it came to cultural engagement by American Christians, as many in the Seven Sisters came to pull away from such a role by the 1960s.[68]

Neither Graham—who first reached national prominence in 1949 following a crusade in Los Angeles at which his ability to connect to audiences was noted in the press[69]—nor Ockenga could provide the leadership needed to win the old battle with modernists, and the conservative-evangelical wing remained splintered. The NAE refused to attack the Federal Council of Churches, despite a growing perception that that organization was increasingly liberal. The NAE also welcomed both Holiness (an offshoot of the wider Wesleyan/Methodist movement) and Pentecostal denominations into membership. The smaller and less influential American Council of Christian Churches (ACCC), founded by the arch-fundamentalist Presbyterian Carl McIntyre, wanted to attack the FCC and distance itself from Pentecostals. Even so, these groups challenged the council's claim to speak for *all* of America's Protestants. Together, they helped convince the more separatist-minded fundamentalists that they could not truly follow God's call if they preached only to themselves and lived in isolation. Rather, the NAE and ACCC helped these fundamentalists embrace the notion that their message should compete as part of modern society, both at home and abroad.[70] As a result, this broad conservative movement eventually found staunch allies among Christians in the Global South.[71] And the modern evangelical movement, one of cultural engagement, was born.

The battle between modernists and fundamentalists is far from over and increasingly focuses on the secularization of culture. While modernists were able to take and keep control of denominational hierarchies within the Seven Sisters by stopping engagement with the fundamentalists, and then increasingly with the moderates, they became less in touch with wider Christian America. Thus, even as their denominational power grew, the old Mainline was becoming less and less mainstream as the second half of the twentieth century wore on.

This bubble mentality, which as the twenty-first century dawned was nearing a bunker mentality in some denominations, contributed to the

Seven Sisters' decline by harnessing Christian modernists to secularism. The modernists embraced the ideas that they were the final arbiters of progress and that religion's role must by attrition diminish in the modern world. An intellectual self-assurance crept in that soon self-justified their conclusions as the only ones that seemed reasonable to them to be reached.[72] Many evangelicals and fundamentalists largely disagreed.

As a result, the democratic spirit of American Christianity exacerbated the Sisters' decline. Christians of both camps easily moved into more accommodating congregations and denominations, where like-minded laity and clergy nourished their thinking one way or another. New parachurch organizations and technology helped foster this trend as well, by helping to connect those believers and congregations together outside denominational constraints; this shift outside of the church proper also contributed to the broader denominational decline. Hence, the two camps had even less cause or need to engage one another. Fundamentalism may have sparked anti-intellectualism among some evangelical Protestants, but the confrontation within American Protestantism over the forces of modernism did something else as well: it produced intellectual snobbery among many in the Seven Sisters.

Thus, as the United States has become a more secular society, Christians and their fellow citizens have had a more difficult time determining when something is a moral imperative, and thus in need of "reform" in the classic evangelical sense, and when something is simply a political issue with no clear moral or religious implications. The polarization that can occur within denominations and congregations when such issues come to the fore is considerable and often breaks along political lines as much as theological ones. And yet, Christians both within and outside of the Seven Sisters are engaging with cultural issues. Cultural engagement carries within it an innate a risk, but *not* being engaged, regardless of which side a church takes on an issue, is also no longer a luxury that can be afforded.[73] The question for the Seven Sisters is twofold: Are they on the loosing side of such engagement, and is finally being engaged again now to little and to late for them?

In the end, the problems facing the Seven Sisters has been more multifaceted than classic decline theory first seems to indicate. The consideration of such factors as consumerism, new forms of communication, and cultural engagement showcases not only how classic decline's features were exacerbated by other factors but also why it has been virtually impossible for the Seven Sisters to recover as the Mainline. With increasing rumblings from the Global South, the Sisters' fall from grace may remain permanent.

6

Unto the Ends of the Earth

*Global Christianity and
Mainline Decline*

The historic squares in Savannah, Georgia, are full of churches. Visitors to Johnson Square are soon drawn to the classic columns of Christ Church. The plaques in front of the building inform readers that this is the mother church of Anglicanism in Georgia and that the congregation was served by both John and Charles Wesley as well as by George Whitefield. Visitors who venture inside will also quickly discover that the congregation is fighting to disassociate itself from the Episcopal Church, and now believes itself apart of an international Anglican renewal movement, steeped in evangelical terms, and led by bishops from Uganda and Nigeria.[1]

Far from Georgia, American missionaries are still spreading the Gospel. In places like Albania and Egypt, Christians from the United States are telling people (sometimes in spite of open hostility) about Jesus, using their own personal witness of their relationship with Christ alongside the Bible and films. They are also engaged in building churches, schools, recreational facilities, and helping with medicine and agriculture.[2] The common denominator between Anglicans in Georgia and evangelicals spreading the Gospel in Albania is that while both are part of the modern realities of Christian missionary activity, neither is operating under the auspices of the Mainline.

As the leading denominations in American Christianity, the Seven Sisters have been at the forefront of fulfilling Christ's Great Commission, to carry the Gospel to all people. As America's power and place in the world grew, the missionary impulse spread to every corner of the globe. By the twenty-first century, however, Global Christianity, specifically from the Southern Hemisphere, was preparing to offer a devastating critique of the Mainline, which would contribute to the continued decline of the Seven Sisters.

God and America

American Christianity has always been a part of global Christianity. Indeed, it is important to remember that Christianity is a global faith, and that American Christians have long viewed themselves as part of that faith in both word and deed.[3] When it comes to missionary activity, this history comes readily into view.

During the colonial period, American Christians were themselves missions, arms of European-based churches. Whether in a transplanted sense, such as with the colonists arriving bringing their faith with them (Congregationalists or Episcopalians), or in outright outreach (whether evangelical or Catholic in orientation), the faith was diverse and strongly connected to Europe, so that many were compelled to look back at their co-religionists across the Atlantic for guidance, support, and inspiration. Spreading and propagating the Good News was part of the impetus for colonization, and it drove Spanish, French, and English efforts in the New World.

Still, it was not very long before American Christians were seeking to spread the faith by making converts of their own. Nearly all denominations, and especially those that came to make up the Seven Sisters, were active in seeking to win Native Americans to the cross of Christ.[4] Among the most famous efforts were the "Praying towns" of Puritan era New England where Christian converts to the Congregational faith lived; wherever white Americans went they took with them the notion that Christianity was not just a hallmark of their civilization but that it would be a civilizing force for people many deemed to be "savages." This belief persisted even as the tribes were often decimated, pacified, and placed on reservations.[5]

As they worked with Natives on the frontier, Christian pioneers themselves were part of the wider world of missions. The Second Great Awakening in the early nineteenth century was, in part, about winning the West for Christ. This was, after all, the theme of many of the sermons preached by Lyman Beecher and his sons, and was at the heart of evangelical Protestantism in one of its more dynamic phases.

The domestic missionary impulse extended to African Americans as well. During the Great Awakenings, black slaves were a focus of evangelical efforts at conversion. Following the Civil War, northern white churches (especially those who were about to forge the Mainline of the Seven Sisters) were active in efforts to aid the former slaves. Baptists and Methodists, with their denominational ties to the South, had an advantage in these activities, but the Congregationalists were also noted for their work on the home mission front in the late nineteenth century.[6]

These efforts, while they did not always bridge the color line when it came to worship, did help foster a broader Christian mission within American Christianity in the late nineteenth and early twentieth century. These efforts corresponded to work not only with immigrant groups of the Social Gospel period (including the famed settlement houses such as Hull House) but to efforts to take the Good News to other nations as well. If working with immigrant groups at home might be seen as fostering this sprit on the small scale (along with blending notions of Protestant Christianity's superiority to other faiths, including Roman Catholicism, and as a bedrock of Americanization), then it is little wonder that American missionaries were soon ready to board ships and go off to foreign lands in large numbers.

The American Missionary Impulse

By the late nineteenth century, Americans believed that they had a special calling to carry God's word around the world. This sense of divine purpose only intensified as American prestige grew globally.[7] Indeed, newfound wealth and power implied that it was God's mission for the United States to redeem the world. And so, American Christians set off around the globe, taking with them the message of Christ. There was a feeling that now was the time to win the world for God. Americans believed, thanks in part to the Kingdom of God theology of the Social Gospel that evangelizing the world could be accomplished in "this generation." They expected great things to happen.[8]

American Christians thought that the problems facing people around the world were largely spiritual in nature and that the answer was spreading Christianity. In doing so, they not only took with them their own cultural norms but also encountered new cultures as well. American missionaries also placed a good deal of emphasis on education within their missionary activities, reflecting a Protestant belief that Christians had to be educated. As a result, missionary schools were often superior to government-funded schools and thus became an attraction to native parents who wanted their children to succeed in an imperial setting.[9]

There was a struggle among and within the Sisters over whether , or at least to what degree, missionary activity should be done by voluntary societies or organized by denominations.[10] As a result, in addition to having denominational boards overseeing them, many missionaries were a part of the American Board of Commissioners for Foreign Missions. Founded in 1810, within a century, there were 102 mission stations under its administration, all around the world.[11] Prior to the Civil War, American evangelicals had gone to help former slaves in the British Empire's Caribbean possessions, making these missionaries among the first to work within an imperial structure. By the late nineteenth century, Presbyterians were active in Egypt; Methodists were evangelizing places like China.[12] And there was also intense missionary activity directed at Africa, including by African American Christians.[13] Furthermore, denominations like the Episcopal Church found themselves able to work effectively not just where the United States was heading but also within the British Empire, thanks to their shared Anglican heritage.[14]

There were numerous attractions to entering a foreign missionary field. For most, it was the feeling of fulfilling the Great Commission, despite the potential dangers.[15] But there is another important factor in considering missions, and that is the role that women played. In many respects, they were the backbone of the movement, both at home and abroad. Women were attracted to becoming missionaries as well as to becoming the spouses of missionaries. Husband-wife teams were quite common and often the most effective at reaching new groups for Christ.[16] Not unlike Prohibition, missionary activity was something that virtually everyone within the Seven Sisters agreed upon. And the stability that family life provided often meant longer terms of missionary service by these couples, turning their time in the field into a lifetime of service, and leaving a lifelong mark on children born and raised in the field.

The people going into the mission field were seen as the "young and future leadership" of America's Protestant churches. Spearheaded by the moral example of Dwight Moody, they saw moral reform and revival as the key to spreading the Gospel and creating a "Christian moral empire." Groups like the Student Volunteer Movement for Foreign Missions, the YMCA, and Christian Endeavor soon made the United States the main source of Christian missionaries globally by the dawn of the twentieth century. They influenced America's foreign policy, were cited as experts by presidents and before Congress, and helped create the very idea of humanitarian foreign aid.[17]

The popularity of missions did not spare American Christians from controversy. The Mainline's missionaries were a part of the modernist-fundamentalist theological debates as well.[18] While in theory, American missionaries may have come from the modernist, moderate, or fundamentalist camp, there is little doubt that those who set out on the mission path tended to have "a strong biblical focus," and so, tended to be more conservative in their theology and doctrine.[19] Even though it is difficult to know with certainty, most American missionaries were probably conservative moderates at the very least, with a good number of fundamentalists as well. That fact was to prove increasingly important, especially as questions about missions and the control of denominational mission boards became more contested.

The theological divide was clearly seen in places like China. Here, liberals were shocked to find how successful conservative missionaries were, and had been, since the mid-nineteenth century. Much of this shock had to do with the orthodox doctrine of such groups as China Inland Mission and the fact that it had nurtured more than a generation of native converts before liberal theologians ever arrived on the scene. Their efforts to take charge of missionary activity were actively resisted, even as both sides attempted to not let the debate distract them from missionary work.[20]

The Presbyterian story is equally revealing. In 1933 fundamentalists, less than a decade removed from their failure to take control of the denominational hierarchy and frustrated by modernist domination of the same, created the Independent Board for Presbyterian Foreign Missions. A few months later Charles J. Woodbridge, a young missionary with a Princeton degree and a ministerial pedigree that stretched back generations, was named as its leader. While serving as a missionary in French Cameroon in 1932, Woodbridge grew incensed with an official from the Presbyterian Board for Missions spoke to natives not on Christ, but on "the Power of Personality." Woodbridge worked with fellow conservatives and fundamentalists, including Carl McIntire, a tireless fighter for the fundamentalist cause, and J. Gresham Machen, one of the original leaders of the fundamentalist cause, in launching the new undertaking.[21] Woodbridge was far from alone in his theology nor in his willingness to strike out on his own.

But these problems lay in the future. In the late nineteenth and early twentieth centuries, the Seven Sisters came to view coordinated action in missionary activity on the part of denominations as paramount.[22] The FCC believed that "Christian unity on the foreign mission field is both desirable and necessary," largely because the task before the nation's churches was so vast. Every missionary was vital, there was no room for denominational competition (or theological arguments) when what was at stake was the salvation of the world. As Robert E. Speer, the secretary of the Board of Foreign Missions of the Presbyterian Church, U.S.A., told the founding meeting of the FCC in 1908, "If we do not seize them [the unsaved] in this generation and claim them for God, they will set and harden in permanently atheistic form."[23]

Even as the missionary moment was arriving, there were forces at play that ultimately cast doubt on it for some within the Seven Sisters and laid the foundation for a foreign critique of American Christianity. As early as 1908, there was a feeling on the part of some within the Mainline that nationalism should, in the long run, trump denominationalism. That is to say, even with missionary efforts on the part of American denominations, which would help propagate denominationalism globally, at the end of the day Christians in Japan would be Japanese Christians first, and American-converted Methodists or Presbyterians second.[24] Thus, mission boards began to put a premium on things beyond spreading the Gospel, such as the culture new Christians were a part of, out of a recognition that denominational names carried with them both blessings and curses.

While this sentiment might be growing among the board members at home, the missionaries in the field were more often than not concerned primarily with the salvation of the lost. American missionaries of virtual all denominations were enjoying a good deal of success. In Latin America, for example, the basis for Protestantism (in what has historically been considered a Roman Catholic portion of the world) was fostered by American missionary organizations or churches (including Pentecostals) led by American-educated Protestants.[25] Soon these American mission-backed churches were thriving, a living testament to the hard work on the part of the missionaries.

But that ever-growing success continued to raise questions for members of mission boards back in the United States. Mission organizations controlled by the Seven Sisters began to pull back from continued missionary work. On the one hand, this was an acknowledgement that the foreign churches were strong enough to survive on their own. On the other, it showcased the worries that many modernists had over charges that American missionaries were little more than imperialists with Bibles. Since American imperialism occurred at the same time as American missionary activity, there was both real and imagined intermingling of the flag and the cross. To modernists, missionaries were part of imperialism even if they all were not imperialistic themselves.[26] Arguing that missionary activity is only a form of imperialism, this in effect shortchanges the faith of both the missionaries and the converts, and many within the Seven Sisters grew increasingly uneasy with both concepts as the twentieth century wore on.[27]

These worries opened the door to questions surrounding whether there was still a need for international missionary activity. In the 1970s many within the Seven Sisters began to wonder if the time had arrived to cease, alter, or at least scale back classic missionary efforts aimed at saving souls, even as they continued to worry about fundamentalist- and Pentecostal-influenced missionaries around the globe—an ironic worry, considering that by scaling back their own efforts they virtually guaranteed that liberal theology would not bear fruit in overseas missionary outposts.[28] An emphasis on home missions took hold, as well as a decision to transform international missionary agencies into organizations focused more strongly on social service or aid than on spreading the Gospel.[29] While hardly unchristian, indeed, many of these organizations were direct outlets for much-needed Christian charity, such aid groups were far removed from the kinds of evangelical efforts these churches had once undertaken.

The Seven Sisters never abandoned evangelistic work, but their efforts also risked being consumed by a reconceptualization of what missionary activity should be. The American Baptists' "Ministry Focus Areas" are a case in point. The seven goals of these Baptist missionaries are:

1. Leading people to faith and starting new churches
2. Training future church leaders
3. Creating economic opportunity and building futures
4. Abolishing human trafficking
5. Promoting health in an HIV/AIDS world
6. Opening the mind, empowering the heart
7. Seeking peace and offering refuge.

The first on this list is obviously classic missionary activity, as is the second to a large degree. But the remaining five might, at best, be seen as outgrowths of missionary activity and, at worse, distractions from the first goal.[30]

A similar sort of hierarchy of missionary priorities can be seen with the United Methodists, although there is also a good deal of language about the "purpose" of the church and the "sacramental nature" of missionary work in Methodist literature.[31] To a degree, Methodists saw a rebirth of missionary activity in the 1990s, following the end of the Cold War.[32] But they also realized they had larger issues before them. Methodists have talked about the need to seek better pastors and stronger churches, blaming a lack of denominational leadership for membership losses of nearly 3 million since 1970, even if the denomination was growing internationally.[33]

Not everyone within the Sisters agreed with the change in missionary focus from saving souls to solely humanitarian work. As some boards, such as that of the United Methodist Church, became less interested (at least in the opinion of some of the laity) in actually engaging in missionary activity, other members of the laity began to take matters into their own hands. In the Methodist case, this prompted the creation of the Mission Society, an organization designed to train, equip, place, and support long-term Methodist evangelical missionaries. The Society has also began working with local churches in the United States to cultivate a sense of the connection beyond that provided for by the denominational hierarchy, creating partnerships with congregations and individual members that make it a parachurch organization rather than a denominationally supported group.[34]

Meanwhile, outside the Sisters, the work of winning the world continued. The Southern Baptists admit to being late to international missionary work (blaming "the Civil War and the South's agrarian economy"), but after World War II, a concerted effort spearheaded by Baker James Cauthen, led to a dramatic improvement of those efforts.[35] Southern Baptists openly talk of the converts they have won via their missionary efforts at both home and abroad since the late 2000s.[36] Likewise, since their emergence in the early twentieth century, the Pentecostal Assemblies of God have consistently affirmed a commitment to global missionary activity as well.[37]

It was also not uncommon for other groups, outside denominational confines, to form. This included New Tribes Mission, founded in 1942 as a Protestant, nondenominational, fundamentalist missions' organization. New Tribes trained its missionaries to do field work in places like South America by emphasizing living *like* the natives, not just *with* the natives.[38] Other parachurch mission organizations include SEND International, which started life as the Far Eastern Gospel Crusade shortly after World War II and is staunchly evangelical and nondenominational. As the Sisters' activities dwindled in the 1980s, these groups thrived. By the dawn of the twenty-first century, the vast majority of American overseas missionaries come from the ranks of fundamentalists, evangelicals, and Pentecostals.[39]

While these organizations still send out long-term missionaries, they also helped pioneer short-term mission trips. These efforts, whether at home or abroad, gave more people, including young professionals, the opportunity to take part in aid and evangelization endeavors. Not unlike their missionary forebears, one of the allures for these short-term missionaries is to be part of such a large "community of believers." Although they have "found misconceptions about Americans in culture," that rarely extends to the Christian faith itself when it is presented to potential converts.[40]

Furthermore, an interesting thing happened in those far-off lands. As the Sisters slowly lost interest in, or transformed their missionary activities officially into humanitarian organizations, the people who had been converted by their earlier efforts continued to grow in their faith. But that spiritual development was in the opposite direction from the Mainline's hierarchies. Increasingly, those converted to Christianity around the globe took a more orthodox stance on matters of faith and doctrine than many within the Sisters. Their churches, especially in Asia and Africa and which have historic connections to the Seven Sisters, tended to be more theologically conservative than their American cousins.[41]

Perhaps not surprisingly, these orthodox Christians of the Global South are growing. Christianity in Africa has risen to nearly 400 million members of the faith, a nearly threefold increase since 1970.[42] These new Christians not only tend to be more doctrinally conservative than many in the Seven Sisters, but they also face cultural circumstances (including persecution) that do not lend themselves to being open to liberal theology. While the spread of the Gospel is something American Christians can take joy in, it also opens up a new facet in our understanding of why the Seven Sisters as an entity is no longer the Mainline.

American Episcopalians in an Anglican Sea

The Church of the Incarnation in Santa Rosa, California, made headlines in January 2007 by announcing that it and many Episcopal congregations were "too boring for the culture wars." The rector of the church, Rev. Matthew Lawrence, as he affirmed his congregation's commitment to both welcoming gays and lesbians as well as to wider theological diversity within the denomination, then went on to say that those who were engaged in fighting against the modernist tide within the Episcopal Church were "extremists" and most congregations that were leaving the denomination are just "little church(es)."[43] Inaccuracies aside, part of what made this rector's proclamation interesting was what he did not mention: the Episcopal Church is part of the Anglican Communion. For in order to understand both the Episcopal Church's current straits and the more general challenges facing the Seven Sisters in the twenty-first century, the local manifestations of what is now a global debate over theological modernism in the aftermath of decline must be understood.

As one of America's colonial churches and a founding member of the Seven Sisters, and because of its place in an international denomination, the

Episcopal Church provides important insights into the turmoil and choices the old Mainline configuration faces as Global South Christianity asserts itself. Perhaps no denomination has felt the sting of decline in all of its forms more so than the American branch of the Anglican Communion.

In many ways, the Episcopal Church is the face of both the old and new decline thesis. The denomination is small, both within the Anglican Communion and within American Christianity. Financially, many of its dioceses and parishes are in trouble, and when this difficulty is coupled with the fact that many of its churches are "grayer" (in terms of demographics) than other Seven Sister denominations, that makes decline even more difficult to reverse.[44]

Despite denominational decline, the modernist wing within the Episcopal Church has sought new ways to implement and expand its agenda since the 1960s and 1970s.[45] Its chief focus since the 1990s has been on garnering wider acceptance for homosexuality, both within and outside the church. It has accomplished this, to a degree, by using passages from the Old and New Testaments to craft an inclusivist message based on God's love, pushing aside both biblical and traditional mores and conventions about condemnation of sin (often both in general and specifically as it relates to homosexuality as mentioned in the Bible). Within the denomination, they have been remarkably successful.[46]

While homosexuals had long been members of Episcopal and other congregations, the denominational hierarchy wished to see them openly a part of the church, not just as members but as celebrated leaders. Modernists first won the right for celibate homosexuals to gain ordination, and then those in open relationships to do the same, by talking about diversity and putting the focus on outreach and the importance of ability, rather than sexual orientation. The culmination of their efforts came with the elevation of Gene Robinson to the office of bishop of the diocese of New Hampshire in 2003.[47]

Episcopalians knew what they were doing when Robinson was ordained. Many anticipated a conservative backlash.[48] As these various moves coincided with wider acceptance of homosexuality in American culture, they seemed to justify the modernists long-held belief that the Seven Sisters needed to adopt secular cultural norms in order to survive. In the process, they largely ignored the worries of traditionalists and even of moderates. Traditionalists then appealed for help from the international Anglican Communion, a major difference from what happened during the fight over female ordination and Prayer Book revision. In response, the Episcopal Church's hierarchy argued that their denomination was "called" to force the conversation about the place of homosexuals in the church, even if the majority within the Communion did not understand or appreciate what the Episcopal Church was doing.[49]

And that majority has taken a hard line against what the Episcopal Church has done. The primates of the Communion's national churches have called on the denomination to confront the ramifications of its decisions, including allowing for some sort of oversight for dissenting traditionalist Episcopalians (a sort of conservative presiding bishop). The modernist wing of the denomination has largely rejected the rationale for the primates' concern, with many Episcopal bishops, while affirming their desire to remain in the Anglican Communion, refusing to accept the outside criticism as valid. Instead, they have demanded that the Communion deal with hatred and violence directed at homosexuals rather than condemn the Episcopal Church for moving forward on promoting homosexual rights.[50] Indeed, this global push-back has caused some resentment with the Episcopal Church hierarchy. Some, because of their commitment to modernist theology, believe that their vision of inclusiveness is paramount to the worries of African and Asian Anglicans in the Global South. They have also sought out alliances with Canadian and Latin American Anglicans with mixed results.[51]

Ironically, the Episcopal Church hierarchy has been able to craft various positions (whether on female ordination or homosexual rights) in opposition to the rest of the Communion because of the position and power of the United States in the world, using American primacy and leadership to do what it wants within the Communion with little fear of ramifications. At the same time, the Episcopal Church hierarchy has often been at odds with the political direction, both at home and abroad, of the United States government. The fact that the Episcopal Church is now having its decisions challenged is new, and has less to do with the arrogance of American foreign policy and much more to do with the decisions Episcopalians themselves have made.[52] The cultural issues that have come to define the Episcopal Church, including politically liberal stances about homosexuality and abortion, may have little chance of building a consensus within either the denomination or the larger Communion the way that civil rights did.[53]

The Episcopal Church's General Conventions have, since the 1990s, become places where the course of the church as well as how to deal with the demands of the Anglican Communion have increasingly been debated. In 2006, this debate included how to respond to the Communion's 2004 Windsor Report, which called upon the Episcopal Church to apologize and repent for "having breached the bonds of affection" with the rest of the Communion by moving ahead with homosexual ordination and rites for same-sex marriages while dragging their collective feet on a proposed covenant for the Anglican Communion, which is designed to strengthen the largely loose bonds of the global denomination. To date, despite talk and debate, little has come of the proposed covenant.[54]

The Anglican Communion is increasingly a key player in the debate. Thanks to the "protective legitimacy" of the Global South, where it is estimated that 75 percent of all Anglicans reside (most of whom are conservative in their faith), many conservative and traditional Episcopalians are now seeking ways to leave the Episcopal Church without leaving the official umbrella of the Communion.[55] This dynamic is different from what happened in the wake of the 1960s and 1970s. Then, during the battles over female ordination and Prayer Book revision, some traditionalists and conservatives formed Concerned Clergy and Laity of the Episcopal Church. The group charged that "radical activists seek to replace biblical truth and godly morality with secular humanism and moral relativism," and was joined in its efforts to halt these changes by such groups as Episcopalians United and the American Anglican Council.[56] In 1990 the newly formed Episcopal Synod of America initially adhered itself to this loose coalition. While they enjoyed international Anglican support, drawing bishops from England, Scotland, Australia, and Melanesia to their founding service, their attempt at trying to renew the denomination was short lived. In 1992, the Synod formed the Episcopal Missionary Church as a rival denomination to the Episcopal Church.[57]

Although little came of these groups, the traditionalist movement this time has external Anglican support: it has not just been individuals but rather entire congregations and dioceses that have voted to leave the Episcopal Church.[58] The dioceses of Fort Worth, Quincy, Central Florida, Springfield, Pittsburgh, San Joaquin, and South Carolina all announced plans to consider "alternative primatial oversight" in the wake of the 2008 General Convention, even though not everyone in their dioceses was ready to make such a step.[59] Lending its support, the Anglican Church of Nigeria announced plans to provide a "safe harbour for all those who can no longer find their spiritual home in those churches [Episcopal Church and Anglican Church of Canada]."[60] This move prompted the archbishop of Canterbury, Rowan Williams, the titular head of the Anglican Communion, to authorize a meeting with American bishops to talk about ways in which those who objected to what the Episcopal Church was doing might stay in the Communion.[61]

The Most Reverend Katharine Jefferts Schori, the first female presiding bishop in the denomination's history, wasted little time in taking action to head off this rupture, though ultimately to little avail. In November 2006, shortly after being vested as presiding bishop, she sent a letter to Bishop John-David Schofield of the diocese of San Joaquin in California, a leader in the traditionalist movement, reminding him that while he might disagree with the decisions of General Convention, he had also taken ordination vows within the denomination. Jefferts Schori implied that she would fight any attempted withdrawal and questioned Schofield's loyalty to the denomination, though not, it should be pointed out, the Anglican Communion. She also told him that if his principles meant he was in disagreement with the denomination, he should resign. When his diocese pressed ahead in December with leaving the Episcopal Church, the presiding bishop was quick to offer a lament at the direction they were headed.[62]

The debate has gone from being just about an issue involving theology or doctrine to one about prestige, property, and money. One Episcopal congregation in Texas has offered to pay more than a million dollars in order to be allowed to withdraw from their diocese and keep their property. Congregations (including some of the most historic) in Virginia have also attempted to leave the Episcopal Church, generating legal battles over land and property. Similar lawsuits have been filed in South Carolina, Georgia, Colorado, and Florida as well. These splits have been far from amicable, with some leaders in the Episcopal Church issuing near racist commentary claiming that "Africans" (because of the ties the American traditionalists have to the Global South) were "occupying" churches. The presiding bishop issued a statement saying that leaving the Episcopal Church would not help the denomination solve the problems facing it, and she also spearheaded efforts to re-form loyal Episcopal congregations within areas that were experiencing breakaway attempts.[63]

In addition to losing members, congregations, and even dioceses, the Episcopal Church has also been hit with clerical defections as a result these theological rifts. Some bishops and priests have left the Episcopal Church to become Roman Catholic (following many laity who are also being welcomed by Rome)[64] or to work more closely with the newly formed Convocation of Anglicans in North America (CANA) being spearheaded by Nigeria's Anglican Church. Jefferts Schori wrote to the Nigerian primate Peter J. Akinola urging him to not install Martyn Minns as bishop of CANA, on grounds that doing so would "violate the ancient customs of the church" and would thus heighten tensions and divisions. Akinola fired back that it was the Episcopal

Church's decisions to violate many of the core doctrines of Christianity that had caused the tensions and divisions within the Anglican Communion to begin with. Installing Minns, conservatives believed, would give traditional American Anglicans a true choice in leadership. The installation occurred in 2007, much to the dismay of the Episcopal hierarchy.[65]

In many ways, this division within the Episcopal Church is the epitome of classic decline. Traditionalists within the denomination do not accept the denominational hierarchy's assertion that the debate is about "rights" or "equality"; rather they see the Episcopal Church as rejecting the traditional teachings of Christianity. Nor do they agree with the presiding bishop that individual salvation is a "heresy" or with the denomination when it crafted an "inclusive" ordination process. Conservative Anglicans find it hard not to see the Episcopal Church as slipping farther outside the mainstream of both the Anglican Communion and of traditional American Christianity based on their own understanding of doctrine, tradition, and scripture.[66]

In this twenty-first century environment, there seems to be less room for compromise. Jefferts Schori has proposed a new position, that of primatial vicar, which can act within the Episcopal Church's existing structure to provide "alternative" oversight to the dissenters. This position is designed to give time to both sides of the debate within the Episcopal Church as well as the Anglican Communion. In some sense this seems a fair compromise, though many have seen it as adding yet another layer of bureaucracy and not going very far in addressing the issues that the dissenters have. Archbishop Williams promised to consider the proposal, but conservative bishops Robert Duncan of Pittsburgh and Jack Iker of Fort Worth were quick to label the plan as largely failing the goal of dealing with the problems facing the denomination. Liberal groups, such as Integrity (a pro-homosexual-rights Episcopal group) believed it was more than the conservatives should have expected.[67]

To his credit, the archbishop of Canterbury has attempted to hold the Communion together. With little actual authority, Archbishop Williams has moved to strengthen the bonds of the Communion while also encouraging dialogue. At the 2008 Lambeth Conference, neither Bishop Robinson nor any of the CANA bishops were invited in an attempt to defuse the situation and allow dialogue to continue.[68] Whether such a moderate line can be held until the next conference, in 2018, or what shape the debate will take between now and then, remains to be seen. Indeed, in 2010 Williams began taking a stronger stand against the Episcopal Church by ordering the removal of Episcopalians from ecumenical commissions in the wake of their denomination's refusal to submit to the Windsor Report and continued ordination of homosexual clergy, including in 2009, when Mary Glasspool was elected bishop of the diocese of Los Angeles. As for Gene Robinson, the bishop who sparked the controversy to begin with, he is slated to retire in 2013.[69]

The Ties That Unbind

The problems confronting the Anglican Communion are just the latest chapter in the history of the decline of the Seven Sisters. The battle raging within the Episcopal Church worries the other Sister denominations who have adopted similar "inclusivist" theology, and so face the possibility of similar battles.[70] Like their Episcopalian counterparts, their denominational leadership seems to have counted on gradual acceptance of the theological and doctrinal changes to keep the laity in line and in the fold.[71]

However, by the Anglican Communion taking up the issue as it has, this has proven impossible for Episcopalians. Other denominations among the Seven Sisters are thus faced with the prospect of their own international denominations voicing dissent over similar ideas, as well as an emboldened conservative/evangelical/traditionalist wing. With the potential implosion of the Episcopal Church, the last days of the Seven Sisters as the Mainline seem to have arrived. For example, the Evangelical Lutheran Church, one of the Episcopal Church's "partners in ministry," is poised for a battle of its own over homosexual clergy, and both the United Methodist and Presbyterian Churches have "renewal" movements within them looking to strengthen the denomination's stands on marriage and homosexuality in a traditionalist way in order to stave off the kind of rupture occurring within the Episcopal Church. In the Methodist case, conservatives are making direct appeals for aid from Methodists in Africa.[72]

American Christians have been active in spreading the Gospel at home and abroad for centuries, but realizing they are a part of an international faith is a concept they have sometimes struggled with. The experience reminds some that the church can all too easily be attached to a culture instead of challenging the status quo via the faith. The message of the Global South, beyond issues of doctrinal orthodoxy, is that decline does not (and in the case of the Seven Sisters did not) have to happen; that the message American missionaries once took to the ends of the earth can promote both faith and growth.[73] Such matters of faith are at the heart of what forges the Mainline, and so, with the decline of the Sisters, we should be looking for new members who better represent that ideal.

7

The Emergence of a New Mainline

As we have seen, the Mainline of the Seven Sisters as defined by the United Methodist, United Church of Christ, Disciples of Christ, Presbyterian, Evangelical Lutheran, Episcopal, and American Baptist churches no longer holds. Moreover, using this old definition negates the current importance of those outside of the Protestant tradition, as well as many within it. A new Mainline for the new millennium is needed and must consist of more representative denominations, in terms of size, worship style, and global membership. America may be pluralistic when it comes to religion but, given the continuing domination of Christianity in the nation's demography as well as public discourse, its diversity and scope need to be acknowledged as we craft a new understanding of the Christian Mainline.[1]

Introducing the New Mainline

Identifying members for a new configuration of the Mainline is not a simple trick to overcome the Seven Sister's decline. Rather, it is a recognition that American Christianity is much more vibrant than it is often given credit for. Crafting a Mainline that incorporates evangelicals, Southern Baptists, and Roman Catholics makes sense. Considering these denominations as part of a new Mainline does not just challenge the way American Christianity is viewed, but it radically changes the perception altogether. Such a reformulation also must include Pentecostals, further diversifying how the faith is understood. Not only will the new Mainline better reflect the actual on-the-ground diversity of Christianity in America and around the world than would continuing to embrace the Seven Sisters model, but it will also highlight one other salient fact: that it is in *these* churches that the majority of American Christians actually worship.

Americans who identify themselves as Christians remain well over 80 percent of the population in the first decades of the twenty-first century, with the faith actually growing between 1990 and 2000. Although religious enthusiasm cooled a bit by 2010, a Gallup Poll found that 54 percent of Americans hold that religion was "very important" in their lives, which is consistent with levels seen in the 1980s.[2] There are still more than twice as many Protestants as Catholics, but the largest denominations are Roman Catholicism (roughly 25 percent of the population—and the largest denomination in thirty-six states), Baptists (at just over 16 percent—the Southern Baptist wing of the Baptist family is the largest denomination in ten states), and Methodist/Wesleyans (at nearly 7 percent of the population). Lutherans comprise around 5 percent of all Americans.[3] The numbers are a bit different if one looks at the number of congregations. Here Southern Baptists lead (with thirteen states), Roman Catholics (in twelve states), Methodists (in twelve states), Latter-day Saints (in eight states), Evangelical Lutherans (in three states), and United Church of Christ (in two states).[4]

Why has a reconfiguration of who is considered part of the American Mainline not been tried before? Evangelicals, perhaps because they are not confined to a single denomination (indeed many still find a home in the old Mainline, which complicates the above statistics), have been left out of the denominational-centric Seven Sister focus. For Southern Baptists, their legacy of the Civil War division and their position in the South has held them back. Roman Catholics historically have not been considered because of the legacy of anti-Catholicism; despite the fact that while such sentiment has not disappeared, it has largely lost the cultural power it had for most of America's history. And Pentecostals, because their worship (and at times, theology) is often so different, have been ignored as a potential part of the Mainline, despite their growth and importance to Christianity both in and outside of the United States.

The Evangelicals and the New Mainline

If there is a remnant of the old Mainline that can most easily adapt to the formulation of a new one, it is the evangelical heart and soul (the American Baptist, United Methodist, Presbyterian, and Disciples of Christ denominations) of the Seven Sisters. Spread out over a variety of other denominations, including the Southern Baptists, evangelicals also comprise the vast majority of megachurches and independent/nondenominational churches in the United States today. That they also have experience being a part of the Mainline is an added bonus. To use them as a foundation only requires that we ignore denominational labels for a moment.[5]

Evangelical Christianity is quite strong in America, despite the denominational decline of the Seven Sisters.[6] A 2004 poll conducted by the *Indianapo-*

lis Star concluded that Hoosiers, right in the heartland of America, believe Christianity to be a "cultural glue" for the state's "social fabric." That glue was not just any version of Christianity but rather one that holds that Christ is the only way to heaven.[7] Similar polls nationally support the notion that evangelicalism remains the dominant force in American culture and religion, transcending both denominational and national boundaries.[8]

As we have seen, there is a great deal of diversity within evangelicalism, running the gamut from liberal moderate to conservative fundamentalist. And while they might disagree on politics, the historic "elastic orthodoxy" of American evangelicalism continues to allow them to work intensely in both the public and private spheres in the name of God.[9] That intensity, which evangelicals bring to their faith, is almost as important as their historic significance in crafting the Mainline of the Seven Sisters. Since evangelicals were the heart of that old Mainline, it makes sense that they would be included in the new formulation. Yet if their path into the new Mainline is in many ways easy, their status within the old Seven Sisters has often been anything but. After the failure to retake denominational hierarchies in the 1920s, evangelicals (who largely made up the moderate wing of American Christianity) watched as fundamentalists remained largely isolated during the 1930s and 40s. The two groups, while not mutually exclusive, were also not united. But, that began to change in the 1940s and '50s thanks to the formation of the National Association of Evangelicals and the work of Billy Graham, who brought the conservative, Protestant evangelical tradition back to the forefront. In many ways, picking up the mantle of revivalists such as Billy Sunday, Graham took the conservative evangelical Protestant message of Christianity to every corner of the nation, and eventually the world.[10]

Although there was little doubt about the doctrinal soundness of his message, some fundamentalists and evangelicals shied away from Graham because of his embrace of pursuing Christian unity, regardless of denominational lines, during his crusades and revivals. At the same time, many in the Seven Sisters condemned him because of his conservative theology and for the potential disruption his crusades could have on a community's churches, as his revivals brought new converts into established congregations (disrupting the status quo) and seemed to encourage congregational consumerism (spurring some people to leave their old congregations to ones more in line with Graham's theology). For his part, Graham became the leading evangelist of the twentieth century, utilizing a wide variety of parachurch organizations, such as Youth for Christ to propagate his message, and becoming a friend and confidant to presidents. In many respects he became America's pastor.[11]

But for all Graham's success, conservative evangelicals did not retake the hierarchies of the Seven Sisters. The postwar modern evangelical movement held fast to the notion of Christ's redeeming sacrifice and the full authority of inspired scripture, and its adherents constituted the main source of Mainline decline, first of all by leaving the Sisters for other congregations and denominations.[12] Rather than retaking the old denominations, evangelical denominational revival was sparked by a "fellow traveler" who had left the Sisters' fold over the trauma of the Civil War.

The Southern Baptists and the Renewal of Protestant America

In Nashville, Tennessee, just a few blocks from the Grand Ole Opry, is the headquarters of the largest Protestant denomination in the United States: the Southern Baptist Convention (SBC). The SBC has its roots in the wider Baptist movement of the seventeenth and eighteenth centuries, which took hold in America in response to the First and Second Great Awakenings. Like many Southern branches of the future Seven Sisters, the Baptist Church split over the issue of slavery as the Civil War approached. Unlike their fellow evangelicals in the Presbyterian and Methodist denominations, the Southern Baptists never reunited with their Northern brethren. Instead, they remained a regional force, in the heart of the Bible Belt, emerging as a national force with the movement of southerners into the North and West in the wake of World War II. By the early 1990s, the SBC had 15 million members and 40,000 churches in all fifty states, and had effectively rebuked and abandoned its past association with racism and segregation.[13]

The denomination's growth is also the story of conservative evangelical success at taking back control of a denominational hierarchy. The SBC demonstrates the importance of cultural battles to American Christians and for American Christianity as well. Evangelicals believe they must engage the culture in order to prove, in some way, Christianity's worth and validate the individual believer's faith. And the SBC has found itself increasingly engaged in doing just that since the onset of the 1960s culture wars.[14]

The SBC is interesting for another reason. It was separate from its fellow evangelical denominations because of the rupture of the Civil War and never reunited with them (or even their fellow Northern Baptists) after the conflict. Because it existed as a regional denomination, in many ways its regionalism protected it and insulated it from much strife, including that of the 1960s; social activism never took hold to any significant degree among either clergy or laity. However, that isolation also prompted members of the SBC to eschew working with Northern evangelicals on projects of mutual interest. Having been forced to create their own institutions in the mid- and late nineteenth century, the SBC felt no urgency to merge their efforts with those of other evangelicals. They felt that they were just fine the way they were.[15]

Well, not exactly. While the SBC was not racked by a theological rift the way most of the Seven Sisters were, the denomination did experience division because of innovations in theology. The SBC was solidly evangelical, with defined moderate and fundamentalist wings, so the debate, when it finally occurred in the late 1970s and early '80s, was really between groups who differed in the degree of their theological conservatism. Most Southern Baptists were of the opinion that liberal theology was destroying denominations in the North. But because of the denomination's growth, there was also a feeling among some moderates that there needed to be greater accommodations with other denominations in order to garner wider acceptance of the SBC beyond the South. In the end, the moderates vacillated once too often on social issues for the fundamentalists, who organized other evangelicals to take control of the denominational hierarchy. The conservative coalition was aided by the national scope of the denomination's growth since World War II, which had been opposed by Northern Baptists and even by some moderates within the SBC.[16] At this point, the nationalization of the denomination put pressure on denominational leaders to be responsive to the laity's demands.[17]

Because of the denomination's makeup, it is perhaps not that surprising that the more conservative evangelical and fundamentalist wings were able to take control of the SBC hierarchy. Thus their victory and subsequent accomplishments at growing the denomination, while also expanding its influence, are worth noting. Nor should it be surprising that most of the SBC's leaders believe the Mainline, as defined by the Seven Sisters, is no more. What they have been able to show is that decline does not have to happen in the classic sense at all. At the end of the day, the SBC is more representative of both Americans and of American Christianity than, say, the Episcopal Church.[18] Both its theology and its size are something that should be taken into account when positing a new Mainline for the twenty-first century.

Evangelicals and the Rise of the Megachurch

Saddleback Church in Lake Forest, California, has become one of the best-known congregations in America. Affiliated with the Southern Baptist Convention, the congregation was founded on Easter 1980 with 205 people in attendance. Three decades later, the church can boast of roughly one out of nine people in the greater South Orange County area calling the congregation their spiritual home.[19] Its pastor, Rick Warren, has become a best-selling author, with two of his books, *The Purpose Driven Church* and *The Purpose Driven Life*, becoming highly influential—not just within evangelical circles but in the wider church as well. Saddleback has pioneered new worship practices, including the concept of simultaneous multiple services to accommodate various music preferences. As a seeker congregation that strives to be welcoming to all visitors and quick to find new members a place in the congregation—before talking much about doctrine and theology, another technique the church has helped popularize—Saddleback attempts to offer attendees relevant sermons, friendly congregations, a place that does not constantly talk about finances, and good childcare. So powerful is its position in American culture that in 2008 it hosted a presidential forum, in some respects the first debate between Senators John McCain and Barack Obama. For all these reasons it has popularized and helped to define in the public mind all that a megachurch can be.[20]

Megachurches are an interesting development in American religious history. On the one hand, they seem to harken back to a time when there was only one church in each community. But in other respects, they are the natural progression of the democratic ethos of American Christianity. They give religious consumers what they want, attracting more and more people to themselves, growing in size by pulling the unchurched in as well as the dissatisfied from other congregations. While such congregations are different, they also have the same forces operating within them as a "normal size" congregation. Megachurches tend to utilize contemporary service styles and often do not "look" like churches either inside or out. Indeed, being a megachurch is the latest model for congregational development. While any group or denomination, including the Seven Sisters, can follow it, the vast majority of megachurches are at least moderate, if not conservative, in their doctrinal statements. Where they rise, the Seven Sisters tend to fall.[21]

This trend was seen long before Warren arrived in Southern California to establish Saddleback. As early as the 1920s, Americans had a glimpse at the megachurch future. In Fort Worth, Texas, the First Baptist Church with J. Frank Norris as its senior pastor could boast of an average attendance of more than 5,000 people. Norris was a conservative theologian and leader of the fundamentalist wing of the Southern Baptist Convention (and later of an independent conservative Baptist movement as well). He led First Baptist for over forty years, sixteen of which he also spent commuting to Detroit, Michigan, where he pastored that city's Temple Baptist Church. By the 1940s the two congregations had a combined membership of around 26,000. One of his legacies was proving the possibilities of the megachurch, long before the term had even been invented.[22]

To those who embrace the model, the megachurch can be seen as the latest innovation in spreading the Gospel. Such large congregations meet the needs of their members, offering them programs, a chance to be part of something big, and a message that "feeds" them spiritually. Megachurches give their members something else as well: a degree of anonymity unheard of in small congregations. This grand scale, on some level, is an attraction to potential members, not unlike the thrill some get from living in a large city, that of being a part while also being unknown. Additionally, megachurches also feed the growth of virtual congregations, have revolutionized church planting (especially the growth of "multisite" congregations), and seem to flourish in suburbia.[23]

According to a 2005 study, there are more than 1,200 Protestant churches in the United States with a weekly attendance of over 2,000. That represents a doubling between 2000 and 2005. A little over half of that number have fewer than 3,000 attendees, with nearly a third having between 3,000 and 5,000 congregants, and the remaining 16 percent with more than 5,000 people. There numbers seem to be growing as well. Nearly half of all megachurches are found in the South, with an additional quarter in the West. Twenty-six percent have some affiliation with a Baptist denomination, while 34 percent are nondenominational. Megachurches typically attract college-educated younger, married couples with children. They are also more multiethnic than traditional congregations.[24] There is little denying that their numbers are impressive. For example, Skip Heitzig's Calvary Chapel of Albuquerque boasts a weekly attendance of 14,000; Joel Osteen's Lakewood Church in Houston has a reported 30,000 members; Frederick K. C. Price's church in Los Angles has 22,000.[25] Such numbers only seem to reinforce the topic of decline when it comes to members of the Seven Sisters.

That being said, there is room to critique the megachurch. Some contend that such congregations are growing by watering down the church's message of the Gospel. Nor can these institutions be relied on as a model to always get things right. Willow Creek, outside of Chicago, one of the nation's premier megachurches, has discontinued its twenty-something ministry, folding it into the main congregation in order to make sure that young members feel a part of the larger church. The "megachurch business model" has been attacked in and of itself for making religion function like a commodity instead of a personal faith.[26] T. D. Jakes, whose Potter's House congregation in Dallas is one of the nation's largest megachurches, demonstrates the potential for other pitfalls with the model as well. As ministries grow they can become as much about self-perpetuation as spreading the Good News. Their size can make them insular to a degree. In some ways, they mimic the problems we have seen with the denominational hierarchies of the Seven Sisters. Furthermore, the senior pastor, the reason many join to begin with or learn about the congregation, is often distant and gone much of the time, keeping the ministry going but not necessarily ministering to the home congregation's needs.[27]

Indeed, running churches like a business and making Sundays about collecting money via tithes and offerings, and to some degree about power and status, strike some as the antithesis of Christianity.[28] The theologian Ronald J. Sider has argued that American Christians, especially evangelicals, routinely fail to live up to their biblical principles in such areas.[29] This is seen perhaps most clearly in the use of the "prosperity gospel" by some megachurches, which promise wealth and health to their adherents as a divine reward for their faith in God and support of the congregation. Some have argued that the megachurch model is an example of the "church marketer" wing of modern evangelicalism, which has tended to see growth as more important than doctrine as evangelicals have increasingly engaged the culture around them. Other evangelicals have flocked to the "emergent church" wing, which minimalizes doctrine altogether.[30] Both wings have attempted to reach modern America via evangelical means, but both can also be seen as modern evangelical attempts to fashion a theology to replace the Kingdom of God from the Social Gospel era.

And yet, as important as the megachurches have become in American life, they do not represent the reality for most Christians. Well over 90 percent of believers belong to or attend churches that have fewer than 1,000 members. Conversely, according to the Hartford Institute for Religion Research's National Congregations Study, "although most congregations are small, most people are in congregations that are large." In other words, the average congregation has only seventy regular attendees, but the average attendee goes to a congregation with four hundred regular participants, neither of which is a "mega" number.[31]

Most Christians are some place in the middle of these numbers. But the importance of the megachurches is that they are solidly evangelical and often times not affiliated with a denomination. As such, they are often not included in the discussion of the Mainline, even as no one doubts their influence on

American Christianity. In the twenty-first century, this subgroup of evangelicals augments the case for the broader evangelical movement being considered a part of what constitutes the Mainline, no matter where they may worship.

The Roman Catholic Church and the New Mainline

St. John's Catholic Church sits in the midst of the convention district of downtown Philadelphia. In its nearly two centuries of existence, it has seen the city grow, decay, and renew itself. A church of the wealthy (it was once the spiritual home of the Drexel family, whose fortune was made in the banking industry, and which counts a saint among its family members) and the miraculous (a statue of Mary survived a fire in the late nineteenth century), it is today a historic church striving to reinvent itself. Its congregation is a mix of parishioners and visitors, elderly and young, native born and immigrant. In that regard it is a good example of the Catholic Church writ large in America, and one of the reasons for this branch of Christendom's success in the New World: It has repeatedly managed to change and adapt to the situation around it without changing its basic tenets.[32] It also helps to make the case for why the largest denomination in Christendom deserves, at last, to be part of the American Mainline.

The Roman Catholic Church is the single largest branch of Christianity in the world and in the United States, and it is an important part of the emerging new Mainline. To put it another way, there are fewer than 160,000 Unitarians in the United States. In any given year, 200,000 adults become Catholic.[33] Up to this point, Catholicism has made little imprint in these pages, but that lack of attention has nothing to do with its vibrancy, nor its historic and important role in American history. Of the nearly 4 million Americans in the 1780s, the Roman Catholic population of the United States was less than 50,000. By the 1860s, thanks to immigration, it was the largest denomination in the country.[34] Catholics have adapted their faith, with its ideas of societal unity, to the American situation rather well, making their denomination fit within a culture that was historically Protestant. Its urban, parish structure made Catholics insular and reluctant to show "concern for those outside their boundaries" despite their growth, but at the same time they were open to the democratic trends in the nation of which they were now a part.[35]

Historically, the Catholic Church's growth was fueled by immigrants. Indeed, the denomination itself was something of an immigrant institution, which makes it different from many, though not all, Protestant denominations in America. Its immigrant membership base meant that Catholics from many nation-states could be found in a single parish, though national parishes (e.g., Polish, German) were also quite common.[36] The church's American hierarchy in the late nineteenth and early twentieth centuries sought to forge "unity amid diversity" by having bishops exert more control over ethnic groups so that they could retain both ethnicity and Catholicism in Protestant America. This dual approach helped lead to the rise of the "Catholic ghetto" (or ethnic neighborhood) in urban areas. Immigrant Catholics found it both necessary (because of Protestant anti-Catholicism) and beneficial (in order to maintain their own ethnic heritage) to devote themselves to their neighborhood parish church and its institutions, often times sacrificing a beautiful home in order to have a beautiful church. Therefore, while there were external forces that helped form the ghetto and kept Catholics from being fully part of wider American society, there were also internal Catholic forces seeking to keep out the larger Protestant culture. Certain community and religious circles on both sides of the Reformation divide had a vested interest in keeping Catholics and Protestants separate.[37]

The ghetto mentality exacerbated tensions between Protestants and Catholics by fostering anti-Protestantism that was equal in its venom to the anti-Catholicism spewed by some Protestants. Editorials in Catholic newspapers called for Protestants to return to the Catholic Church if they sought true reverence in religious life, labeled Lutherans as bigots, and asserted that Protestant Sunday schools were anti-Catholic indoctrination institutions. They also argued that Protestantism at its best was a "weak" faith when compared to Catholicism, and at its worst, promoted paganism. Protestant revivals were reviled, and Protestants were said to not have true religion. In short, it is not surprising that the Catholic Church was not invited to sit with the Seven Sisters to forge their version of the Mainline.[38]

The two branches of Christianity were not ignorant of one another, however. There was a great deal of interaction between them on every day of the week but Sunday, and a tradition of Catholics and Protestants working together at the local for philanthropic ends.[39] Many Catholics were eager to unite with Protestants against the problems facing America and the wider Christian culture, but it is important to note that these two branches of Christianity often took different approaches toward societal problems. When it came to the content of Hollywood motion pictures, for example, Protestants sought Sunday theater closings while Catholics sought outright censorship. Catholics eventually compromised with the creation of a "movie czar" to keep the studios in their place during the early and mid-twentieth century; this was the inception of the movie rating system.[40]

In many ways, it was World War II and the suburbanization of America after the conflict, coupled with the nation's involvement in the Cold War, which at last broke the Catholic ghetto. As Catholics and Protestants became neighbors in the suburbs, as they fought against common external foes, the boundaries between them began at long last to disappear.[41] This was a revolutionary moment, signaling the beginning of the end of institutional Protestant anti-Catholicism. With John F. Kennedy's election in 1960, the nation never looked back. Indeed, by the twenty-first century, Catholics were a majority of the United States Supreme Court, and were leaders in state-houses, governors' mansions, and in the halls of Congress in both parties. So ubiquitous is Catholicism today that you can even find chapels in shopping malls.[42]

The more a part of American society and culture Catholics have become, the more scrutiny there has been on how the denomination operates. This is especially the case of the laity, most of whom are farther away from an immigrant past and increasingly willing to bristle at decisions made by the church hierarchy. Other tensions are also seen in the way native-born American Catholics have dealt with Hispanic immigration. The flow of immigrants from Latin and South America, where many, in both Catholic and Protestant traditions, have embraced charismatic worship styles, holds the potential to transform American Christianity in very real ways. But the wrestling with potential changes in doctrine, theology, and worship between the new and old ways of doing things has only just begun.[43]

In some respects, this is nothing new for the Roman Catholic Church. It has had its struggles with theological controversies and changes in its liturgy and worship style before. For example, Catholics have a long history of arguing for a just society, which has to do with a large portion of America's working class historically being a part of the Catholic faith tradition. As a result, the denomination has often sought to take a stand for worker's right, even when it was unpopular to do so.[44] This history complicated the American Catholic relationship to liberation theology when it emerged from Latin and South America in the 1970s and '80s.[45] But the largest challenge and change was the Second Vatican Council (Vatican II) in the 1960s and 1970s. The reforms unleashed by Pope John XXIII created major shifts in how Catholics understood their church. Gone was the use of Latin in the Mass, and indeed, gone was how the Mass was celebrated. The resulting reorientation of Catholic worship practice and increased interaction between priest and laity completely altered how Catholics the world over experienced church life. Embraced by some and decried by others, Vatican II's repercussions echo to the present, not unlike the Episcopal Church's ever-ongoing revision of the Book of Common Prayer.[46]

Perhaps the greatest challenge the American Catholic Church has faced in recent years is the sexual abuse scandal involving priests and young parishioners. As horrible as the revelations were and as devastating (including financially) as the resulting battles have been, the scandal has also showcased the Americanization of the Catholic Church in many ways. The scandal happened in part because of the closed and somewhat secretive world the clergy and bishops live in. The coverup, complete with payoffs and the moving around of "problem" priests, was perhaps an attempt to try to protect the priesthood as a vocation. Some have said it presents an opportunity for reform (including calls for a third Vatican Council) since so many different groups can use it as a rallying point. The scandal has led to challenges to the celibacy rule (in order to garner more recruits) as well as notions of a grand conspiracy of epic proportions offered up by both liberals and conservatives.[47]

As important as the scandal is, the Catholic Church's experience with it is somewhat reflected in the experiences of other American Christians. Coupling the debate over reform in the wake of scandal with how the lay members of the Catholic Church react to the church's teaching on birth control, or how the hierarchy handles divorce and annulments, it is hard not to see the Catholic Church as very much an American institution. The laity expects to be listened to and for change of some sort to happen.[48]

The Americanization of the Roman Catholic Church is quite complete. There is no reason not to count them among the modern Mainline. Not doing so not only fails to acknowledge the majority status of the globally largest group of Christians but also promotes a skewed, if not intolerant view of the Christian faith in America. Their inclusion allows for a much more diverse consideration of Christianity, complete with a rich intellectual, theological, and doctrinal tradition.

Furthermore, Catholics and evangelical Protestants are coming together in surprising ways.[49] This rapprochement is one of the more interesting developments of the Religious Right's involvement in politics. It has contributed to the continued diminishing of anti-Catholicism in American life. A religious alliance of this sort helps overcome the perceived (both correctly and not) intellectual deficiencies of evangelical Protestantism, while also defusing much past anti-Catholicism and much anti-Protestantism as well. In many ways they have been brought together by their shared orthodoxy in the face of modernist and secular advances in American society.[50] Still, the two branches of American Christianity seem to find plenty of common cause when it comes to social issues, even though there are still theological and doctrinal differences that remain and that matter. Protestants have long noted their unease with Roman Catholicism's claim to be the "true" church, for example. And Catholics remain perplexed by the diversity of Protestant denominations. But, Catholics and evangelical Protestants have made strides to overcome the "Reformation problem," and embrace one another as members of the same faith, even if they are not members of the same church. Bringing them together in the new articulation of the Mainline makes a good deal of sense.[51]

The Pentecostals and the New Mainline

The large number of American evangelicals, including the largest Protestant denomination in the nation, and the Roman Catholic Church, representing the largest branch of Christendom, are obvious candidates to include in the twenty-first century's composition of the Mainline. The other new addition might prove to be a bit controversial though. Pentecostalism, including holiness and charismatics, is largely an American creation that has swept the globe. Perhaps no one personifies both the potential and the pitfalls of the mainstreaming of Pentecostalism more than T. D. Jakes. As the sociologist Shayne Lee points out in his biography of the man thought by some to be America's next Billy Graham, Jakes has built a megachurch empire based on his message, showmanship, utilization of television, and marketing. And, he has helped bring Pentecostalism into the consciousness of the mainstream of American Christianity.[52]

American Pentecostalism had its start with the interracial Azusa Street revival in Los Angeles, which lasted from 1906 until 1909. At that time, the revival met continuously and thrived without a public relations arm, spread by word of mouth.[53] Like Jakes, who is the movement's current face, one of the revivals founders, William Joseph Seymour, was also an African American. Born in 1870, Seymour moved from Louisiana to Indianapolis to Cincinnati, and finally to Houston before eventually making his way to Los Angeles. During his cross-country trek, Seymour spent time as a Methodist, Holiness, and eventually Pentecostal. Along the way he had met Charles Fox Parham, who was white (and somewhat racist), but who had helped convince him that the Pentecostal way was the surest road to Christ.[54]

Azusa Street was described as a place where "God was working mightily." The movement that started there drew people from the Seven Sisters who (not unlike Seymour himself in some ways) were seeking something other than the doctrinal battles and interdenominational squabbling of the early twentieth century, a search they described as looking for "authentic Christianity." Though many talked about old time religion, much of what they did and enjoyed about the movement was, indeed, new. These innovations included a feeling of having been a part of a unique and important revelation from God, the renewal of spiritual gifts (including speaking in tongues), and of being locked in spiritual warfare with the forces of Satan. As a result, while the founders of Pentecostalism did not set out to craft a new type of Christianity or make new denominations, that is exactly what happened as the revival gave way to the world beyond Azusa Street.[55]

Pentecostals sought to restore Christianity to its roots, and that meant an emphasis on evangelization, preparing for Christ's return, "holy healing," and the ability to speak in tongues. In some respects, they were answering a lack of emphasis on the Holy Spirit in most other branches of American Christianity, and as they emerged on the scene they faced opposition from both the Seven Sisters and from fundamentalists. Another characteristic of Pentecostal worship services was/is their "emotional exuberance," with loud "amens" being shouted in the midst of the sermons, spontaneous singing and dancing, and exaltation being the hallmarks of worship. Pentecostalism was so attractive as a means of renewal that it bred the charismatic movement, which spread the belief that the Holy Spirit could bring spiritual gifts and renewal to Christians beyond Pentecostal churches, finding its way into the Seven Sisters and even into the Catholic Church by century's end.[56]

Pentecostals have blended a wide variety of evangelical traditions with a focus on experiencing the Holy Spirit and a determination to use any technological means to spread the Gospel of Christ. Understanding that their heritage is a complex one, they have flourished both in the United States and around the globe—including Central and South America.[57] From a historical perspective, the Pentecostals have three branches. The first comes from the Methodist/Holiness tradition (with the leading denominational example being the Church of God in Christ [COGIC]). The second drew from Baptist heritage, with the Assemblies of God being the best example. And then there are the United Pentecostals, who broke with the Assemblies of God between 1914 and 1916 over the Trinity and the development of Oneness doctrine.[58]

Oneness teaching is the most controversial element of Pentecostalism because it takes issue with the traditional Trinitarian understanding of the Christian conception of God. Instead of three "persons" making up God, Oneness Pentecostals believe that there is only God, who has been called three different names at different points in history. Critics of the doctrine point out the alteration of historic Christian teaching. Moreover, they note that this approach, as propagated by T. D. Jakes and others, seems also to present a very watered-down Christianity, one built on feeling rather than substance and designed to increase revenues, not to save souls. In short, it is a secularized version of the faith fit for a postmodern America.[59] Its advocates tend to downplay its doctrinal significance, and for most Pentecostals this does not define nor is it a part of their faith.

A more significant doctrinal issue is the place the so-called prosperity gospel has found within Pentecostalism, and by extension, within many Protestant churches as well. At its core, this doctrine tells believers that if they give generously of their time, talent, and treasure, God will not only bless them in the next life but in this one as well. Specifically, they will reap spiritual and material rewards for serving the church. Some denominations, such as the National Baptist Church (the largest black Baptist organization in the nation, which was founded in 1880), have openly condemned the prosperity gospel.[60] Of the four largest megachurches in the nation, the three headed by Joel Osteen, T. D. Jakes, and Creflo Dollar have all embraced the prosperity doctrine to varying degrees. The fourth, as *Christianity Today* noted in 2010, is headed by Rick Warren, who is a critic of the movement. It should be noted that evangelicals, and indeed most American Christians, have spent little time talking about either personal finances or social inequality in a nonpartisan way, thus opening the door for such a doctrine. To do so would require that they confront the very difficult question of what it means to be a Christian in the wealthiest nation in the world.[61] At the same time, many of the proponents of the prosperity gospel have fallen on hard times. Supporters note that some advocates, especially televangelists who have watched as their churches have lost members and their ministries decline, are not experiencing difficulty because of their embrace of prosperity gospel, but rather because of personal shortcomings and sin in the lives of the ministers involved.[62] Whoever is correct, it did not stop some critics, as Hanna Rosin of *The Atlantic* noted, from laying the blame of the Great Recession of 2008/9 at the feet of the prosperity gospel movement.[63]

Not all Pentecostals subscribe to either of these more controversial doctrines of Oneness or the prosperity gospel, but they all have enjoyed dramatic growth since 1906. Indeed, although it started as a largely localized event, by the end of the twentieth century Pentecostalism had spanned denominations and influenced virtually every other branch of Christianity in America through the charismatic movement, booming in membership during the 1970s and 1980s. This large and growing movement has become a global branch of Christianity staggering in its size (an estimated 500 million members) and diverse in its appearance, cutting across race and class boundaries. The racial diversity that Pentecostalism brings to the table marks it (and by extension the new Mainline) as quite different from the denominations of the Seven Sisters. At its core then, modern Pentecostalism recognizes the power that the Holy Spirit can bring to today's church and the Christian faithful, and is represented by a number of thriving denominations and megachurches.[64]

Thus, even with doctrinal controversies, any new Mainline must include a Pentecostal wing. From a denominational perspective perhaps the best choice is the Assemblies of God. Founded in 1914, by 2007 the Assemblies of God counted 2.8 million members in the United States, making it larger than the Episcopal Church by at least a million members, with an additional 54 million members worldwide—or just a bit smaller than the entire Anglican Communion. While the Assemblies of God was itself segregated for a time earlier in the twentieth century, it is now "the largest white and Hispanic Pentecostal denomination in the United States" and represents a racial diversity, which has been a part of the movement since Azusa Street that puts most other Protestant denominations to shame. Furthermore, from its inception the Assemblies of God has reached out to the broader evangelical movement. In 1942 these efforts were rewarded when the denomination was asked to join the National Association of Evangelicals.[65]

The Assemblies of God, then, fits nicely within the broad evangelical movement. As part of the wider Pentecostal movement, the size and global influence of this branch of Christianity deserves respect. Coupled with their present utilization of powerful contemporary trends such telecommunications and megachurches, Pentecostalism's importance requires their inclusion in the twenty-first century Mainline.[66]

A New Beginning

The overview has highlighted the changed nature of American Christianity in the opening decades of the twenty-first century. Including the Southern Baptist Convention and Roman Catholicism in the newly conceived Mainline offers a means to recapture the old denominational spirit of the Mainline, from a "majority of believers point of view" as well as from a pietistic/liturgical perspective, but from very different denominational starting points. When evangelicals of all denominations and Pentecostals are also included, these strands of American Christianity bear witness to the complexity and diversity of the faith and its interaction with culture and life. This new Mainline reminds us that American Christianity is part of a global faith. And since the Mainline of the Seven Sisters was never monolithic in thought, theology, or doctrine, it is hardly surprising that the new Mainline is not of one mind in these areas either. The new configuration of the Mainline not only showcases where Americans tend to worship but also the doctrinal beliefs that the majority of Americans adhere to as bedrocks of their faith.

Just because the Seven Sisters are no longer appropriately considered part of the Mainline does not mean that they are no longer important to American history or religious experience. Instead, the new Mainline speaks to the continued vibrancy of the faith, the democratic ethos of American Christianity, and the reality of denominational decline. But the reconfiguration also reminds us that the Mainline itself is a lineup of believers that has changed over the course of American history. The twenty-first century is no exception.[67]

Notes

NOTES TO INTRODUCTION

1. Throughout this book the words "American" and "United States" will be used to refer to the United States of America. The author is aware of the differences, and trusts his readers are as well, but also recognizes that historically both have been used interchangeably by both citizens and historians of the nation under study.

2. The Pennsylvania Railroad's executives built houses in Philadelphia's suburbs, equipped with their own rail stations so that they could come downtown to work. The track these houses and suburbs were on was the railroad's main line, and the term "mainline," which already had a resonance with those in Pennsylvania, may have become attributed to the founders of the FCC, the Seven Sisters, as well.

3. "Documented: The Decline of America's Largest Denominations," http://www.mondaymorninginsight.com, 24 February 2009.

4. For example, Dean M. Kelley, *Why Conservative Churches Are Growing* (New York: Harper, 1972); Thomas C. Reeves, *The Empty Church: The Suicide of Liberal Christianity* (New York: Free Press, 1996); Dave Shiflett, *Exodus: Why Americans are Fleeing Liberal Churches for Conservative Christianity* (New York: Sentinel, 2005).

5. Robert Putnam has explored this concept to a degree in his most recent book. See Robert D. Putnam and David E. Campbell, *American Grace: How Religion Divides and Unites Us* (New York: Simon and Schuster, 2010).

6. G. K. Berry, *The Eight Leading Churches: Their History and Teaching* (St. Louis, MO: Christian Board of Publication, 1914).

7. Martin E. Marty, foreword to *Righteous Empire: The Protestant Experience in America* (New York: Dial Press, 1970).

8. David Sehat, *The Myth of American Religious Freedom* (New York: Oxford University Press, 2011). Much of Sehat's analysis is steeped in notions of order, control, and authority of a majority oppressing (or ignoring) a minority or minorities. He rarely deals with doctrine or theology, other than in strictly political terms.

9. For example, see Leonard J. Arrington and Davis Bitton, *The Mormon Experience: A History of the Latter-day Saints* (New York: Vintage Books, 1979); Rodney Stark and William Sims Bainbridge, *Religion, Deviance, and Social Control* (New York: Routledge, 1996), 106; Stephen J. Stein, *Communities of Dissent: A History of Alternative Religions in America* (New York: Oxford University Press, 2003); Robert A. Orsi, *Thank You, St. Jude: Women's Devotion to the Patron Saint of Hopeless Causes* (New Haven, CT: Yale University Press, 1996).

10. Substituting the word "Mainstream," as some have done, is hardly beneficial to either academic or general discussion of the Mainline because it casts those outside the fold not just as a minority but also as radical in some way.

11. John Micklethwait and Adrian Wooldridge, *God Is Back: How the Global Revival of Faith Is Changing the World* (New York: Penguin, 2009), 192–93.

NOTES TO CHAPTER 1

1. *Daily Mail* (London), 5 May 2007.

2. Thomas Cahill, *Mysteries of the Middle Ages: The Rise of Feminism, Science, and Art from the Cults of Catholic Europe* (New York: Nan A. Talese, 2006), 179–83; Diarmaid MacCulloch, *The Reformation: A History* (New York: Viking, 2004), 52–55.

3. MacCulloch, *Reformation*, 10, 15, 26–34, 40; Paul R. Lucas, *American Odyssey, 1607–1789* (Englewood Cliffs, NJ: Prentice Hall, 1984), 10–11.

4. Cahill, *Mysteries of the Middle Ages*, 192–95.

5. Ibid., 133–34, 166; Thomas F. Madden, *The New Concise History of the Crusades* (Lanham, MD: Rowman and Littlefield, 2005).

6. Edmund S. Morgan, *American Heroes: Profiles of Men and Women who Shaped Early America* (New York: W. W. Norton, 2009), 3–20.

7. Samuel Eliot Morison, *Admiral of the Ocean Sea: A Life of Christopher Columbus* (Boston: Little, Brown, 1991); Lucas, *American Odyssey*, 3.

8. John Edwards, *Ferdinand and Isabella* (New York: Longman, 2004). It should be noted that the Spanish Crown also expelled or forced the conversion of all Jews residing in Spain during these years as well.

9. Perry Miller, *Errand into the Wilderness* (Cambridge, MA: Belknap Press, 1964), vii. See also Alfred Crosby, *Columbian Exchange: Biological and Cultural Consequences of 1492* (New York: Praeger, 2003).

10. MacCulloch, *Reformation*, 111–36, 147–53, 189–92; Martin E. Marty, *Martin Luther: A Life* (New York: Penguin, 2008); Roland H. Bainton, *Here I Stand: A Life of Martin Luther* (New York: Hendrickson Publishing, 2009).http://www.amazon.com/Martin–Luther–Life-Penguin-Lives/dp/0143114301/ref=sr_1_13?ie=UTF8&s=books&qid=1256615527&sr=8-13

11. MacCulloch, *Reformation*, 189–92, 230–45, 259–61, 296–300.

12. Ibid., 341–43; Lucas, *American Odyssey*, 16–17; "Martin Luther and John Calvin," http://www.reformedreflections.ca, 3 April 2011.

13. Alister E. McGrath, *Christianity's Dangerous Idea: The Protestant Revolution—A History from the Sixteenth Century to the Twenty-First* (New York: HarperOne, 2007).

14. "95 Theses–Luther," http://www.iclnet.org/pub/resources/text/wittenberg/luther/web/ninetyfive.html, 31 October 2009.

15. MacCulloch's *Reformation* is an indispensable source for this discussion.

16. Victor Davis Hanson, *Carnage and Culture: Landmark Battles in the Rise of Western Power* (New York: Anchor, 2001), 170–232.

17. Bartolome de Las Casa, "Las Casas," http://www.lascasas.org/, 31 October 2009; Judith McLaughlin, *Sacred Feminine: Sacred Images of the Southwest and the Development of the Feminine Principles in New Mexico Folkloric Art* (Los Ranchos, NM: Rio Grande Books, 2009).

18. MacCulloch, *Reformation*, 327–29.

19. Stephen Toulmin, *Cosmopolis: The Hidden Agenda of Modernity* (Chicago: University of Chicago Press, 1992); MacCulloch, *Reformation*, 327–29.

20. Richard White, *The Middle Ground: Indians, Empires, and Republics in the Great Lakes Region, 1650–1815* (New York: Cambridge University Press, 1991); Jon Butler, *The Huguenots in America, A Refugee People in New World Society* (Cambridge, MA: Harvard University Press, 1983).

21. Carla Gardina Pestana, *Protestant Empire: Religion and the Making of the British Atlantic World* (Philadelphia: University of Pennsylvania Press, 2009).

22. Cahill, *Mysteries of the Middle Ages*, 132; MacCulloch, *Reformation*, 193–99; "John Wycliffe," http://www.christianitytoday.com/ch/131christians/moversandshakers/wycliffe.html?start=2, 25 August 2011.

23. Diarmaid MacCulloch, *Thomas Cranmer* (New Haven, CT: Yale University Press, 1996).

24. MacCulloch, *Reformation*, 272–86, 322–24; Alison Weir, *The Children of Henry VIII* (New York: Ballantine Books, 1996).

25. Miller, *Errand Into the Wilderness*, 100–103, 122–23; Jon Butler, *Awash in a Sea of Faith: Christianizing the American People* (Cambridge, MA: Harvard University Press, 1990), 38–51, 127–28; Rhys Isaac, *The Transformation of Virginia, 1740–1790* (Chapel Hill: University of North Carolina Press, 1999); Michael Kranish, *Flight from Monticello: Thomas Jefferson at War* (New York: Oxford University Press, 2010), 8; Thomas S. Kidd, *God of Liberty: A Religious History of the American Revolution* (New York: Basic Books, 2010), 49–51; Bret Tarter, "Reflections on the church of England in Colonial Virginia," *Virginia Magazine of History and Biography* 112 no.4 (2004): 338–71.

26. Lucas, *American Odyssey*, 31, 38; Robert Middlekauff, *The Mathers: Three Generations of Puritan Intellectuals, 1596–1728* (Berkeley: University of California Press, 1999), 49. For a very enjoyable account of all things Puritan, see Sarah Vowell, *The Wordy Shipmates* (New York: Riverhead Books, 2008).

27. Hugh Trevor-Roper, *The Crisis of the Seventeenth Century: Religion, the Reformation, and Social Change* (Indianapolis: Liberty Fund, 1967), 318–58; MacCulloch, *Reformation*, 485–515. King James I was also the monarch when an official version of the Bible was commissioned in England, eponymously named the King James Version, which further angered Puritans because they were largely excluded from the translation process and had to watch as the KJV replaced their beloved Geneva Bible. See Alister McGrath, *In the Beginning: The Story of the King James Bible and How It Changed a Nation, a Language, and a Culture* (New York: Anchor, 2002).

28. David Hackett Fischer, *Albion's Seed: Four British Folkways in America* (New York: Oxford University Press, 1989); Francis J. Bremer, *John Winthrop: America's Forgotten Founding Father* (New York: Oxford University Press, 2003); Edmund S. Morgan, *The Puritan Dilemma: The Story of John Winthrop* (New York: Longman, 1999); Morgan, *American Heroes*, 54–60; Theodore Dwight Bozeman, *To Live Ancient Lives: The Primitivist Dimension in Puritanism* (Chapel Hill: University of North Carolina Press, 1988); Theodore Dwight Bozeman, *The Precisianist Strain: Disciplinary Religion and Antinomina Backlash in Puritanism to 1638* (Chapel Hill: University of North Carolina Press, 2003); David D. Hull, *A Reforming People: Puritanism and the Transformation of Public Life in New England* (New York: Alfred A. Knopf, 2011), 23

29. William Bradford, *Of Plymouth Plantation, 1620–1647* (New York: Modern Library, 1981); Nathaniel Philbrick, *Mayflower: A Story of Courage, Community, and War* (New York: Viking, 2006); Edwin S. Gaustad, *Liberty of Conscience: Roger Williams in America* (Grand Rapids, MI: William B. Eerdmans Publishing, 1991), 14; Nick Bunker, *Making Haste from Babylon: The Mayflower Pilgrims and Their World, a New History* (New York: Alfred A Knopf, 2010).

30. Miller, *Errand into the Wilderness*, 17; Morgan, *American Heroes*, 24–25; Middlekauff, *The Mathers*, 41; Morgan, *American Heroes*, 90; Perry Miller, *Roger Williams: His Contribution to the American Tradition* (Indianapolis: Bobbs-Merrill, 1953), 22; Hull, *Reforming People*, 86.

31. Miller, *Errand into the Wilderness*, 63–64, 84, 91.

32. Perry Miller, *The New England Mind: The Seventeenth Century* (New York: Macmillan, 1939), viii; Perry Miller, *The New England Mind: From Colony to Province* (Cambridge, MA: Harvard University Press, 1953), 25; Hull, *Reforming People*, 97–101.

33. Miller, *From Colony to Province*, 93–113, 278–87; Edmund S. Morgan, *Visible Saints: The History of a Puritan Idea* (Ithaca, NY: Cornell University Press, 1965); Trevor-Roper, *Crisis of the Seventeenth Century*, 229; Miller, *Errand into the Wilderness*, 160; Middlekauff, *The Mathers*, 87; Thomas S. Kidd, *The Great Awakening: The Roots of Evangelical Christianity in Colonial America* (New Haven, CT: Yale University Press, 2007), 6–7; Philip F. Gura, *Jonathan Edwards: America's Evangelical* (New York: Hill and Wang, 2005), 12–15.

34. Miller, *Errand into the Wilderness*, 7, 23; Perry Miller, *Nature's Nation* (Cambridge, MA: Belknap Press, 1967), 14–16; Eve LaPlante, *Salem Witch Judge: The Life and Repentance of Samuel Sewall* (New York: HarperOne, 2007), 25, 38, 59, 69, 203–5.

35. James F. Cooper Jr., *Tenacious of Their Liberties: The Congregationalists in Colonial Massachusetts* (New York: Oxford University Press, 1999), 11, 13, 19.

36. Morgan, *American Heroes*, 90–101; Lucas, *American Odyssey*, 39–40; Bremer, *Winthrop*, 297.

37. Miller, *Errand into the Wilderness*, 146; Miller, *From Colony to Province*, 120; Miller, *Roger Williams*, 25; Gaustad, *Liberty of Conscience*, 25, 34–37, 77–78; Edwin S. Gaustad, *Roger Williams* (New York: Oxford University Press, 2005), 6–7, 95.

38. Morgan, *American Heroes*, 139–76; Miller, *Roger Williams*, 241–53.

39. Lucas, *American Odyssey*, 43; Butler, *Awash in a Sea of Faith*, 51–55; "George Calvert," http://mdroots.thinkport.org/library/georgecalvert.asp, 25 August 2011.

40. Michael Kammen, *Colonial New York: A History* (New York: Oxford University Press, 1996).

41. Mary Beth Norton, *In the Devil's Snare: The Salem Witchcraft Crisis of 1692* (New York: Vintage Books, 2002); Middlekauff, *The Mathers*, 148–61; Trevor-Roper, *Crisis of the Seventeenth Century*, 88–93, 107–18, 127–77; Miller, *From Colony to Province*, 191–208; Morgan, *American Heroes*, 112–29.

42. Missing, in large part, from this mix was the Lutheran Church, which eventually achieved Mainline status at the dawn of the twentieth century.

43. MacCulloch, *Reformation*, 674; Trevor-Roper, *Crisis of the Seventeenth Century*, 188–99. This included such American colonists as Cotton Mather and Jonathan Edwards.

44. Richard S. Westfall, *Never at Rest: A Biography of Isaac Newton* (New York: Cambridge University Press, 1983); Roger Woolhouse, *Locke: A Biography* (New York: Cambridge University Press, 2007).

45. James A. Herrick, *The Radical Rhetoric of the English Deists: The Discourse of Skepticism, 1680–1750* (Columbia: University of South Carolina Press, 1997); John C. Biddle, "Locke's Critique of Innate Principles and Toland's Deism," *Journal of the History of Ideas* 37 (September 1976): 411–22.

46. Miller, *From Colony to Province*, 464, 471; Herrick, *Radical Rhetoric of the English Deists*; Roger L. Emerson, "Heresy, the Social Order, and English Deism," *Church History* 37 (December, 1968): 389–403.

47. Francis J. McConnell, *John Wesley* (New York: Abingdon Press, 1939); Richard E. Brantley, *Locke, Wesley, and the Method of English Romanticism* (Gainesville: University of Florida Press, 1984); Stuart C. Henry, *George Whitefield: Wayfaring Witness* (New York: Abingdon Press, 1957); Butler, *Awash in a Sea of Faith*, 186–91; Mark A. Noll, *The Rise of Evangelicalism: The Age of Edwards, Whitefield, and the Wesleys* (Downers Grove, IL: InterVarsity Press, 2004); J. Wesley Bready, *England: Before and After Wesley* (New York: Harper, 1938); David Hempton, *Methodism: Empire of the Spirit* (New Haven, CT: Yale University Press, 2005), 13; Kidd, *Great Awakening*, 42–44.

48. Miller, *Errand into the Wilderness*, 156; Kidd, *Great Awakening*, xvi.

49. Kidd, *Great Awakening*, 55–116; Walter J. Fraser Jr., *Savannah in the Old South* (Athens: University of Georgia Press, 2003), 21; R. Lawrence Moore, *Touchdown Jesus: The Mixing of Sacred and Secular in American History* (Louisville, KY: Westminster John Knox Press, 2003), 18–20; Thomas S. Kidd, *God of Liberty: A Religious History of the American Revolution* (New York: Basic Books, 2010), 21; Edgar Legare Pennington, "John Wesley's Georgia Ministry," *Church History* 8 (September 1939): 231–54.

50. George M. Marsden, *Jonathan Edwards: A Life* (New Haven, CT: Yale University Press, 2003); Miller, *Errand into the Wilderness*, 167, 175; Kidd, *Great Awakening*, 9–23; Philip F. Gura, *Jonathan Edwards: America's Evangelical* (New York: Hill and Wang, 2005), 18–19, 97–109; Edgar Legare Pennington, "John Wesley's Georgia Ministry," *Church History* 8 (September 1939): 231–54; Frederick Dreyer, "Evangelical Thought: John Wesley and Jonathan Edwards," *Albion* 19 (Summer 1987): 177–92.

51. Perry Miller, *Nature's Nation* (Cambridge, MA: Belknap Press, 1967), 32–33; Kidd, *Great Awakening*, 1, 40–54; Middlekauff, *The Mathers*, 96–138.

52. MacCulloch, *Reformation*, 363–65; Miller, *Errand into the Wilderness*, 56–57.

53. Kidd, *Great Awakening*, xiv–xv, 117–70; Lucas, *American Odyssey*, 191; Butler, *Awash in a Sea of Faith*, 180–81; Gura, *Jonathan Edwards*, 71–84.

54. William Hague, *William Wilberforce: The Life of the Great Anti-Slave Trade Campaigner* (New York: Harcourt, 2008). See also Kidd, *Great Awakening*.

55. Jeffry H. Morrison, *John Witherspoon and the Founding of the American Republic* (Notre Dame, IN: University of Notre Dame Press, 2005); Daniel L. Dreisbach, Mark D. Hall, and Jeffry H. Morrison, eds., *The Founders on God and Government* (Lanham, MD: Rowman and Littlefield, 2004); Thomas S. Engeman and Michael P. Zuckert, eds., *Protestantism and the American Founding* (Notre Dame, IN: University of Notre Dame Press, 2004); Carl Bridenbaugh, *Miter and Scepter: Transatlantic Faiths, Ideas, Personalities, and Politics, 1689–1775* (New York: Oxford University Press, 1967); Ellis Sandoz, ed., *Political Sermons of the American Founding Era, 1730–1805*, vol. 1 (Indianapolis, IN: Liberty Fund, 1998).

56. Butler, *Awash in a Sea of Faith*, 194–98.

57. James B. Bell, *A War of Religion: Dissenters, Anglicans, and the American Revolution* (New York: Palgrave, 2008).

58. Kidd, *Great Awakening*, 288–89, 294–98; Kidd, *God of Liberty*, 82–95.

59. Kidd, *God of Liberty*, 5.

60. Morrison's *John Witherspoon* is a good source for this discussion.

61. "Roots: 1736–1816," http://www.umc.org, 25 August 2010.

62. Kidd, *God of Liberty*, 38–40, 167–68.

63. Forrest Church, *So Help Me God: The Founding Fathers and the First Great Battle Over Church and State* (New York: Harcourt, 2007); Jon Meacham, *American Gospel: God, the Founding Fathers, and the Making of a Nation* (New York: Random House, 2007); John A. Ragosta, *Wellspring of Liberty: How Virginia's Religious Dissenters Helped Win the American Revolution and Secured Religious Liberty* (New York: Oxford University Press, 2010); Ron Chernow, *Washington: A Life* (New York: Penguin, 2010), 130–33; Kidd, *God of Liberty*, 223–24, 241.

64. Ira Stoll, *Samuel Adams: A Life* (New York: Free Press, 2008); Kidd, *God of Liberty*, 11–16.

65. David Sehat, *The Myth of American Religious Freedom* (New York: Oxford University Press, 2011), 4; Walter Stahr, *John Jay: Founding Father* (New York: Hambledon and London, 2006); Kidd, *Great Awakening*, 290; Kranish, *Flight from Monticello*, 9–10. As Kranish notes, Patrick Henry was raised Anglican and remained Anglican. But his mother, Sarah, left the Anglican fold to become a Presbyterian during the First Great Awakening thanks in large part of the preaching of Samuel Davies, a Presbyterian evangelist.

66. Morrison, *John Witherspoon*.

67. Ron Chernow, *Alexander Hamilton* (New York: Penguin, 2005).

68. Church, *So Help Me God*; Meacham, *American Gospel*; John Micklethwait and Adrian Wooldridge, *God Is Back: How the Global Revival of Faith Is Changing the World* (New York: Penguin, 2009).

69. Kidd, *God of Liberty*, 6, 227.

NOTES TO CHAPTER 2

1. Harriet Beecher Stowe, *Uncle Tom's Cabin or, Life among the Lowly* (New York: Penguin, 1986), 41.

2. David Sehat, *The Myth of American Religious Freedom* (New York: Oxford University Press, 2011), 2.

3. Edmund S. Morgan, *American Heroes: Profiles of Men and Women who Shaped Early America* (New York: W. W. Norton, 2009), 177–94; Martin E. Marty, *Righteous Empire: The Protestant Experience in America* (New York: Dial Press, 1970), 69–70; John B. Boles, *The Great Revival: 1787–1805* (Lexington: University Press of Kentucky, 1996), 1, 12–13.

4. George C. Rable, *God's Almost Chosen Peoples: A Religious History of the American Civil War* (Chapel Hill: University of North Carolina Press, 2010), 36.

5. "Freedom of Religion," http://www.hsp.org/default.aspx?id=1251, 27 October 2009.

6. Thomas S. Kidd, *The Great Awakening: The Roots of Evangelical Christianity in Colonial America* (New Haven, CT: Yale University Press, 2007), 268, 286, 311–16, 322.

7. Boles, *Great Revival*, x, 10, 19.

8. Debby Applegate, *The Most Famous Man in America: The Biography of Henry Ward Beecher* (New York: Doubleday, 2006), 57; Ernest Lee Tuveson, *Redeemer Nation: The Idea of America's Millennial Role* (Chicago: University of Chicago Press, 1974); Jon Butler, *Awash*

in a Sea of Faith: Christianizing the American People (Cambridge, MA: Harvard University Press, 1990), 258–70.

9. Kidd, *Great Awakening*, 184–87, 299–301; Paul R. Lucas, *American Odyssey, 1607–1789* (Englewood Cliffs, NJ: Prentice Hall, 1984), 106; Edwin S. Gaustad, *Liberty of Conscience: Roger Williams in America* (Grand Rapids, MI: William B. Eerdmans Publishing, 1991), 208.

10. David Baines-Griffiths, *Wesley the Anglican* (New York: Macmillan, 1919); William Larkin Duren, *Francis Asbury: Founder of American Methodism and Unofficial Minister of State* (New York: Macmillan, 1928); Frederick C. Gill, *Charles Wesley: The First Methodist* (New York: Abingdon Press, 1964), 187–202; Butler, *Awash in a Sea of Faith*, 237–41; Russell E. Richey, *Methodist Connectionalism: Historical Perspectives* (Nashville, TN: United Methodist General Board of Higher Education, 2009); John Wigger, *American Saint: Francis Asbury and the Methodists* (New York: Oxford University Press, 2009); "The Churches Grow: 1817–1843," http://www.umc.org, 25 August 2010.

11. James F. Cooper Jr., *Tenacious of Their Liberties: The Congregationalists in Colonial Massachusetts* (New York: Oxford University Press, 1999), 68–71; Lucas, *American Odyssey*, 106; Hugh Trevor-Roper, *The Crisis of the Seventeenth Century: Religion, the Reformation, and Social Change* (Indianapolis: Liberty Fund, 1967), 363–64; "Presbyterian Historical Society: A Brief History of the Presbyterian Church in this Country," http://www.history.pcusa.org, 25 August 2010.

12. Nathan O. Hatch, *The Democratization of American Christianity* (New Haven, CT: Yale University Press, 1989).

13. Dickson D. Bruce Jr., *And They All Sang Hallelujah: Plain-Folk Camp-Meeting Religion, 1800–1845* (Knoxville: University of Tennessee Press, 1974).

14. Charles G. Finney, *How to Experience Revival* (New Kensington, PA: Whitaker House, 1984); "Charles Finney," http://www.christianitytoday.com/ch/131christians/evangelistsandapologists/finney.html, 31 October 2009; "A Wolf in Sheep's Clothing," http://www.spurgeon.org/~phil/articles/finney.htm, 31 October 2009.

15. Boles, *Great Revival*, 183.

16. "About Us–Our History," http://www.ame-church.com, 27 August 2010; Richard Newman, *Freedom's Prophet: Bishop Richard Allen, the AME Church, and the Black Founding Fathers* (New York: New York University Press, 2009); Marty, *Righteous Empire*, 24–33; Walter J. Fraser Jr., *Savannah in the Old South* (Athens: University of Georgia Press, 2003), 150.

17. "Seventh Day Adventists," http://www.religionfacts.com/christianity/denominations/seventh_day_adventist.htm, 27 October 2009.

18. Jan Shipps, *Mormonism: The History of a New Religious Tradition* (Chicago: University of Illinois Press, 1987).

19. Thomas W. Grafton, *Alexander Campbell: Leader of the Great Reformation of the Nineteenth Century* (St. Louis, MO: Christian Publishing Company, 1897); Charles Crossfield Ware, *Barton Warren Stone: Pathfinder of Christian Union* (St. Louis, MO: Bethany Press, 1932); "History of the Disciples," http://www.disciples.org, 25 August 2010; Boles, *Great Revival*, 143, 158.

20. Paul E. Johnson, *A Shopkeeper's Millennium: Society and Revivals in Rochester, New York, 1815–1837* (New York: Hill and Wang, 2004); Timothy L. Smith, *Revivalism and Social Reform: American Protestantism on the Eve of the Civil War* (Baltimore, MD: Johns Hopkins

University Press, 1989); Daniel Walker Howe, *The Political Culture of the American Whigs* (Chicago: University of Chicago Press, 1984); Rodney Stark, *For the Glory of God: How Monotheism led to Reformations, Science, Witch-hunts, and the End of Slavery* (Princeton, NJ: Princeton University Press, 2003), 365; Mark A. Noll, ed., *Religion and American Politics: From the Colonial Period to the 1980s* (New York: Oxford University Press, 1990); Jon Meacham, *American Gospel: God, the Founding Fathers, and the Making of a Nation* (New York: Random House, 2006); Harry S. Stout, *Upon the Altar of the Nation: A Moral History of the Civil War* (New York: Viking Press, 2006).

21. Milton Rugoff, *The Beechers: An American Family in the Nineteenth Century* (New York: Harper and Row, 1981); Applegate, *Most Famous Man in America*; Constance Mayfield Roarke, *Trumpets of Jubilee: Henry Ward Beecher, Harriet Beecher Stowe, Lyman Beecher, Horace Greeley, P. T. Barnum* (New York: Harcourt, Brace, 1927); Lyman Beecher Stowe, *Saints, Sinners, and Beechers* (Indianapolis, IN: The Bobbs-Merrill Company, 1934). If there was a challenger to Beecher as America's most famous preacher, it would have been Boston's Trinity Episcopal Church's pastor Phillips Brooks.

22. Christine Leigh Heyrman, *Southern Cross: The Beginnings of the Bible Belt* (Chapel Hill: University Of North Carolina Press, 1997); Kidd, *Great Awakening*, 214, 217, 234–35, 249; Butler, *Awash in a Sea of Faith*, 129–63; Emory M. Thomas, *The Confederate Nation: 1861–1865* (New York: Harper Perennial, 2011), 21–23.

23. The Friends were the first Christian denomination to condemn slavery as an institution and to require members to either free their slaves or leave the church altogether.

24. Henry Mayer, *All on Fire: William Lloyd Garrison and the Abolition of Slavery* (New York: W. W. Norton, 1998); David S. Reynolds, *John Brown, Abolitionist: The Man Who Killed Slavery, Sparked the Civil War, and Seeded Civil Rights* (New York: Vintage Books, 2005); Eve LaPlante, *Salem Witch Judge: The Life and Repentance of Samuel Sewall* (New York: HarperOne, 2007), 224–30; Heyrman, *Southern Cross*, 92–93, 155; Fraser, *Savannah in the Old South*, 142.

25. Rable, *God's Almost Chosen Peoples*, 23–24; Mayer, *All on Fire*, 376; "The Slavery Question and Civil War: 1844–1865," http://www.umc.org, 25 August 2010.

26. Abraham Lincoln, "Second Inaugural Address," http://www.bartleby.com/124/pres32.html, 27 October 2009.

27. James H. Moorhead, *American Apocalypse: Yankee Protestants and the Civil War, 1860–1869* (New Haven, CT: Yale University Press, 1978); Mark A. Noll, *The Civil War as Theological Crisis* (Chapel Hill: University of North Carolina Press, 2006); Drew Gilpin Faust, *This Republic of Suffering: Death and the American Civil War* (New York: Random House, 2008); Randall M. Miller, Harry S. Stout, Charles Reagan Wilson, eds., *Religion and the American Civil War* (New York: Oxford University Press, 1998); Rable, *God's Almost Chosen Peoples*, 7, 204–10.

28. George M. Marsden, *The Evangelical Mind and the New School Presbyterian Experience* (New Haven, CT: Yale University Press, 1970), 240–42; Gaines M. Foster, *Moral Reconstruction: Christian Lobbyists and the Federal Legislation of Morality, 1865–1920* (Chapel Hill: University of North Carolina Press, 2002).

29. *Christianity Today*, September 2006, 32–38; Charles Spurgeon, *Grace: God's Unmerited Favor* (New Kensington, PA: Whitaker House, 1996); "Charles Spurgeon Archive," http://www.spurgeon.org/, 31 October 2009; Applegate, *Most Famous Man in America*, 470. Robert Orsi also made this statement in the July/August 2006 issue of *Historically Speaking*, 9–10.

30. Edward Caldwell Moore, *The Spread of Christianity in the Modern World* (Chicago: University of Chicago Press, 1919); Cyril J. Davey, *The March of Methodism: The Story of Methodist Missionary Work Overseas* (New York: Philosophical Library, 1951); John Micklethwait and Adrian Wooldridge, *God Is Back: How the Global Revival of Faith Is Changing the World* (New York: Penguin, 2009), 224–25, 232–34.

31. Kevin Phillips, *William McKinley*, The American Presidents Series: *The 25th President, 1897–1901* (New York: Times Books, 2003).

32. Elias B. Sanford, *Origin and History of the Federal Council of the Churches of Christ in America* (Hartford, CT: S. S. Scranton, 1916), 259–60; Elias B. Sanford, ed., *Federal Council of the Churches of Christ in America: Report of the First Meeting of the Federal Council, Philadelphia, 1908* (New York: Revell Press, 1909), 267–73.

33. "Federal Council of the Churches of Christ in America," http://www.history.pcusa.org, 25 August 2010; Sanford, *Federal Council*, iii.

34. Sanford, *Federal Council*, 507; "Federal Council of the Churches of Christ in America," http://www.history.pcusa.org, 25 August 2010.

35. Sanford, *Federal Council*, vi; Marty, *Righteous Empire*, 183–84.

36. Samuel S. Hill, Charles H. Lippy, and Charles Reagan Wilson, eds., *Encyclopedia of Religion in the South* (Macon, GA: Mercer University Press, 2005), 273. The founding members were the Baptist Churches of the United States, the Free Baptist General Conference, the National Baptist Convention (African), the Christians (The Christian Connection), the Congregational Churches, the Congregational Methodist Churches, the Disciples of Christ, the Evangelical Association, the Evangelical Synod of North America, the Friends, the Evangelical Lutheran Church, the Methodist Episcopal Church, the Methodist Episcopal Church South, the Primitive Methodist Church, the Colored Methodist Episcopal Church in America, the Methodist Protestant Church, the African Methodist Episcopal Church, the African Methodist Episcopal Zion Church, the General Conference of the Mennonite Church of North America, the Moravian Church, the Presbyterian Church in the U.S.A., the Welsh Calvinistic Methodist or Presbyterian Church, the Reformed Presbyterian Church, the United Presbyterian Church, the Protestant Episcopal Church, the Reformed Church in America, the Reformed Church of the U.S.A., the Reformed Episcopal Church, the Seventh-Day Baptist Churches, the Swedish Lutheran Augustana Synod, the United Brethren in Christ, and the United Evangelical Church. See Sanford, *Federal Council*, 512–13.

37. Jane Addams' work at Hull House is an example.

38. Sanford, *Federal Council*, 87–88.

39. E. Clifford Nelson, ed., *The Lutherans in America* (Philadelphia: Fortress Press, 1975); "Lutheran Roots in America," http://www.elca.org, 25 August 2010; Marty, *Righteous Empire*, 125. World War I helped spur various Lutheran synods (first Norwegian and then German) to merge. These mergers ebbed and flowed, culminating in the 1960s and 1970s when the American Lutheran Church (German), the United Evangelical Lutheran Church (Danish), and the Evangelical Lutheran Church (Norwegian) merged to form the American Lutheran Church. Another round of mergers between German, Slovak, Icelandic, Swedish, Finish, and Danish Lutherans then formed the Lutheran Church in America. In the 1980s, work began to form the Evangelical Lutheran Church in America.

40. Karen Abbott, *Sin in the Second City: Madams, Ministers, Playboys, and the Battle for America's Soul* (New York: Random House, 2008); Mike Dash, *Satan's Circus: Murder,*

Vice, Police Corruption, and New York's Trial of the Century (New York: Three Rivers Press, 2007); William R. Moody, *The Life of Dwight L. Moody* (Chicago: Fleming H. Revell, 1900); D. L. Moody, *Heaven Awaits* (New Kensington, PA: Whitaker House, 1982); Margaret Lamberts Bendroth, *Fundamentalists in the City: Conflict and Division in Boston's Churches, 1885–1950* (New York: Oxford University Press, 2005); Daniel Mark Epstein, *Sister Aimee: The Life of Aimee Semple McPherson* (New York: Harvest, 1993); Marty, *Righteous Empire*, 103, 107–10, 162–63.

41. Edward J. Renehan Jr., *Commodore: The Life of Cornelius Vanderbilt* (New York: Basic Books, 2009); David Nasaw, *Andrew Carnegie* (New York: Penguin, 2007); Ron Chernow, *Titan: The Life of John D. Rockefeller, Sr.* (New York: Vintage, 2004); Jean Strouse, *Morgan: American Financier* (New York: Harper Perennial, 2000).

42. Timothy Miller, *Following in His Steps: A Biography of Charles M. Sheldon* (Knoxville: University of Tennessee Press, 1987), 159, 164–72; Robert M. Crunden, *Ministers of Reform: The Progressives Achievement in American Civilization, 1889–1920* (Urbana: University of Illinois Press, 1984), ix; John Whiteclay Chambers II, *The Tyranny of Change: America in the Progressive Era, 1890–1920* (New Brunswick, NJ: Rutgers University Press, 2000), 144, 164; Paul Boyer, *Urban Masses and Moral Order in America, 1820–1920* (Cambridge, MA: Harvard University Press, 1997), 195–99.

43. James H. Moorhead, *World without End: Mainstream American Protestant Visions of the Last Things, 1880–1925* (Bloomington: Indiana University Press, 1999).

44. George M. Marsden, *Fundamentalism and American Culture: The Shaping of Twentieth-Century Evangelicalism, 1870–1925* (New York: Oxford University Press, 1982), 70–71, 87, 242–43; Bradley J. Longfield, *The Presbyterian Controversy: Fundamentalists, Modernists, and Moderates* (New York: Oxford University Press, 1991), 3.

45. D. G. Hart, *That Old Time Religion in America: Evangelical Protestantism in the Twentieth Century* (Chicago: Ivan R. Dee, 2002), 31; Kevin J. Corn, *Forward Be Our Watchword: Indiana Methodism and the Modern Middle Class* (Indianapolis: University of Indianapolis Press, 2008); Dale A. Johnson, "The Methodist Quest for an Educated Ministry," *Church History* 51 (September 1982): 304–20.

46. Marsden, *Fundamentalism and American Culture*, 12, 17, 38, 125.

47. Ibid., 48–51; Longfield, *The Presbyterian Controversy*, 220–21.

48. Perry Miller, *Errand into the Wilderness* (Cambridge. MA: Belknap Press, 1964), 235.

49. Walter Rauschenbusch, *A Gospel for the Social Awakening* (New York: Association Press, 1950), 31, 81; Charles Howard Hopkins, *The Rise of the Social Gospel in American Protestantism, 1865–1915* (New Haven, CT: Yale University Press, 1967), 12, 280–317; Donald K. Gorrell, *The Age of Social Responsibility: The Social Gospel in the Progressive Era, 1900–1920* (Macon, GA: Mercer University Press, 1988), ix; Douglas Jacobson and William Vance Trollinger Jr., eds., *Re-Forming the Center: American Protestantism, 1900 to the Present* (Grand Rapids, MI: William B. Eerdmans Publishing, 1998), 1–14, 317; Martin E. Marty, *Pilgrims in Their Own Land: 500 Years of Religion in America* (Boston: Little, Brown, 1984), 375–77; Paul A. Carter, *The Decline and Revival of the Social Gospel: Social and Political Liberalism in American Protestant Churches, 1920–1940* (Ithaca, NY: Cornell University Press, 1956), 12–13; Charles S. MacFarland, ed., *Christian Unity at Work: The Federal Council of the Churches of Christ in America in Quadrennial Session at Chicago, Illinois, 1912* (New York: Federal Council of Churches, 1913), 253; Robert H. Wiebe, *Businessmen and Reform: A Study of the Progressive Movement* (Cambridge, MA: Harvard University Press, 1962), 17.

50. Foster, *Moral Reconstruction*.

51. Philip Williams, *Walls that Human Hands Have Raised: A History of Central Avenue United Methodist Church* (Indianapolis: Central Avenue United Methodist Church, 2000), 7; First Quarterly Conference, 10 December 1917, Minutes and Board Meetings 1864–1918 book, Archives of Meridian Street United Methodist Church, Indianapolis, Indiana.

52. Cassandra Tate, *Cigarette Wars: The Triumph of "the Little White Slaver"* (New York: Oxford University Press, 1999); Egal Feldman, "Prostitution, the Alien Woman and the Progressive Imagination, 1910–1915," *American Quarterly* 19 (Summer 1967): 192–206; Robert E. Riegel, "Changing American Attitudes toward Prostitution (1800–1920)," *Journal of the History of Ideas* 29 (July–September, 1968): 437–52; Richard H. Shryock, "Sylvester Graham and the Popular Health Movement, 1830–1870," *Mississippi Valley Historical Review* 18 (September 1931): 172–83.

53. Sanford, *Origin and History*, 259–60; Sanford, *Federal Council*, 267–73; Department of Social Service, 29 October 1913, 29 January, 20 March, 8 October 1914, 1913–1914, Folder 1, Box 1, Indianapolis Church Federation Executive Committee Minutes, Indiana Historical Society, Indianapolis, Indiana; *Indianapolis News*, 30 November, 2 December, 5 December 1914, 23 January, 30 January, 12 June 1915, 20 February, 28 October, 4 November 1916, 2 November 1918; *Indianapolis Star*, 8 January, 24 January, 27 January, 31 January, 8 March 1910; 3 July, 13 July, 14 July, 15 July, 16 July, 20 July, 1 October, 19 October 1912; Edwin L. Becker, *From Sovereign to Servant: The Church Federation of Greater Indianapolis, 1912–1987* (Indianapolis: Church Federation of Greater Indianapolis, 1987), 9.

54. *Noblesville Daily Ledger*, 20 July, 27 July 1914, 11 March, 23 October 1915.

55. Much of the following discussion on Prohibition is drawn from Jason S. Lantzer, *Prohibition is Here to Stay: The Reverend Edward S. Shumaker and the Dry Crusade in America* (Notre Dame, IN: University of Notre Dame Press, 2009).

56. Micklethwait and Wooldridge, *God Is Back*, 90.

57. K. Austin Kerr, *Organized for Prohibition: A New History of the Anti-Saloon League* (New Haven, CT: Yale University Press, 1985), 2–3, 8, 25, 90; Richard F. Hamm, *Shaping the Eighteenth Amendment: Temperance Reform, Legal Culture, and the Polity, 1880–1920* (Chapel Hill: University of North Carolina Press, 1995), 132–36; Edward Behr, *Prohibition: Thirteen Years that Changed America* (New York: Arcade, 1996), 56–57; Richard Jensen, *The Winning of the Midwest: Social and Political Conflict, 1888–1896* (Chicago: University of Chicago Press, 1971); Ann-Marie E. Szymanski, *Pathways to Prohibition: Radicals, Moderates, and Social Movement Outcomes* (Durham, NC: Duke University Press, 2003), 1–5.

58. Ann-Marie Szymanski, "Dry Compulsions: Prohibition and the Creation of State-Level Enforcement Agencies," *Journal of Policy History* 11 (1999): 115–46.

59. Francis I. Moats, "The Rise of Methodism in the Middle West," *Mississippi Valley Historical Review*, 15 (June 1928): 69–88; Jack J. Detzler, *The History of the Northwest Indiana Conference of the Methodist Church, 1852–1951* (Nashville, TN: Parthenon Press, 1953), 97; Emory Stevens Bucke, ed., *The History of American Methodism*, vol. 3 (New York: Abingdon Press, 1964), 335; James H. Timberlake, *Prohibition and the Progressive Movement, 1900–1920* (Cambridge, MA: Harvard University Press, 1963), 20.

60. E. Glenn Hinson, *A History of Baptists in Arkansas, 1818–1978* (Little Rock: Arkansas Baptist State Convention, 1979), 217–18; Wayne Flynt, *Alabama Baptists: Southern Baptists in the Heart of Dixie* (Tuscaloosa: University of Alabama Press, 1998), 209; *Baptist World*, 27 July 1911.

61. Jack S. Blocker Jr., *American Temperance Movements: Cycles of Reform* (Boston: Twayne, 1989), 54; Executive Committee, 14 January 1919, 1918–1919, Folder 3, Box 1, Indianapolis Church Federation Executive Committee Minutes, Indiana Historical Society, Indianapolis, Indiana.

62. Herbert Hoover to F. A. Govett, 28 June 1922, Prohibition 1922–1924 file, Box 486, Commerce Series, Herbert Hoover Papers, Herbert Hoover Presidential Library.

63. *Western Christian Advocate*, 7 January, 21 January, 7 July 1920; General Board of Church and Society, "The United Methodist Building," http://www.umc-gbcs.org/75th-book.htm, 20 September 2002; *Ninety-Third Session of the Indiana Annual Conference of the Methodist Episcopal Church*, 1924; Charles E. Canup, "The Temperance Movement in Indiana," *Indiana Magazine of History* 16 (June 1920): 151.

64. Michael McGerr, *A Fierce Discontent: The Rise and Fall of the Progressive Movement in America, 1870–1920* (New York: Free Press, 2003), 315.

65. Deirdre M. Moloney, *American Catholic Lay Groups and Transatlantic Social Reform in the Progressive Era* (Chapel Hill: University of North Carolina Press, 2002).

66. Richard Hofstadter, *The Age of Reform: From Bryan to FDR* (New York: Vintage Books, 1955), 181–82; James Cannon Jr., *Bishop Cannon's Own Story: Life as I Have Seen It* (Durham, NC: Duke University Press, 1955), 337.

67. Marvin R. O'Connell, *Edward Sorin* (Notre Dame, IN: University of Notre Dame Press, 2001), 707; John F. Quinn, *Father Mathew's Crusade: Temperance in Nineteenth-Century Ireland and Irish America* (Boston: University of Massachusetts Press, 2002), 172, 182–83, 186; Joseph C. Gibbs, *History of the Catholic Total Abstinence Union of America* (Philadelphia: Penn Printing House, 1907); Joan Bland, *Hibernian Crusade: The Story of the Catholic Total Abstinence Union of America* (Washington, DC: Catholic University of America Press, 1951), 135–36, 245, 274; John Radzilowski, *The Eagle and the Cross: A History of the Polish Roman Catholic Union of America, 1873–2000* (New York: Columbia University Press, 2003), 127–31.

68. Robert E. Burns, *Being Catholic, Being American: The Notre Dame Story, 1842–1934* (Notre Dame, IN: University of Notre Dame Press, 1999), 262–69, 310–22, 335–36; *Indiana Catholic and Record*, 21 April 1922.

69. Bulletins, 16 December 1923, 6 April 1924, 25 October 1925, Bulletins 1923–1926 book, Bulletins, 16 January, 23 January, 19 June 1927, Bulletins 1927–1929 book, Bulletins, 23 February, 11 May, 18 May 1930, Bulletins 1930–1932 book, MSUMC Archives; *Ninety-Fifth Session of the Indiana Annual Conference of the Methodist Episcopal Church*, 1926; Larry Engelmann, *Intemperance: The Lost War against Liquor* (New York: Free Press, 1979), 78–81, 149; James A. Morone, *Hellfire Nation: The Politics of Sin in American History* (New Haven, CT: Yale University Press, 2003), 320–23; Catherine Gilbert Murdock, *Domesticating Drink: Women, Men, and Alcohol in America, 1870–1940* (Baltimore. MD: Johns Hopkins University Press, 1998), 36; Norman H. Clark, *Deliver Us from Evil: An Interpretation of American Prohibition* (New York: W. W. Norton, 1976), 140; Behr, *Prohibition*, 162, 167, 241.

70. Irving Fisher, *The Noble Experiment.* (New York: Alcohol Information Committee, 1930); Behr, *Prohibition*, 233; Clark, *Deliver Us from Evil*, 167; John C. Burnham, *Bad Habits: Drinking, Smoking, Taking Drugs, Gambling, Sexual Misbehavior, and Swearing in American History* (New York: New York University Press, 1993), 31.

71. David E. Kyvig, *Repealing National Prohibition* (Kent, OH: Kent State University Press, 2000), xxv.

72. Albert W. Wardin Jr., *Tennessee Baptists: A Comprehensive History, 1779–1999* (Brentwood, TN: Executive Board of the Tennessee Baptist Convention, 1999), 415, 425; Howard Hyde Russell to Lincoln-Lee Chain supporters, 29 June 1933, Reel 12, American Issue Publishing Papers, Temperance and Prohibition Papers; Frances Hendrickson, *Hoosier Heritage: Women's Christian Temperance Union, 1874–1974* (Indianapolis: WCTU of Indiana, 1974), 91–92; Resolution on Temperance and Prohibition, June 1935; Untitled Resolution, June 1936; Resolution on the Liquor Situation, June 1938, Southern Baptist Convention Resolutions, http://www.sbc.net/resolutions, 3 February 2004.

73. Elkhart County Prohibition Committee Letter, 22 October 1960; Mrs. Galen Bowman to Joe Ludd, 17 August 1962; Indiana Prohibition Committee Letter, 14 January 1967, Folder 1, Box 1; Letter, J. Ralston Miller to the Rev. Lee Cory, 19 April 1962; W. E. Yeater to Robert L. Gildea, 11 June 1966, Folder 28, Box 1, Prohibition Party of Indiana Papers, Manuscripts Division, Indiana State Library, Indianapolis, Indiana.

74. Robert A. Hohner, *Prohibition and Politics: The Life of Bishop James Cannon, Jr.* (Columbia: University of South Carolina Press, 1999), 289; Robert Moats Miller, *Harry Emerson Fosdick: Preacher, Pastor, Prophet* (New York: Oxford University Press, 1985), 432–33; Rev. E. Y. Mullins to W. O. Carver, 23 October 1907, Folder 41, Box 4, William O. Carver Papers, SBC Archives; Robert Dean McNeil, *Valiant for Truth: Clarence True Wilson and Prohibition* (Portland: Oregonians Concerned about Addiction Problems, 1992), 75–76, 124.

75. M. Nelson McGeary, *Gifford Pinchot: Forester, Politician* (Princeton, NJ: Princeton University Press, 1960), 382–83; Russell Pulliam, *Publisher: Gene Pulliam, Last of the Newspaper Titans* (Ottawa, IL: Jameson Books, 1984), 109–10; Henry Z. Scheele, *Charlie Halleck: A Political Biography* (New York: Exposition Press, 1966), 35, 38–41, 53; Roger K. Newman, *Hugo Black: A Biography* (New York: Pantheon Books, 1994), 39–45, 63–65, 89–129, 148, 239–63.

76. Donald Meyer, *The Protestant Search for Political Realism, 1919–1941* (Middletown, CT: Wesleyan University Press, 1988), 11–12.

77. Engelmann, *Intemperance*, 194; Morone, *Hellfire Nation*, 282; Boyer, *Urban Masses*, 285–287; Jonathan Zimmerman, *Distilling Democracy: Alcohol Education in America's Public Schools, 1880–1925* (Lawrence: University of Kansas Press, 1999); Kerr, *Organized for Prohibition*, 9–10, 243, 246, 276–77; McGerr, *Fierce Discontent*, 317.

78. Micklethwait and Wooldridge, *God Is Back*, 90.

79. Miller, *Harry Emerson Fosdick*.

80. Edward J. Larson, *Summer for the Gods: The Scopes Trial and America's Continuing Debate Over Science and Religion* (New York: Basic Books, 2006), 34; Marsden, *Fundamentalism and American Culture*, 3–5, 43–44, 118–23; Jeffery L. Sheler, *Believers: A Journey into Evangelical America* (New York: Viking, 2006), 56; Longfield, *Presbyterian Controversy*, 20–21, 27–30, 69, 124; Marty, *Righteous Empire*, 217.

81. Robert Middlekauff, *The Mathers: Three Generations of Puritan Intellectuals, 1596–1728* (Berkeley: University of California Press, 1999), 280–96; Adam Hamilton, *Confronting the Controversies: Biblical Perspectives on Tough Issues* (Nashville, TN: Abingdon Press, 2005), 39–53; *Social Principles of the United Methodist Church, 2005–2008* (Washington, DC: United Methodist Church General Board of Church and Society, 2004), 7; Tony Williams, *The Pox and the Covenant: Mather, Franklin, and the Epidemic that Changed America's Destiny* (New York: Source Books, 2010).

82. Stark, *For the Glory of God*, 197; Rodney Stark and William Sims Bainbridge, *The Future of Religion, Secularization, Revival, and Cult Formation* (Berkeley: University of California Press, 1985), 14.

83. Larson, *Summer for the Gods*, 23, 32; Barry Werth, *Banquet at Delmonico's: Great Minds, the Gilded Age, and the Triumph of Evolution in America* (New York: Random House, 2009).

84. Christine Rosen, *Preaching Eugenics: Religious Leaders and the American Eugenics Movement* (New York: Oxford University Press, 2004).

85. Longfield, *Presbyterian Controversy*, 54–55; Larson, *Summer for the Gods*, 39–47.

86. Robert Hastings Nichols, "Fundamentalism in the Presbyterian Church," *Journal of Religion*, 5 (January 1925): 14–36. Traditionally, Christians had referred to Christ's Second Coming as the Millennium: the book of Revelation speaks of Christ's rule for a thousand years. By the late nineteenth and early twentieth centuries, Christians were debating whether that was a literal reign, if it meant the church's progress and triumph in the world, and if believers would be "raptured" to Heaven before or after it started. The arguments between pre- and post-Millenialists continues to the present.

87. Longfield, *Presbyterian Controversy*, 9–11, 115.

88. Marsden, *Fundamentalism and American Culture*, 91–92, 164, 174–75.

89. Longfield, *Presbyterian Controversy*, 87–89, 141–47, 157, 214–15, 223; Marty, *Righteous Empire*, 219.

90. Larson, *Summer for the Gods*, 116, 121.

91. Ibid., 88–95, 197; Hart, *That Old Time Religion in America*, 25.

92. Larson, *Summer for the Gods*, 224, 233; Joel A. Carpenter, *Revive Us Again: The Reawakening of American Fundamentalism* (New York: Oxford University Press, 1997), xi.

93. Larson, *Summer for the Gods*, 229–31; Hamilton, *Confronting the Controversies*, 39–53; C. S. Lewis, *Mere Christianity* (New York: Touchstone, 1996), 32; *Social Principles of the United Methodist Church*, 2005–2008 (Washington, DC: United Methodist Church General Board of Church and Society, 2004), 7.

94. Marsden, *Fundamentalism and American Culture*, 188–94; Larson, *Summer for the Gods*, 233–34; R. Lawrence Moore, *Touchdown Jesus: The Mixing of Sacred and Secular in American History* (Louisville, KY: Westminster John Knox Press, 2003), 46–50. Perhaps the best example of this is William Bell Riley. See, William V. Trollinger Jr., *God's Empire: William Bell Riley and Midwestern Fundamentalism* (Madison: University of Wisconsin Press, 1991).

95. Marsden, *Fundamentalism and American Culture*, 103–8, 165, 172, 178–79; Longfield, *Presbyterian Controversy*, 233–35; "World War and More Change: 1914–1939," http://www.umc.org, 25 August 2010.

96. Micklethwait and Wooldridge, *God Is Back*, 79.

NOTES TO CHAPTER 3

1. "Christ Church," http://www.nycago.org/Organs/NYC/html/ChristMethodist.html, 25 January 2011; "Sanctuary," http://www.christchurchnyc.org/tour.html, 25 January 2011.

2. David Sehat, *The Myth of American Religious Freedom* (New York: Oxford University Press, 2011), 227, 235–54.

3. Darren Dochuk, *From Bible Belt to Sunbelt: Plain-Folk Religion, Grassroots Politics, and the Rise of Evangelical Conservatism* (New York: W. W. Norton, 2011), 45.

4. Sermon, 4 May 1969, Folder 19, Box 5, Record Group 1, and September/October *Positiv*, 1 publications—Positiv box, Record Group 3, St. Paul's Archives; *Trinity News*, Trinity 1970, Newsletter: Trinity News Box, Trinity Archives.

5. Sehat, *Myth of American Religious Freedom* , 229; Daniel K. Williams, *God's Own Party: The Making of the Christian Right* (New York: Oxford University Press, 2010), 39; Dochuk, *From Bible Belt to Sunbelt*, 41; Samuel C. Kincheloe, *Research Memorandum on Religion in the Depression* (New York: Arno Press, 1972); Martin E. Marty, *Righteous Empire: The Protestant Experience in America* (New York: Dial Press, 1970), 234; Erik S. Gellman and Jarod Roll, *The Gospel of the Working Class: Labor's Southern Prophets in New Deal America* (Chicago: University of Illinois Press, 2011).

6. James Hudnut-Beumler, *Looking for God in the Suburbs: The Religion of the American Dream and its Critics, 1945–1965* (New Brunswick: Rutgers University Press, 1994); Robert S. Ellwood, *The Fifties Spiritual Marketplace: American Religion in a Decade of Conflict* (New Brunswick: Rutgers University Press, 1997); Williams, *God's Own Party*, 27.

7. Alan Petigny, "Two Great Myths About the 1950s," *Historically Speaking* (April 2010): 2–6; *Church Militant*, November 1955; Wade Clark Roof, *Community and Commitment: Religious Plausibility in a Liberal Protestant Church* (New York: Elsevier, 1978), 40, 45; Robert S. Ellwood, *The Sixties Spiritual Awakening: American Religion Moving from Modern to Postmodern* (New Brunswick: Rutgers University Press, 1994), 37–38, 47–48; Wade Clark Roof and William McKinney, *American Mainline Religion: Its Changing Shape and Future* (New Brunswick: Rutgers University Press, 1989), 22; John Micklethwait and Adrian Wooldridge, *God Is Back: How the Global Revival of Faith is Changing the World* (New York: Penguin, 2009), 90–97; "Norman Vincent Peale," http://normanvincentpeale.wwwhubs. com/, 1 November 2009; Robert S. Ellwood, *1950: Crossroads of American Religious Life* (Louisville, KY: Westminster John Knox Press, 2000).

8. Andrew S. Finstuen, *Original Sin and Everyday Protestants: The Theology of Reinhold Niebuhr, Billy Graham, and Paul Tillich in an Age of Anxiety* (Chapel Hill: University of North Carolina Press, 2009); the historian Arthur Schlesinger Jr. bemoaned the fact that Richard Niebuhr, whom he considered to be the greatest American theologian of the twentieth century, was neglected by both conservatives and liberals. See *New York Times*, 18 September 2005.

9. David W. Lotz, ed., *Altered Landscapes: Christianity in American, 1935–1985* (Grand Rapids, MI: William B. Eerdmans Publishing, 1989), 26; Roof, *Community and Commitment*, 3; Raymond W. Albright, *A History of the Protestant Episcopal Church* (New York: Macmillan, 1964), 359–61.

10. Timothy F. Sedgwick and Philip Turner, eds., *The Crisis in Moral Teaching in the Episcopal Church* (Harrisburg: Morehouse Publishing, 1992), 77; Robert W. Prichard, *A History of the Episcopal Church* (Harrisburg, PA: Morehouse Publishing, 1991), 243; John L. Kater Jr., "Experiment in Freedom: The Episcopal Church and the Black Power Movement," *Historical Magazine of the Protestant Episcopal Church* 48 (March 1979): 68–69.

11. David E. Sumner, *The Episcopal Church's History: 1945–1985* (Wilton, CT: Morehouse Publishing, 1987), 36; Thomas C. Reeves, *The Empty Church: Does Organized Religion Matter Anymore?* (New York: Free Press, 1998), 136; James F. Findlay, Jr., *Church People in the Struggle: The National Council of Churches and the Black Freedom Movement, 1950–1970* (New York: Oxford University Press, 1993), 16–17.

12. Reeves, *Empty Church: Does Organized Religion Matter*, 137; Sumner, *Episcopal Church's History*, 38; Rev. Mary Ringwald, correspondence with author, 17 February 1998; Episcopal Society for Cultural and Racial Unity, pamphlet, 1965.

13. *Church Militant*, June 1963; Findlay, *National Council*, 3, 14, 25; Mark Newman, *Divine Agitators: The Delta Ministry and Civil Rights in Mississippi* (Athens: University of Georgia Press, 2004).

14. "Letter from a Birmingham Jail," http://www.africa.upenn.edu/Articles_Gen/Letter_Birmingham.html, 27 October 2009.

15. Dochuk, *From Bible Belt to Sunbelt*, 277; Williams, *God's Own Party*, 6, 33, 43–48

16. Ellwood, *Sixties Spiritual*, 70–71; Kit and Frederica Konolige, *The Power of Their Glory: America's Ruling Class, The Episcopalians* (New York: Wyden Books, 1978), 20; Paul Moore, *Presences: A Bishop's Life in the City* (New York: Farrar, Straus and Giroux, 1997), 122–23; David L. Holmes, *A Brief History of the Episcopal Church* (Valley Forge: Trinity Press International, 1993), 131; Gloria Kemper, interview with author, 9 November 1998; *Church Militant*, October 1961.

17. Rev. Gordon Chastain, interview with author, 2 October 1998; Bishop Stewart Wood, interview with author, 19 January 1999; Rev. Carol Mader (10 o'clock Group), interview with author, 20 January 1999; Alice Roettger, interview with author, 21 January 1999; Nicholas J. Demerath III and Phillip E. Hammond, *Religion in Social Context: Tradition and Transition* (New York: Random House, 1969), 218–19; *Indianapolis News*, 29 August 1959; *Church Militant*, April 1965; Findlay, *National Council*, 96.

18. Hadden, *Gathering Storm*, 112, 121, 175; Rev. Robert Giannini, interview with author, 25 March 1999.

19. Carl R. Stockton, *Christ Church Cathedral: Sesquicentennial, 1837–1987* (Indianapolis, IN: Christ Church Cathedral, 1987), 23; Findlay, *National Council*, 64; Russell B. Pulliam, correspondence with author, 9 April 1999; *Indianapolis Star*, 20 October 1975; Alice Roettger, interview with author, 21 January 1999; Gary Lowe, correspondence with author, 14 April 1999. See also, Jason S. Lantzer, "Crisis on the Circle: Christ Church Cathedral Confronts the 1960s," *Journal of Anglican and Episcopal History* 68 (December 1999): 489–513.

20. Kater, "Experiment in Freedom: The Episcopal Church and the Black Power Movement," 69–70; Anderson, *Movement*, 117, 132, 158; Philip Berrigan, *A Punishment for Peace* (London: Macmillan, 1969), 3, 7, 28, 64; McCartney, *Black Power*, 3, 95, 102–3, 108; Leon Howell and Vivian Lindermayer, eds., *Ethics in the Present Tense: Readings from Christianity and Crisis, 1966–1991* (New York: Friendship Press, 1991), 23; Wilmore, *Black Religion*, 201–2.

21. Forman, *Black Revolutionaries*, 457; *Church Militant*, December 1966, September 1968, November 1968; Howell and Lindermayer, *Ethics*, 22, 24–25; James Forman, *High Tide of Black Resistance and other Political and Literary Writings* (Seattle: Open Hand Publishers, Incorporated, 1994), 121–31; Patterson, *Grand Expectations*, 654; Anderson, *Movement*, 157; ESCRU, The Church and the Riots: Guidelines for Diocesan Strategy in Northern Urban Areas, 1966.

22. Sermon, 12 March 1972, Folder 20; Sermons, 15 November 1964 and 19 February 1967, Folder 21; Sermon, 26 January 1969, Folder 19, Box 5, Record group 1, St. Paul's Archives; James Forman, *The Making of Black Revolutionaries* (Washington, DC: Open Hand Publications, 1985), 458; James Haskins, *Profiles in Black Power* (Garden City, NY: Doubleday, 1972); Moore, *Presences,* 208.

23. Anderson, *Movement*, 168–69; Forman, *High Tide*, 131; Kater, "Experiment," 74–76; Sumner, *Episcopal Church's History*, 48; Bentley, *Florida*, 194–95; Sedgwick and Turner, *Moral Teaching*, 77–78; Catherine M. Prelinger, ed., *Episcopal Women: Gender, Spirituality, and Commitment in an American Mainline Denomination* (New York: Oxford University Press, 1992), 138–40; Bishop Paul Moore, interview with author, 29 January 1999; Moore, *Presences*, 201–3.

24. Vestry meeting, 2 April 1967, vestry minutes 2 April 1967 folder, Box 1, Archives of All Saints Episcopal Church; vestry meeting, 5 November 1967, St. Christopher's vestry Book 2: 1966–1974, Archives of St. Christopher's; vestry meeting, 13 December 1968, vestry minutes 1955–1969 folder, St. Matthew's Archives.

25. *Christopher*, April 1968, Archives of St. Christopher's.

26. Hadden, *Gathering Storm*, 59, 104; Kater, "Experiment," 72–73.

27. Wilmore, *Black Religion*, 235; Ellwood, *Sixties Spiritual*, 275–77; McCartney, *Black Power*, 143, 149; Forman, *Black Revolutionaries*, 544–48; Booty, *Crisis*, 60; Rosemary Radford Ruether, *Liberation Theology: Human Hope Confronts Christian History and American Power* (New York: Paulist Press, 1972), 127–44.

28. Reeves, *Empty Church: Does Organized Religion Matter*, 138; Haskins, *Profiles*, 135.

29. Reeves, *Empty Church: Does Organized Religion Matter*, 138–40; See BEC Dialogue Committee Folder, Massachusetts Conference Materials, Box 1, Congregational Library and Archive, Boston, Massachusetts.

30. Findlay, *National Council*, 200–203; Booty, *Crisis*, 61; Haskins, *Profiles*, 136.

31. Vestry meeting, 26 May 1969, vestry meeting minutes, 1965–1971, Box 1/1, CCC Archives; *Cathedral News*, 30 May 1969 and 24 October 1969, Cathedral News Folder, 1968–1971, box 8/2/1, CCC Archives; *Church Militant*, June 1969; Alice Roettger, interview with author, 21 January 1999; Ehrgott to vestry, letter, 14 July 1969; 1969 vestry minutes and Treasurer Reports, Box 1, Nativity Archives; Sermon, 15 June 1969, Folder 19, Box 5, Record group 1, St. Paul's Archives; Alfred Tsang, correspondence with author, 1 March 1999; Patricia Herndon, interview with author, 7 April 1999; Forward Incorporated information, in author's collection.

32. Sumner, *Episcopal Church's History*, 51–53; Prichard, *History*, 260–61; Kater, "Experiment," 72; Moore, *Presences*, 204; Wilmore, *Black Religion*, 234; John D. Beatty, *Beyond These Stones: A History of Trinity Episcopal Church , Fort Wayne, Indiana* (Fort Wayne, IN: Trinity Episcopal Church, 1994), 206–7; Paul M. Washington, *"Other Sheep I Have": The Autobiography of Father Paul M. Washington* (Philadelphia: Temple University Press, 1994), 87–95; Robert J. Center, *Our Heritage: A History of the First Seventy-Five Years of the Diocese of Northern Indiana* (South Bend: Peterson Printing, 1973), 64.

33. Kater, "Experiment," 77; Findlay, *National Council*, 207; Haskins, *Profiles*, 137. Mainline churches across the nation felt compelled to respond to the manifesto but were frightened by the rhetoric. The Indianapolis Church Federation, though it never endorsed the manifesto, did call it a "symbol of remaining unmet needs of minority groups." See Becker, *Sovereign*, 106–7; Findlay, *National Council*, 212.

34. Forman, *Black Revolutionaries*, 549; Wilmore, *Black Religion*, 240–41.

35. Vestry Meetings, 9 September 1968 and 11 November 1968, 1968 vestry minutes Folder, vestry minutes Box 1960–1969, Trinity Archives.

36. Findlay, *National Council*, 142–43, 205–7, 220; Reeves, *Empty Church: Does Organized Religion Matter*, 140; Konolige, *Power of Their Glory*, 34; Sumner, *Episcopal Church's History*,

48–50; Bryan V. Hills, *Can Two Walk Together Unless They be Agreed?: American Religious Schisms in the 1970s* (Brooklyn: Carlson Publishing, 1991), 102; Kater, "Experiment," 80; *Indianapolis News*, 27 September 1969; *Cathedral News*, 12 September 1969, Cathedral News Folder, 1968–1971, Box 8/2/1, CCC Archives; Church Militant, September 1969, November 1969; Booty, *Crisis*, 61; *Church Militant*, June 1969; Center, *Heritage*, 68.

37. Findlay, *National Council*, 173, 213; Prichard, *History*, 242; Sermon, 29 August 1971, Folder 21, Box 5, Record group 1, St. Paul's Archives; James Gilbert, *Chance*, 106; Robert Emmett Curran, "History of a Changing Neighborhood," *America* (15 June 1968): 773–75; Jeanne Atkins, interview with author, 2 November 1998; *Indianapolis Star*, 12 December 1982; *Koinonia* newsletter, May 1977, 1977 folder, Newsletters box, St. Alban's Archives; Roof, *Community and Commitment*, 163, 169; Dean M. Kelley, *Why Conservative Churches are Growing: A Study in Sociology of Religion* (New York: Harper and Row, 1972), 98; Patterson, *Grand Expectations*, 732; Canon Mary Ringwald, correspondence with author, 16 September 1998; "Questions and Answers About Desegregation in New Castle County, 1975"; Hadden, *Gathering Storm*, 130, 135; Frank R. Westie, "The American Dilemma: An Empirical Test," *American Sociological Review* 30 (August 1965): 531–32; Gunnar Myrdal, *An American Dilemma: The Negro Problem and Modern Democracy*, 2 vols. (New York: Harper and Brothers, 1944).

38. Niebuhr, *Moral Man*, 252–54; Alice Roettger, interview with author, 21 January 1999; Wilmore, *Black Religion*, 237.

39. John Booty, *The Episcopal Church in Crisis* (Cambridge: Cowley Publishers, 1988), 73; James T. Patterson, *Grand Expectations: The United States, 1945–1974* (New York: Oxford University Press, 1996), 8, 80, 436; Ellwood, *Sixties Spiritual Awakening*, 23, 58; David W. Lotz, ed., *Altered Landscapes; Christianity in America, 1935–1985* (Grand Rapids, MI: William B. Eerdmans Publishing, 1989), 352; Robert D. Schulzinger, *A Time For War: The United States and Vietnam, 1941–1975* (New York: Oxford University Press, 1997), 88, 124; Terry H. Anderson, *The Movement and the Sixties* (New York: Oxford University Press, 1995), 120; *Church Militant*, February 1961; William Scarlet, ed., *The Christian Demand for Social Justice* (New York: Signet, 1949); Alice Roettger, interview with author, 21 January 1999.

40. Williams, *God's Own Party*, 21–28, 78–80; Dochuk, *From Bible Belt to Sunbelt*, 147–166; Norman Berdischevsky, "The Religious Left, J. B. Matthews and the Censure of Senator McCarthy," http://www.newenglishreview.org, 28 March 2011.

41. Sedgwick and Turner, eds., *Crisis in Moral Teaching*, 96–97, 103; Reeves, *Empty Church: Does Organized Religion Matter*, 140; Lantzer, "Crisis on the Circle," 489–513.

42. Michael B. Friedland, "Giving a Shout for Freedom: The Reverend Malcolm Boyd, the Right Reverend Paul Moore, Jr., and the Civil Rights and Antiwar Movements of the 1960s and 1970s," Vietnam Generation Journal (March 1994), http://lists.village.virginia.edu/sixties.Texts.Scholarly/Freidland_Boyd_01.html, (11 January 1999).

43. Forman, *High Tide of Black Resistance*, 102–3; Roof and McKinney, *American Mainline Religion*, 28; Berrigan, *Peace*, 13; Findlay, *National Council*, 182; Becker, *From Sovereign to Servant*, 75–77; Schulzinger, *War*, 236; Mitchell K. Hall, *Because of Their Faith: CALCAV and Religious Opposition to the Vietnam War* (New York: Columbia University Press, 1990); Friedland, "Giving a Shout," 11 January 1999. By the end of 1966, Boyd was made a member of the CALCAV's national committee, none of whose members served at the parish level within their respective denominations.

44. Jerry Belknap, interview with author, 28 October 1998; Gloria Kemper, interview with author, 9 November 1998; Bishop Stewart Wood, interview with author, 19 January 1999; Margaret Barnard, interview with author, 16 February 1999; Rev. Donald Jones, interview with author, 16 November 1998; Schulzinger, *War*, 239; St. James Episcopal Church (New Castle, IN), "St. James Episcopal Church," http://www.avcnet.com/stjames/. (11 January 1999); Rev. Frederic P. Williams, interview with author, 23 February 1999; William Osborn, correspondence with author, 1 March 1999; vestry meeting, 28 July 1967, vestry minutes 1955–1969 folder, St. Matthew's Archives; *Trinity News*, Late Trinity Season 1967, Newsletters: Trinity News Box, Trinity Archives; Russell B. Pulliam, correspondence with author, 9 April 1999.

45. Rauch to Moore, letter, 24 February 1967, vestry correspondence folder, Box 1/3, CCC Archives; *Trinity News*, Trinity 1969, Newsletters: Trinity News Box, Trinity Archives.

46. Anderson, *Movement*, 208; Patterson, *Grand Expectations*, 599; Berrigan, *Peace*, 20–21; *Indianapolis News*, 9 October 1967.

47. Robert W. Prichard, *A History of the Episcopal Church* (Harrisburg, PA: Morehouse Publishing, 1991), 260–61; Moore, *Presences*, 204–6; Hall, *CALCAV*, 90.

48. Fred Munds, interview with author, 19 January 1999; John Oaks, correspondence with author, 22 March 1999; Rev. Carol Mader (10 o'clock Group), interview with author, 20 January 1999; vestry meeting, 12 September 1969 and 3 October 1969, vestry meeting minutes, brown folder, Miscellaneous box, and Newsletters, February and March 1968, 1968 folder, Newsletters box, St. Alban's Archives; Jeanne Atkins, interview with author, 2 November 1998; Schulzinger, *War*, 215–17, 233–34.

49. *Church Militant*, June 1971; Kelley, "Long Island," 109–15, 174–75; Reeves, *Empty Church: Does Organized Religion Matter*, 140.

50. Reeves, *Empty Church: Does Organized Religion Matter*, 140–42.

51. Book of Common Prayer (1928) and (1979); Alice Roetteger, interview with author, 21 January 1999; Friedland, "Giving a Shout," 11 January 1999.

52. Holmes, *A Brief History of the Episcopal Church*, 12; Hills, *Can Two Walk*, 100–101.

53. Hills, *Can Two Walk*, 102–3; *Indianapolis News*, 7 October 1967; Konolige, *Power of Their Glory*, 161–62.

54. Hills, *Can Two Walk*, 101–2; *Church Militant*, September 1964; Lotz, ed., *Altered Landscapes*, 30–31.

55. Booth, *Indianapolis*, 110; Catherine Prelinger, ed., *Episcopal Women: Gender, Spirituality, and Commitment in an American Mainline Denomination* (New York: Oxford University Press, 1992), 21, 25, 52–53; Heather Huyck, "Indelible Change: Women Priests in the Episcopal Church," *Historical Magazine of the Protestant Episcopal Church* 51 (December 1982): 385, 392–95; J. Carleton Hayden, "New Men, Strange Faces, Other Minds: The Human Rights Revolution, 1954–1978," *Historical Magazine of the Protestant Episcopal Church* 49 (March 1980): 71–73, 79–81; Hills, *Can Two Walk*, 109–10; *New York Times*, 30 July 1974; Jacqueline Field-Bibb, *Women Towards Priesthood: Ministerial Politics and Feminist Praxis* (New York: Cambridge University Press, 1991), 294–95; Rev. Mary Ringwald, correspondence with author, 17 February 1998 and 16 September 1998; Sumner, *Episcopal Church's History*, 9–11; Paula D. Nesbitt, *Feminization of the Clergy in America: Occupational and Organizational Perspectives* (New York: Oxford University Press, 1997), 37–38; Prichard, *History of the Episcopal Church*, 255–57.

56. Vestry Meeting, 12 March 1973, 1973 vestry minutes Folder, vestry minutes Box 1970–1979, Trinity Archives.

57. *Christopher*, October 1969 and October 1973, Archives of St. Christopher's; Hills, *Can Two Walk*, 110–11; *Church Militant*, June 1973.

58. Sumner, *Episcopal Church's History*, 21; Hills, *Can Two Walk*, 112–16; Washington, *"Other Sheep I Have"*, 162–72; Field-Bibb, *Priesthood*, 295; Huyck, "Indelible," 389–92; *Church Militant*, December 1964, November 1972, June 1974, and September 1974; Booth, *Indianapolis*, 111; Nesbitt, *Feminization*, 4; James Elliot Lindsley, *This Planted Vine: A Narrative History of the Episcopal Diocese of New York* (New York: Harper and Row, 1984), 316–22; Konolige, *Power of Their Glory*, 34; John Booty, *The Episcopal Church in Crisis* (Cambridge: Cowley Publishers, 1988), 65–72.

59. Rev. Carol Mader (10 o'clock Group), interview with author, 20 January 1999; Craine to Taylor, letter, 2 May 1973, vestry minutes 1973–1982 folder, St. Matthew's Archives; *Church Militant*, September 1973, March 1974, April 1974, November 1976 and December 1976; vestry meeting, 25 March 1974, vestry minutes 1973–1982 folder, St. Matthew's Archives; Clergy newsletter, 27 February 1975, Clergy newsletter folder, Box 2, Archives of All Saints Episcopal Church; vestry meetings, 20 April 1975 and 11 May 1975, 1975 vestry minutes folder, Box 1; Clergy newsletter, 24 April 1975, Clergy newsletter folder, Box 2, Archives of All Saints Episcopal Church; Bishop Stewart Wood, interview with author, 19 January 1999; *Indianapolis Star*, 2 July 1975; Church Militant, December 1977/January 1978; vestry meetings, 27 September 1971 and 24 May 1972, vestry minutes 1970–1972 folder, St. Matthew's Archives; Booth, *Indianapolis*, 111, 173, 241–42; Rev. Tanya Beck, correspondence with author, 16 June 1999; "The Sounds of All Saints," November/December 1976, News 1976 folder, Box 1, Archives of All Saints Episcopal Church; Rev. Gordon Chastain, interview with author, 2 October 1998; Jerry Belknap, interview with author, 28 October 1998; Alice Roettger, interview with author, 21 January 1999.

60. *Church Militant*, June 1976 and October 1976; Hills, *Can Two Walk*, 116–17; Sumner, *Episcopal Church's History*, 12.

61. Vestry meeting 3 January 1977, vestry minutes 1973–1982 folder, St. Matthew's Archives; ECW meeting, 17 January 1977, ECW minutes, Green Box, St. Alban's Archives; 2 January 1977 bulletin, Bulletin box, St. Alban's Archives; Gloria Kemper, interview with author, 9 November 1998; Rev. Gordon Chastain, interview with author, 2 October 1998; Rev. Jack Eastwood, interview with author, 5 February 1999; Margaret Barnard, interview with author, 16 February 1999; Bishop Edward Jones, interview with author, 8 April 1999; Rev. Tanya Beck, correspondence with author, 16 June 1999; Rev. Jack Eastwood, interview with author, 5 February 1999; Margaret Barnard, interview with author, 16 February 1999; Bishop Donald J. Davis, correspondence with author, 3 March 1999; Robert Goodlett, interview with author, 11 March 1999; Booth, *Indianapolis*, 163; *Indianapolis Star*, 2 January 1977 and 3 January 1977; *Indianapolis News*, 3 January 1977; vestry meeting, 2 January 1977, 1977 vestry minutes folder, Box 1; "The Sounds of All Saints," January 1977, News 1977 folder, Box 1, Archives of All Saint's Episcopal Church; Robert Goodlett, interview with author, 11 March 1999; 1976 Annual Report, Annual Report folder, Box 1, Archives of All Saints Episcopal Church; Fred Munds, interview with author, 19 January 1999; Alice Roettger, interview with author, 21 January 1999; Robert Goodlett, interview with author, 11 March 1999; Field-Bibb, *Priesthood*, 295, 297; Hills, *Can Two Walk*, 103, 124–25; David L. Holmes, *A Brief History of the Episcopal Church* (Valley Forge, PA.: Trinity Press Inter-

national, 1993), 173. Craine was too ill to perform the service himself, and asked Bishop Donald J. Davis, a former Indianapolis parish priest and then bishop of the diocese of Northwestern Pennsylvania to stand in for him.

62. Vestry meeting, 17 April 1977, 1976 vestry minutes, Box 1, Nativity Archives; Fred Munds, interview with author, 19 January 1999; Ed Champa, correspondence with author, 1 March 1999; Rose Lane, correspondence with author, 2 March 1999; Linda Dernier, correspondence with author, 3 March 1999.

63. Kelley, "Diocese of Long Island," 127–34.

64. Mark Oppenheimer, *Knocking on Heaven's Door: American Religion in the Age of Counterculture* (New Haven. CT: Yale University Press, 2003), 130–71; Richard Cimino and Don Lattin, *Shopping for Faith: American Religion in the New Millennium* (San Francisco: Jossey-Bass, 1998), 89–94.

65. Catherine A. Brekus, *Strangers and Pilgrims: Female Preaching in America, 1740–1845* (Chapel Hill: University of North Carolina Press, 1998); Clifford Putney, *Muscular Christianity: Manhood and Sports in Protestant America, 1880–1920* (Cambridge, MA: Harvard University Press, 2003).

66. "Promise Keepers," http://www.promisekeepers.org/, 27 October 2009.

67. Prichard, *History*, 251–54, 257–60; C. G. Brown, "Divided Loyalties? The Evangelicals, The Prayer Book, and the Articles," *Historical Magazine of the Protestant Episcopal Church* 44 (June 1975); 189; Sumner, *Episcopal Church's History*, 107; Ephraim Radner and George R. Sumner, eds., *Reclaiming Faith: Essays on Orthodoxy in the Episcopal Church and the Baltimore Declaration* (Grand Rapids. MI: William B. Eerdmans Publishing, 1993), 43–44.

68. Erik Routley, *Hymns and the Faith* (Greenwich, CT: Seabury Press, 1956); Rev. Frederic P. Williams, interview with author, 23 February 1999.

69. Lotz, *Altered*, 111; William H. Petersen, "The Tensions of Anglican Identity in PECUSA: An Interpretive Essay," *Historical Magazine of the Protestant Episcopal Church* 47 (December 1978): 445; Hills, *Can Two Walk*, 104–9; *Church Militant*, December 1967 and May 1976, June 1968, and February 1969; G. B. Landrigan, correspondence with author, 1 March 1999; Gary Lowe, correspondence with author, 14 April 1999; Russell B. Pulliam, correspondence with author, 9 April 1999; *Koinonia* newsletter, February 1977, 1977 folder, Newsletters box, St. Alban's Archives; Jeanne Atkins, interview with author, 2 November 1998; Rose Lane, correspondence with author, 2 March 1999.

70. *Indianapolis News*, 27 February 1968; Rev. Frederic P. Williams, interview with author, 23 February 1999.

71. Robert Bruce Mullin, *Episcopal Vision/American Reality: High Church Theology and Social Thought in Evangelical America* (New Haven. CT: Yale University Press, 1986); "Welcome to The Church of Saint Mary the Virgin"; *Angelus*, 19 July 2009, both in author's collection. The church of Saint Mary the Virgin is located near Times Square in New York City and was founded in 1868 to promote the High Church tradition within the Episcopal Church.

72. G. B. Landrigan, correspondence with author, 1 March 1999; Joyce Krause, correspondence with author, 23 March 1999; Fred Munds, interview with author, 19 January 1999; Rev. Carol Mader (10 o'clock Group), interview with author, 20 January 1999; Annual Meeting (17 January 1971) and Report on Trial Liturgy (15 January 1973), Annual Report folder; vestry meetings, 23 November 1970 and 26 April 1971, vestry minutes

1970–1972 folder, St. Matthew's Archives; Liturgy Trial Questionnaire folder, Box 4, Archives of All Saints Episcopal Church; Bishop Stewart Wood, interview with author, 19 January 1999; Rev. Jack Eastwood, interview with author, 5 February 1999; Margaret Barnad, interview with author, 16 February 1999; Robert Goodlett, interview with author, 11 March 1999; Robert Goodlett, interview with author, 11 March 1999.

73. Hills, *Can Two Walk*, 105–8; *Church Militant*, December 1972 and November 1974; Stephen H. Applegate, "The Rise and Fall of the Thirty-Nine Articles: An Inquiry into the Identity of the Protestant Episcopal Church in the United States," *Historical Magazine of the Protestant Episcopal Church* 50 (December 1981): 420–21.

74. Jerry Belknap, interview with author, 28 October 1998; Gloria Kemper, interview with author, 9 November 1998; Alice Roettger, interview with author, 21 January 1999; G. B. Landrigan, correspondence with author, 1 March 1999; Douglas E. Rogers, correspondence with author, 15 April 1999; Phyllis A. Dexter, correspondence with author, 3 March 1999.

75. Fred Munds, interview with author, 19 January 1999; Bishop Stewart Wood, interview with author, 19 January 1999; Alice Roettger, interview with author, 21 January 1999; Rev. Robert Giannini, interview with author, 25 March 1999; Holmes, *History*, 17, 121, 126–28; Mullin, *Episcopal Vision/American Reality*; Radner and Sumner, *Reclaiming Faith*, 24–37; C.G. Brown, "Christocentric Liberalism in the Episcopal Church," *Historical Magazine of the Protestant Episcopal Church* 37 (March 1967): 7–9, 11–15, 24–29, 33–35.

76. "Trinity Topics" February/March 2006, Bloomington, Indiana.

77. For discussion and comparison of the two, see John Fenwick and Bryan Spinks, *Worship in Transition: The Liturgical Movement in the Twentieth Century* (New York: Continuum, 1995).

78. Bishop Paul Moore, interview with author, 29 January 1999; Robert Goodlett, interview with author, 11 March 1999; G. B. Landrigan, correspondence with author, 2 March 1999; Rev. Robert Giannini, interview with author, 25 March 1999.

79. Beatty, *Stones*, 216–17; Ron Kaser, *St. John's, Bristol: A Parish History (1843–1989)* (Bristol, IN: Bristol Banner Books, 1989), 77; Rev. Frank McKee, correspondence with author, 15 May 1999; Rev. Henry Randolph, correspondence with author, 22 March 1999; Rev. Joseph Illes, correspondence with author, 29 March 1999; George Imus, correspondence with author, 6 May 1999; Booth, *Indianapolis*, 140, 143, 150, 156, 158–59, 204; Douglas Bess, *Divided We Stand: A History of the Continuing Anglican Movement* (Riverside, CA: Tractarian Press, 2002).

80. Anonymous, correspondence with author, 7 March 1999; Standing Commission on Liturgy and Music, "Liturgy and Music," http://www.dfms.org/governance/general-convention/2000-IBs/LitandMus.html, (9 February 1999). There has even been talk of a Rite III, which would be geared toward young people.

81. 1975 and 1976 rector's annual reports, vestry annual reports 1970s, Archives of St. Paul's Episcopal Church, Indianapolis.

82. Radner and Sumner, eds., *Reclaiming Faith*, xi; Wade Clark Roof, *Community and Commitment: Religious Plausibility in a Liberal Protestant Church* (New York: Elsevier, 1978), 4. For dramatic examples of "Mainline Decline," see James W. Lewis, *The Protestant Experience in Gary, Indiana, 1906–1975: At Home in the City* (Knoxville: University of Tennessee Press, 1992); Milton J. Coalter, John M. Mulder, and Louis B. Weeks, eds., *The Mainstream Protestant "Decline": The Presbyterian Pattern* (Louisville, KY: Westminster John Knox Press, 1990).

83. Kelley, *Why Conservative Churches are Growing*, vii–viii, 20–26.

84. Patterson, *Grand Expectations*, 785; Kelley, *Conservative*, 9; Nicholas J. Demerath III and Phillip E. Hammond, *Religion in Social Context: Tradition and Transition* (New York: Random House, 1969), 172, 187; Bishop Paul Moore, interview with author, 29 January 1999; Jerry Belknap, interview with author, 28 October 1998; Vallet and Zech, *Funding*, 11–12; Holmes, *A Brief History*, 166; John Booty, *The Episcopal Church in Crisis* (Cambridge: Cowley Publishers, 1988), 62.

85. *Church Militant*, April 1971; Wade Clark Roof and William McKinney, *American Mainline Religion: Its Changing Shape and Future* (New Brunswick: Rutgers University Press, 1989), 211; Bishop Stephen Sykes, correspondence with author, 16 September 1998.

86. Sumner, *Episcopal Church's History*, 161; Vallet and Zech, *Funding*, 11; Lotz, *Altered Landscapes*, 11; *Church Militant*, January 1970 and February 1970; L. C. Rudolph, *Hoosier Faiths: A History of Indiana's Churches and Religious Groups* (Bloomington: Indiana University Press, 1995), 170.

87. St. Stephen's Episcopal Church, Philadelphia, Visit by author, 11 July 2007; Kelley, *Conservative*, 92, 136; Lotz, *Altered*, 38–39; Reeves, *Empty Church: Does Organized Religion Matter*, 28; Findlay, *Church People in the Struggle*, 222–23; Phyllis A. Dexter, correspondence with author, 3 March 1999.

88. Charles Y. Glock and Rodney Stark, *Religion and Society in Tension* (Chicago: Rand McNally, 1965), 306; Rodney Stark and Charles Y. Glock, *American Piety: The Nature of Religious Commitment* (Berkeley: University of California Press, 1968), 221–24; Rodney Stark and William Sims Bainbridge, *A Theory of Religion* (New York: Peter Lang, 1987), 11–12 .

89. Rev. Frederic P. Williams, interview with author, 23 February 1999; Linda Dernier, correspondence with author, 3 March 1999; Bishop Edward Jones, interview with author, 8 April 1999; Rev. Robert Giannini, interview with author, 25 March 1999; Rev. Bradley McCormick, correspondence with author, 19 November 1998; Bishop William C. R. Sheridan, correspondence with author, 20 May 1999; The Cathedral Church of St. James, "1998 Epiphany VI," http://www.nd.edu/~ktrembat/wwwEDNIN/Parish/CSJ/dox/krt.sermon.15feb98.html, (11 November 1998).

90. Robert Boak Slocum and Don S. Armentrout, *Discovering Common Mission: Lutherans and Episcopalians Together* (2003); Roof and McKinney, *Mainline*, 237–43; The Episcopal diocese of Pennsylvania, "Bennison Investiture," http://www.diopa.org/sermon.html, (11 September 1998); Moore, *Presences*, 90–91, 255–58; Konolige, *Power of the Their Glory*, 366–69; Thomas C. Reeves, correspondence with author, 23 October 1998.

NOTES TO CHAPTER 4

1. Deborah Mathias Gough, *Christ Church, Philadelphia: The Nation's Church in a Changing City* (Philadelphia: University of Pennsylvania Press, 1995).

2. Kenneth Heineman, *God Is a Conservative: Religion, Politics, and Morality in Contemporary America* (New York: New York University Press, 2005).

3. Mark A. Noll and Luke E. Harlow, eds., *Religion and American Politics: From the Colonial Period to the Present* (New York: Oxford University Press, 2007).

4. Adam Hamilton, *Confronting the Controversies: Biblical Perspectives on Tough Issues* (Nashville. TN: Abingdon Press, 2005), 57–90, 111–25; Social Principles of the United

Methodist Church, 2005–2008 (Washington, DC: United Methodist Church General Board of Church and Society, 2004), 11–12, 32; Pope John Paul II, *Memory and Identity: Conversations at the Dawn of a Millennium* (New York: Rizzoli, 2005), 134–35; Dave Shiflett, *Exodus: Why Americans Are Fleeing Liberal Churches for Conservative Christianity* (New York: Sentinel, 2005), 132, 164; Peter Irons, *God on Trial: Landmark Cases from America's Religious Battlefields* (New York: Penguin, 2007); John Micklethwait and Adrian Wooldridge, *God Is Back: How the Global Rise of Faith Will Change the World* (New York: Penguin, 2009), 98–99, 326–35.

5. Bruce T. Murray, *Religious Liberty in America: The First Amendment in Historical and Contemporary Perspective* (Amherst: University of Massachusetts Press, 2008).

6. Daniel K. Williams, *God's Own Party: The Making of the Christian Right* (New York: Oxford University Press, 2010), 64–67.

7. Louis H. Pollak, "Lawyer Sawyer," *University of Pennsylvania Law Review* 148 (November 1999): 26–37.

8. "Fourth Day: 13 March 1959," 24119 File 16, Box 2261, Record Group 21, Records of the U.S. District Court, Eastern District of Pennsylvania, Civil Case Files 1938–1963, National Archives, Philadelphia, Pennsylvania; David Bruton, email with author, 2 May 2008, David Bruton interview with author, 8 May 2008; David W. Maxey, email with author, 1 May 2008.

9. *New York Times*, 5 August 1999; David Bruton interview with author, 8 May 2008.

10. *Philadelphia Inquirer*, 13 November 2003.

11. "Third Day: 25 November 1958," 24119 File 11, Box 2261, Record Group 21, Records of the U.S. District Court, Eastern District of Pennsylvania, Civil Case Files 1938–1963, National Archives, Philadelphia, Pennsylvania.

12. Consisting of one judge from the U.S. Court of Appeals and two federal district court judges, during much of the twentieth century three-judge panels of this type were used to determine cases with important constitutional issues, with decisions available for direct appeal to the U.S. Supreme Court.

13. "Fourth Day: 13 March 1959," 24119 File 16, Box 2261, Record Group 21, Records of the U.S. District Court, Eastern District of Pennsylvania, Civil Case Files 1938–1963, National Archives, Philadelphia, Pennsylvania; *Schempp v. School District of Abington*, 201 F. Supp. 815, February 1962

14. "Pretrial Conference: 20 December 1960," 24119 File 38, Box 2262, Record Group 21, Records of the U.S. District Court, Eastern District of Pennsylvania, Civil Case Files 1938–1963, National Archives, Philadelphia, Pennsylvania.

15. "Hearing on Amended Complaint: 17 October 1961," 24119 File 48, Box 2262, Record Group 21, Records of the U.S. District Court, Eastern District of Pennsylvania, Civil Case Files 1938–1963, National Archives, Philadelphia, Pennsylvania; *Schempp v. School District of Abington*, 201 F. Supp. 815, February 1962.

16. "Argument: 18 December 1961," 24119 File 50, Box 2262, Record Group 21, Records of the U.S. District Court, Eastern District of Pennsylvania, Civil Case Files 1938–1963, National Archives, Philadelphia, Pennsylvania.

17. Seymour I. Toll, *A Judge Uncommon: A Life of John Biggs, Jr.* (Philadelphia: Legal Communications LTD, 1993), 289–90. As Toll relates, Biggs was a religious skeptic and doubted if organized religion had a place in influencing public life in the United States.

18. *Schempp v. School District of Abington Township*, 201 F. Supp. 815, February 1962.

19. *Philadelphia Inquirer*, 13 November 2003.

20. Irons, *God on Trial*, 30–33.

21. *School District of Abington v. Schempp*, 374 U.S. 203, 83 S. Ct. 1506, 1963. The majority opinion also made clear that "Nondevotional use of the Bible in the Public Schools" was allowed, indeed, it had to be part of some classroom curriculums.

22. Bruce J. Dierenfield, *Battle Over School Prayer: How Engel v. Vitale Changed America* (Lawrence: University of Kansas Press, 2007); Martin E. Marty, *Righteous Empire: The Protestant Experience in America* (New York: Dial Press, 1970), 249–250.

23. David Sehat, *The Myth of American Religious Freedom* (New York: Oxford University Press, 2011), 258–62.

24. *Lemon v. Kurtzman*, 310 F. Supp. 35, November 1969; *New York Times*, 5 August 1999; Louis H. Pollak, "Lawyer Sawyer," *University of Pennsylvania Law Review* 148 (November 1999): 37–44.

25. *Lemon v. Kurtzman*, 403 U.S. 602, 91 S. Ct. 2105, June 1971.

26. *Lemon v. Kurtzman*, 348 F. Supp. 300, February 1972.

27. *Lemon v. Kurtzman*, 411 U.S. 192, 93 S.Ct. 1463, April 1973. Three of the justices would have made Lemon II retroactive.

28. *Lemon v. Sloan*, 340 F. Supp. 1356, April 1972.

29. *Sloan v. Lemon*, 413 U.S. 825, 93 S. Ct. 2982, June 1973.

30. *Meek v. Pittinger*, 374 F. Supp. 639, February 1974; Judge Louis Bechtle, email correspondence with author, 10 July 2008.

31. *Meek v. Pittinger*, 374 F. Supp. 639, February 1974. The irony of course is that Higginbotham's salary as a federal judge was paid by the taxpayers.

32. *Meek v. Pittinger*, 421U.S. 349, 95 S.Ct. 1753, 1975.

33. Honorable Harvey Bartle III, *First Among Equals*, forthcoming history of the Federal District Court for Eastern Pennsylvania.

34. Clark Hodgson, email correspondence with author, 20 October 2007.

35. Ibid.

36. Ibid.; *Valley Forge Christian College v. Americans United for Separation of Church and State*, 454 U.S. 464, 12 January 1982; Judge J. William Ditter, interview with author, 10 March 2009. Ditter told the author that he took some satisfaction in being upheld by the U.S. Supreme Court.

37. In 1957, the Congregational Church (which had earlier merged with the Christian Church) and the Evangelical and Reformed Church (also the product of earlier mergers), formed the United Church of Christ. More than a decade later, in 1968, the United Methodist Church was formed with the merger of the Methodist Church (which had reunited after the Civil War and then included the more conservative Methodist Protestant Church in an earlier merger) and the Evangelical United Brethren Church (itself a merger of two denominations, the Evangelical Church and the United Brethren Church, which had Wesleyan roots among largely German Americans.

38. John B. Judis, "The Chosen Nation: The Influence of Religion on U.S. Foreign Policy," *Carnegie Endowment for International Peace Policy Brief* 37 (March 2005); Madeline Albright, *The Mighty and the Almighty: Reflections on America, God, and World Affairs* (New York: HarperCollins, 2006); Jeff Manza and Clem Brooks, "The Religious Factor in U.S. Presidential Elections, 1960–1992," *American Journal of Sociology* 103 (July 1997): 38–81.

39. D. Michael Lindsay, *Faith in the Halls of Power: How Evangelicals Joined the American Elite* (New York: Oxford University Press, 2007), 54; Sehat, *Myth of American Religious Freedom*, 255–58; Williams, *God's Own Party*, 75.

40. Yanek Mieczkowski, *Gerald Ford and the Challenges of the 1970s* (Lexington: University Press of Kentucky, 2005); Dochuk, *From Bible Belt to Sunbelt*, 371; Williams, *God's Own Party*, 106–32.

41. Dochuk, *From Bible Belt to Sunbelt*, 367–68; John C. Green, *The Faith Factor: How Religion Influences American Elections* (Westport, CT: Praeger, 2007), xi; Lindsay, *Faith in the Halls of Power*, 15–18. Perhaps most famously, Carter gave an interview to *Playboy Magazine* in which he talked about having lustful thoughts about women other than his wife.

42. Williams, *God's Own Party*, 125–27, 133–34.

43. Ronald Reagan, *An American Life* (New York: Pocket Books, 1999); Lindsay, *Faith in the Halls of Power*, 18–20; Dochuk, *From Bible Belt to Sunbelt*, 259–74; Williams, *God's Own Party*, 187.

44. D. G. Hart, *That Old Time Religion in America: Evangelical Protestantism in the Twentieth Century* (Chicago: Ivan R. Dee, 2002), 144–47; Lindsay, *Faith in the Halls of Power*, 56; "About Liberty," http://www.liberty.edu/index.cfm?PID=6921, 4 May 2010; Alister E. McGrath, *Christianity's Dangerous Idea: The Protestant Revolution–A History from the Sixteenth Century to the Twenty-First* (New York: HarperOne, 2007), 329.

45. "Youth for Christ," http://www.yfc.net/Brix/yfcusa/public, 21 November 2010; "Campus Crusade for Christ," http://www.ccci.org/, 21 November 2010; Williams, *God's Own Party*, 120–21; Dochuk, *From Bible Belt to Sunbelt*, 210; Jason VanHorn, correspondence with author, 24 January 2011; Jayson Hartman, correspondence with author, 24 January 2011.

46. C. S. Lewis, *Mere Christianity* (New York: Touchstone, 1996), 79–81; Milton J. Coalter, John M. Mulder, and Louis B. Weeks, eds., *The Presbyterian Predicament: Six Perspectives* (Louisville, KY: Westminster/John Knox Press, 1990), 107; Williams, *God's Own Party*, 1–2.

47. Daniel Sack, *Whitebread Protestants: Food and Religion in American Culture* (New York: St. Martin's Press, 2000), 124.

48. Americans United, http://www.au.org, 1 October 2009.

49. Micklethwait and Wooldridge, *God Is Back*, 102–17.

50. Jeffery L. Sheler, *Believers: A Journey into Evangelical America* (New York: Viking, 2006), 265–68; Dave Shiflett, *Exodus: Why Americans Are Fleeing Liberal Churches for Conservative Christianity* (New York: Sentinel, 2005), 74; Benedict XVI, *God Is Love* (Washington, DC: U.S. Conference of Catholic Bishops, 2006), 32–42.

51. Sheler, *Believers*, 16, 35, 80; *Christianity Today*, editorial, online, 23 April 2007; Dan Gilgoff, *The Jesus Machine: How James Dobson, Focus on the Family, and Evangelical America are Winning the Culture War* (New York: St. Martin's Press, 2007); Shayne Lee and Phillip Sinitiere, *Holy Mavericks: Evangelical Innovators and the Spiritual Marketplace* (New York: New York University Press, 2009); Lindsay, *Faith in the Halls of Power*, 27–29; Peter Goodwin Heltzel, *Jesus and Justice: Evangelicals, Race, and American Politics* (New Haven, CT: Yale University Press, 2009).

52. Sheler, *Believers*, 234, 244–45, 269; Mark G. Toulouse, *God in Public: Four Ways American Christianity and Public Life Relate* (Louisville, KY: Westminster-John Knox Press,

2006); Victor Gold, *Invasion of the Party Snatchers: How the Holy-Rollers and the Neo-Cons Destroyed the GOP* (Naperville, IL: Sourcebooks, 2007); Mel White, *Religion Gone Bad: The Hidden Dangers of the Christian Right* (New York: Penguin, 2006).

53. Williams, *God's Own Party*, 202–5, 211.

54. Episcopal News Service, 16 February 2007.

55. *Social Principles of the United Methodist Church*, 2005–2008 (Washington, DC: United Methodist Church General Board of Church and Society, 2004), 33–34; Drew Christiansen, "Catholic Peacemaking, 1991–2005: The Legacy of Pope John Paul II," *Review of Faith and International Affairs* 4 (Fall 2006): 21–28; Thomas J. Massaro and Thomas A. Shannon, *Catholic Perspectives on Peace and War* (Lanham, MD: Rowman and Littlefield, 2003).; C. S. Lewis, *The Weight of Glory* (New York: Touchstone, 1996), 58–69.

56. Philip Jenkins, *The Next Christendom: The Coming of Global Christianity* (New York: Oxford University Press, 2003), 142–49; *Social Principles of the United Methodist Church*, 2005–2008 (Washington, DC: United Methodist Church General Board of Church and Society, 2004), 30–31; T. S. Eliot, *Christianity and Culture* (New York: Harvest, 1976), 76; Hamilton, *Confronting the Controversies*, 21–37; Mary L. Mapes, *A Public Charity: Religion and Social Welfare in Indianapolis, 1929–2002* (Indianapolis: Indiana University Press, 2004); Mary J. Oates, *The Catholic Philanthropic Tradition in America* (Indianapolis: Indiana University Press, 1995).

57. William Martin, *With God on Our Side: The Rise of the Religious Right in America* (New York: Broadway Books, 1996), 384–85; David S. Gutterman, *Prophetic Politics: Christian Social Movements and American Democracy* (Ithaca. NY: Cornell University Press, 2005); Walter Russell Mead, "God's Country?" *Foreign Affairs* 85 (September/October 2006): 24–43; *Indianapolis Star*, 12 August, 4 November 2006. Stephen L. Carter, *God's Name in Vain: The Wrongs and Rights of Religion in Politics* (New York: Basic Books, 2000); *Christianity Today*, June 2006, 44–47.

58. Richard Cimino and Don Lattin, *Shopping for Faith: American Religion in the New Millennium* (San Francisco: Jossey-Bass, 1998), 139.

59. C. S. Lewis, *Mere Christianity* (New York: Touchstone, 1996), 45–46; Thomas Cahill, *Desire of the Everlasting Hills: The World Before and After Jesus* (New York: Doubleday, 1999); Episcopal News Service, 23 January 2007.

60. John Danforth, *Faith and Politics: How the "Moral Values" Debate Divides America and How to Move Forward Together* (New York: Viking, 2006); *Christianity Today*, August 2006, 40, and September 2006, 28–29; Mary Jo Weaver and R. Scott Appleby, *Being Right: Conservative Catholics in America* (Indianapolis: Indiana University Press, 1995); Mary Jo Weaver, *What's Left?: Liberal American Catholics* (Indianapolis: Indiana University Press, 1999).

61. Michael Gerson and Peter Wehner, *City of Man: Religion and Politics in a New Era* (Chicago: Moody Publishers, 2010).

62. Michael Kazin, *A Godly Hero: The Life of William Jennings Bryan* (New York: Alfred A. Knopf, 2006).

63. Bill Press, *How the Republicans Stole Christmas: The Republican Party's Declared Monopoly on Religion and What Democrats can do to Take It Back* (New York: Doubleday, 2005).

64. Ronald J. Sider, *The Scandal of Evangelical Politics: Why Are Christians Missing the Chance to Really Change the World* (New York: Baker Books, 2008); John Micklethwait and Adrian Wooldridge, *God Is Back: How the Global Revival of Faith is Changing the World*

(New York: Penguin, 2009), 128–31; Jim Wallis, *God's Politics: Why the Right Gets it Wrong and the Left Doesn't Get It* (New York: HarperSanFrancisco, 2006), xvii, 3; Williams, *God's Own Party*, 100–101.

65. Tony Campolo, *Red Letter Christians: A Citizen's Guide to Faith and Politics* (New York: Regal Books, 2008); Tony Campolo, *Choose Love Not Power: How to Right the World's Wrongs from a Place of Weakness* (New York: Regal Books, 2009).

66. For discussion of the movement, see Luke Timothy Johnson, *The Real Jesus: The Misguided Quest for the Historical Jesus and the Truth of the Traditional Gospels* (New York: HarperSanFrancisco, 1997).

67. John Shelby Spong, *Living in Sin?: A Bishop Rethinks Human Sexuality* (New York: HarperSanFrancisco, 1990); Spong, *Born of a Woman: A Bishop Rethinks the Virgin Birth and the Treatment of Women by a Male Dominated Church* (New York: HarperSanFrancisco, 1992); Spong, *The Sins of Scripture: Exposing the Bible's Texts of Hate to Reveal the God of Love* (New York: HarperSanFrancisco, 2006); Spong, *Here I Stand: My Struggle for a Christianity of Integrity, Love, and Equality* (New York: HarperSanFrancisco, 2001); Spong, *Why Christianity Must Change or Die: A Bishop Speaks to Believers in Exile* (New York: HarperSanFrancisco, 1999); xvii; Spong, *Resurrection: Myth or Reality? A Bishop's Search for the Origins of Christianity* (New York: HarperSanFrancisco, 1994); Spong, *Rescuing the Bible from Fundamentalism: A Bishop Rethinks the Meaning of Scripture* (New York: HarperSanFrancisco, 1991).

68. Concerned Clergy and Laity of the Episcopal Church, "Online Publications: The Archbishop of Canterbury Urged to Bar Bishop Spong from the Lambeth Conference," http://www.episcopalian.org/cclec/paper-londontimes.htm, 24 October 1998; Peter C. Moore, ed., *Can a Bishop be Wrong?: Ten Scholars Challenge John Shelby Spong* (Harrisburg, PA: Morehouse Publishing, 1998), xxi; The Episcopal diocese of Newark, "Biography of John Shelby Spong," http://www.intac.com/~rollins/jsspong/jssbio.html, 27 October 1998; Spong, "A Call for a New Reformation," http://www.intac.com/~rollins/jsspong/reform. html, 4 September 1998; Bishop Michael Nazir-Ali, "A New Way to Speak to God?— Bishop Michael responds to Bishop Spong," http://www.anglican.org.uk/rochester/docs/ anewway.htm, 4 September 1998; Bishop Stephen Sykes, correspondence with author, 16 September 1998; N. T. Wright, *Who Was Jesus?* (Grand Rapids, MI: William B. Eerdmans Publishing, 1992), 18, 65–92; Shiflett, *Exodus*, 51.

69. Randall Balmer, *Thy Kingdom Come: How the Religious Right Distorts the Faith and Threatens America—An Evangelical's Lament* (New York: Basic Books); Michelle Goldberg, *Kingdom Coming: The Rise of Christian Nationalism* (New York: W. W. Norton); Mel White, *Religion Gone Bad: The Hidden Dangers of the Religious Right* (New York: Tarcher, 2006); Christopher Hedges, *American Fascists: The Christian Right and the War on America* (New York: Free Press, 2008); Kevin Phillips, *American Theocracy: The Peril and Politics of Radical Religion, Oil, and Borrowed Money in the 21st Century* (New York: Viking, 2006); Steven Bruce, *The Rise and Fall of the New Christian Right: Conservative Protestant Politics in America, 1978–1988* (Oxford: Clarendon Press, 1988), 182.

70. Ramesh Ponnuru, "Secularism and Its Discontents," *National Review*, 27 December 2004, 32–35.

71. Allan J. Lichtman, *White Protestant Nation: The Rise of the American Conservative Movement* (New York: Atlantic Monthly Press, 2008); William Martin, *With God on Our Side: The Rise of the Religious Right in America* (New York: Broadway Books, 1996).

72. Williams, *God's Own Party*, 9, 267, 275–76.

73. Colleen Carroll, *The New Faithful: Why Young Adults are Embracing Christian Orthodoxy* (Chicago: Loyola Press, 2002); *Christianity Today*, August 2006, 39–40. For an alternative view, see David Kinnaman and Gabe Lyons, *unChristian: What a New Generation Really Thinks about Christianity . . . and Why It Matters* (New York: Baker Books, 2007).

74. Lindsay, *Faith in the Halls of Power*, 20.

75. Ibid., 21–24.

76. Phillips, *American Theocracy*; Lindsay, *Faith in the Halls of Power*, 24–27; Williams, *God's Own Party*, 245–67.

77. Indeed, one needs look no farther than the man who was the senior pastor of the president's church in Chicago, the Reverend Jeremiah Wright. See "Jeremiah Wright, "http://abcnews.go.com/Blotter/DemocraticDebate/story?id=4443788&page=1, 26 January 2011.

78. Thomas Frank, *What's the Matter with Kansas: How Conservatives Won the Heart of America* (New York: Holt, 2005). Others have argued that evangelicals stayed firmly within the Republican camp. See Williams, *God's Own Party*, 8.

79. Williams, *God's Own Party*, 269, 273–75.

80. N. T. Wright, *Simply Christian: Why Christianity Makes Sense* (New York: HarperSan Francisco, 2006), 123; *USA Today*, 5 May 2008; *Christianity Today*, August 2006, 14–15.

NOTES TO CHAPTER 5

1. Daniel F. Evans, *At Home in Indiana for One Hundred Seventy-five Years: The History of Meridian Street United Methodist Church, 1821–1996* (Indianapolis: Guild Press, 1996).

2. Hart M. Nelsen and Mary Ann Maguire, "The Two Worlds of Clergy and Congregations: Dilemma for Mainline Denominations," *Sociological Analysis* 41 (Spring 1980): 74–80.

3. Glenn Span, "Theological Transition within Methodism: The Rise of Liberalism and the Conservative Response," *Methodist History* 43 (April 2005): 198–212; David Hempton, *Methodism: Empire of the Spirit* (New Haven, CT: Yale University Press, 2005), 183; Joel A. Carpenter, *Revive Us Again: The Reawakening of American Fundamentalism* (New York: Oxford University Press, 1997), 43–47, 53; "Movement Toward Union: 1940–1967," http://www.umc.org, 25 August 2010.

4. Kevin J. Corn, *Forward Be Our Watchword: Indiana Methodism and the Modern Middle Class* (Indianapolis: University of Indianapolis Press, 2008).

5. "New to the UCC?," http://www.ucc.org, 25 August 2010; Richard Cimino and Don Lattin, *Shopping for Faith: American Religion in the New Millennium* (San Francisco: Jossey-Bass, 1998), 65; *Indianapolis Star*, 14 November 2010.

6. Reginald W. Bibby, "Why Conservative Churches Really Are Growing: Kelley Revisited," *Journal for the Scientific Study of Religion* 17 (June 1978): 129–37; Benton Johnson, "Liberal Protestantism: End of the Road?," *Annals of the American Academy of Political and Social Science* 480 (July 1985): 39–52; Benton Johnson, Dean R. Hoge, and Donald A. Luidens, "Mainline Churches: The Real Reason for Decline," *First Things* 31 (March 1993): 13–18; Michael Hout, Andrew Greeley, and Melissa J. Wilde, "The Demographic Imperative in Religious Change in the United States," *American Journal of Sociology* 107 (September 2001): 468–500; Kenneth Inskeep, "Mainline Decline: Understanding the Membership Drop," *Lutheran* (April 2006).

7. G. Jeffrey MacDonald, *Thieves in the Temple: The Christian Church and the Selling of the American Soul* (New York: Basic Books, 2010).

8. Cimino and Lattin, *Shopping for Faith*, 10, 23, 68; Phyllis A. Dexter, correspondence with author, 3 March 1999.

9. Hartford Institute for Religion Research, "The National Congregations Study by Dr. Mark Chaves," http://hirr.hartsem.edu/org/faith_congregations_research_ncs.html, 17 February 2005; Daniel Sack, *Whitebread Protestants: Food and Religion in American Culture* (New York: St. Martin's Press, 2000), 61–65, 80–83.

10. "The Call to Love the City," Rev. Stephen P. Bauman, Christ Church United Methodist, New York City, 12 July 2009.

11. C. S. Lewis, *The Weight of Glory* (New York: Touchstone, 1996), 119–21; "Bowling Alone," http://www.bowlingalone.com/, 31 October 2009.

12. Jay P. Dolan, *In Search of an American Catholicism: A History of Religion and Culture in Tension* (New York: Oxford University Press, 2002), 130: Etan Diamond, *Souls of the City: Religion and the Search for Community in Postwar America* (Indianapolis: Indiana University Press, 2003); Philip Jenkins, *The Next Christendom: The Coming of Global Christianity* (New York: Oxford University Press, 2003), 194, 197–98, 213.

13. Rodney Stark and Charles Y. Glock, *American Piety: The Nature of Religious Commitment* (Berkeley: University of California Press, 1968), 220–21; Hempton, *Methodism*, 200.

14. Episcopal News Service, 3 January 2007.

15. Priests entering the Roman Catholic Church in 2007 were overwhelmingly Catholic since birth (94 percent), coming from homes where both parents were also Catholic (83 percent). Mary L. Gautier and Mary E. Bendyna, "The Class of 2007: Survey of Ordinands to the Priesthood: A Report to the Secretariat for Vocations and Priestly Formation United States Conference of Catholic Bishops," Center for Applied Research in the Apostolate, Georgetown University, March 2007.

16. *Christian Century*, "No Shows: The Decline in Worship Attendance," 22 September 2010.

17. Mark Oppenheimer, *Knocking on Heaven's Door: American Religion in the Age of Counterculture* (New Haven, CT: Yale University Press, 2003), 2.

18. William G. McLoughlin Jr., *Modern Revivalism: Charles Gradison Finney to Billy Graham* (New York: Ronald Press, 1959), 150–51, 166–67, 342; Leigh Eric Schmidt, *Hearing Things: Religion, Illusion, and the American Enlightenment* (Cambridge, MA: Harvard University Press, 2000); James H. Timberlake, *Prohibition and the Progressive Movement, 1900–1920* (Cambridge, MA: Harvard University Press, 1963), 10, 16; Dickson D. Bruce, *And They All Sang Hallelujah: Plain-Folk Camp-Meeting Religion, 1800–1845* (Knoxville: University of Tennessee Press, 1974); Roger Robins, "Vernacular American Landscape: Methodists, Camp Meetings, and Social Respectability," *Religion and American Culture* 4 (Summer 1994): 169, 172; T. J. Jackson Lears, *No Place of Grace: Antimodernism and the Transformation of American Culture, 1880–1920* (Chicago: University of Chicago Press, 1994), 24; Arthur Shumaker, interview with author, 24 March 2000; Bruce Catton, *Waiting for the Morning Train: An American Boyhood* (Detroit, MI: Wayne State University Press, 1987), 29.

19. Carpenter, *Revive Us Again*, 259; *Indianapolis Star*, 24 March 2007; "We Confess: A Newsletter of the Confessing Movement with the United Methodist Church," March/April 2007; Arthur Emery Farnsley II, *Southern Baptist Politics: Authority and Power in the*

Restructuring of an American Denomination (University Park: Penn State University Press, 1994), ix, 129; Robert Boak Slocum and Don S. Armentrout, eds., *Discovering Common Mission: Lutherans and Episcopalians Together* (New York: Church Publishing, 2003).

20. Milton J. Coalter, John M. Mulder, and Louis B. Weeks, eds., *The Presbyterian Predicament: Six Perspectives* (Louisville, KY: Westminster/John Knox Press, 1990), 67–68; Cimino and Lattin, *Shopping for Faith*, 97–98, 113.

21. Alister E. McGrath, *Christianity's Dangerous Idea: The Protestant Revolution–A History from the Sixteenth Century to the Twenty-first* (New York: HarperOne, 2007), 402–7.

22. Hartford Institute for Religion Research, "The National Congregations Study by Dr. Mark Chaves," http://hirr.hartsem.edu/org/faith_congregations_research_ncs. html, 17 February 2005; "Another word for church," http://www.churchmarketingsucks. com/2009/08/another-word-for-church/, 21 November 2010; Darren Dochuk, *From Bible Belt to Sunbelt: Plain-Folk Religion, Grassroots Politics, and the Rise of Evangelical Conservatism* (New York: W. W. Norton, 2011), 35, 141.

23. "Facts about Sand Hill Christian Church," pamphlet in author's collection.

24. Jeffery L. Sheler, *Believers: A Journey into Evangelical America* (New York: Viking, 2006), 62.

25. Thomas S. Kidd, *The Protestant Interest: New England after Puritanism* (New Haven, CT: Yale University Press, 2004).

26. Sheler, *Believers*, 49.

27. Edith L. Blumhofer, *Aimee Semple McPherson: Everybody's Sister* (Grand Rapids, MI: William B. Eerdmans, 1993); Donald Warren, *Radio Priest: Charles Coughlin, The Father of Hate Radio* (New York: Free Press, 1996); "Moody Radio," http://www.moodyradio.org/, 28 October 2009; "The Foursquare Church," http://www.foursquare.org, 27 September 2010; Daniel K. Williams, *God's Own Party: The Making of the Christian Right* (New York: Oxford University Press, 2010), 16–17; Joel A. Carpenter, "Fundamentalist Institutions and the Rise of Evangelical Protestantism, 1929–1942," *Church History* 49 (March 1980): 70–72.

28. Tona J. Hangen, *Redeeming the Dial: Radio, Religion, and Popular Culture in America* (Chapel Hill: University of North Carolina Press, 2002); Edith L. Blumhofer, *Restoring the Faith: The Assemblies of God, Pentecostalism, and American Culture* (Chicago: University of Chicago Press, 1993), 7, 251;Timothy H. B. Stoneman, "Preparing the Soil for Global Revival: Station HCJB's Radio Circle, 1949–1959," *Church History* 76 (March 2007): 114–55; Carpenter, *Revive Us Again*, 125–40; D. Michael Lindsay, *Faith in the Halls of Power: How Evangelicals Joined the American Elite* (New York: Oxford University Press, 2007), 123–24.

29. Michele Rosenthal, *American Protestants and TV in the 1950s: Responses to a New Medium* (New York: Macmillan, 2007).

30. Dolan, *In Search of an American Catholicism*, 175; "Fulton J. Sheen," http://www. museum.tv/eotvsection.php?entrycode=sheenfulton, 21 November 2010.

31. "TBN: Trinity Broadcasting Network," http://www.tbn.org/index.php/3.html, 2 March 2006; *Christianity Today*, August 2006, 21–22; John Micklethwait and Adrian Wooldridge, *God Is Back: How the Global Revival of Faith is Changing the World* (New York: Penguin, 2009), 230–32; Jeffrey K. Hadden and Anson Sharpe, *Televangelism: Power and Politics on God's Frontier* (New York: Henry Holt, 1988); Blumhofer, *Restoring the Faith*, 255–56; Milton J. Coalter, John M. Mulder, and Louis B. Weeks, eds., *The Presbyterian Predicament: Six Perspectives* (Louisville, KY: Westminster/John Knox Press, 1990), 50; R. Lawrence Moore, *Touchdown Jesus: The Mixing of Sacred and Secular in American History*

(Louisville, KY: Westminster John Knox Press, 2003), 67–68; Barry R. Litman and Elizabeth Bain, "The Viewership of Religious Television Programming: A Multidisciplinary Analysis of Televangelism," *Review of Religious Research* 30 (June 1989): 329–43.

32. Jim Bakker, *I Was Wrong* (New York: Thomas Nelson, 1997); Jimmy Swaggart Ministries, http://www.jsm.org, 31 October 2009; David Edwin Harrell Jr., *Oral Roberts: An American Life* (Indianapolis: Indiana University Press, 1985); "Jerry Falwell," http://www.falwell.com, 31 October 2009; "Pat Robertson," http://www.cbn.com, 31 October 2009; "D. James Kennedy," http://www.coralridge.org, 31 October 2009; "Robert Schuller," http://www.crystalcathedral.org, 31 October 2009.

33. Jason S. Lantzer, "A World Wide Communion and the World Wide Web: The Use of Email Surveys in Studying the Anglican Communion," *Journal of the American Association for History and Computing* (April 2001)

34. Bishop Michael Hare Duke, retired bishop of the diocese of St. Andrew's, Scotland, correspondence with author, 22 May 2000.

35. Lantzer, "A World Wide Communion and the World Wide Web."

36. Ibid.

37. Ibid.; Bishop James Tengatenga, correspondence with author, 1 June 2000.

38. *Christianity Today*, June 2006, 17–18, 24–32; "Who Killed Jesus?," *Newsweek*, 16 February 2004, 44–53; Bruce Marchiano, *In the Footsteps of Jesus: One Man's Journey Through the Life of Christ* (Eugene, OR: Harvest House, 1997); Paula Fredriksen, ed., *On the Passion of the Christ* (Berkeley: University of California Press, 2006); "The 25 Most Controversial Movies of All Time," *Entertainment Weekly*, 16 June 2006, 35–39. Also on the list were *The Da Vinci Code* (13) and The Last Temptation of Christ (6).

39. For just a few examples, see Hal Lindsey, *The Late Great Planet Earth* (Grand Rapids, MI: Zondervan, 1970); John Hagee, *Jerusalem Countdown: A Warning to the World* (Lake Mary, FL: Frontline, 2006); Joyce Meyer, *Look Great, Feel Great: 12 Keys to Enjoying a Healthy Life Now* (New York: Warner Faith, 2006); Joyce Meyer, *Battlefield of the Mind* (New York: Warner Faith, 1995); Frederick K. C. Price, *Answered Prayer Guaranteed!: The Power of Praying with Faith* (Lake Mary, FL: Charisma House, 2006); Philip Jenkins, *The New Faces of Christianity: Believing the Bible in the Global South* (New York: Oxford University Press, 2006), 96; Philip Yancey, *The Jesus I Never Knew* (Grand Rapids, MI: Zondervan, 1995). One might also take a look at Tim LaHaye and Jerry B. Jenkins' *Left Behind* series as well.

40. *Erasmus Institute News*, Spring 2007.

41. Rodney Stark and William Sims Bainbridge, *The Future of Religion, Secularization, Revival, and Cult Formation* (Berkeley: University of California Press, 1985), 1–3.

42. Hempton, *Methodism*, 196–98; Callum G. Brown, *The Death of Christian Britain* (London: Routledge, 2001); Cimino and Lattin, *Shopping for Faith*, 2–3; Stephen Toulmin, *Cosmopolis: The Hidden Agenda of Modernity* (Chicago: University of Chicago Press, 1992); Richard John Neuhaus, "Secularization Doesn't Just Happen," *First Things* (March 2005): 58–61; Coalter, Mulder, and Weeks, eds., *Presbyterian Predicament*, 53; Dolan, *In Search of an American Catholicism*, 154, 160; Sam Harris, *Letter to a Christian Nation* (New York: Knopf, 2006); Daniel C. Dennett, *Breaking the Spell: Religion as a Natural Phenomenon* (New York: Penguin, 2006); Richard Dawkins, *The God Delusion* (New York: Houghton Mifflin, 2006); Madeleine Albright, "Faith and Diplomacy," *Review of Faith and International Affairs* 4 (Fall 2006): 3; "The Secularization of Justification," http://www.modernreformation.org, 24 September 2010; Williams, *God's Own Party*, 134–43.

43. Gene Edward Veith, "A Nation of Deists," http://ww.worldmag.com/articles/10775, 26 October 2009.

44. Steven Bruce, *The Rise and Fall of the New Christian Right: Conservative Protestant Politics in America, 1978–1988* (Oxford: Clarendon Press, 1988), 183–89; Bernard E. Meland, *Faith and Culture* (Carbondale: Southern Illinois Press, 1972); Paul Tillich, *Dynamics of Faith* (New York: Harper and Row, 1956); Bernard E. Meland, *The Secularization of Modern Cultures* (New York: Oxford University Press, 1966), 12–13, 19.

45. Samuel P. Huntington, *The Clash of Civilizations and the Remaking of World Order* (New York: Simon and Schuster, 2003); Benjamin R. Barber, *Jihad vs. McWorld: How Globalization and Tribalism are Reshaping the World* (New York: Ballantine Books, 1996). This is what some scholars have alleged has happened in Europe.

46. Steve Bruce, *God Is Dead: Secularization in the West* (New York: Wiley-Blackwell, 2002).

47. Pope Benedict XVI and Marcello Pera, *Without Roots: The West, Relativism, Christianity, and Islam* (New York: Basic Books, 2006), 65–66, 70, 109; Owen Chadwick, *The Secularization of the European Mind in the 19th Century* (New York: Cambridge University Press, 1995); Toulmin, *Cosmopolis*; N. T. Wright, *Simply Christian: Why Christianity Makes Sense* (New York: HarperSan Francisco, 2006), 13, 20–21; Ruth A. Tucker, *Left Behind in a Megachurch World: How God Works Through Ordinary Churches* (Grand Rapids, MI: Baker Books, 2006), 11.

48. Lindsay, *Faith in the Halls of Power*, 75; David Sehat, *The Myth of American Religious Freedom* (New York: Oxford University Press, 2011), 185–87.

49. *Indiana Catholic and Record*, 29 September 1911, 2 August 1912; Jay P. Dolan, *The American Catholic Experience: A History from Colonial Times to the Present* (Garden City, NY: Doubleday, 1985), 267–68, 276–77; *Baptist World*, 12 September 1912.

50. See for example, "HSLDA," http://www.hslda.org/Default.asp?bhcp=1, 5 May 2010.

51. John T. McGreevy, *Catholicism and American Freedom: A History* (New York: W. W. Norton, 2003), 183.

52. Carpenter, "Fundamentalist Institutions," 66–69; *Christianity Today*, 28 August 2008.

53. "Harvard," http://www.hno.harvard.edu/guide/intro/index.html, 4 January 2007; Perry Miller, *Nature's Nation* (Cambridge, MA: Belknap Press, 1967), 154–55.

54. "Tracing Princeton's Religious Tradition," http://www.princeton.edu/main/news/archive/S13/84/00C39/, 27 October 2009; *Victoria Advocate*, 7 May 2005.

55. "William and Mary Reaches Cross Compromise," http://www.foxnews.com/story/0,2933,257138,00.html, 6 March 2007.

56. Three such examples in the author's home state of Indiana may suffice: The University of Indianapolis (now loosely affiliated with the United Methodist Church), Franklin College (which maintains an affiliation with the American Baptist Convention), and Butler University (founded as a Disciples of Christ college, but in the mid-twentieth century spun off the seminary into its own entity—Christian Theological Seminary—and took unaffiliated status).

57. Naomi Schaefer Riley, *God on the Quad: How Religious Colleges and the Missionary Generation are Changing America* (New York: St. Martin's Press, 2005), 115–33, 203; "Baylor," http://www.baylor.edu, 4 January 2007; James Tunstead Burtchaell, *The Dying of the Light: The Disengagement of Colleges and Universities from their Christian Churches* (Grand Rapids. MI: William B. Eerdmans Publishing, 1998).

58. Rev. John I. Jenkins, "Academic Freedom and Catholic Character: An Invitation to Reflection and Response," Address to the Faculty, 23 January 2006, http://president. nd.edu/academic-freedom/address_text.shtml, 2 March 2006; *New York Times*, 18 February 2006; Rev. John I. Jenkins, "Closing Statement on Academic Freedom and Catholic Character," http://alumni.nd.edu/closingstatement.html, 5 April 2006.

59. Rev. John I. Jenkins, "My Love for the Place," *Notre Dame Magazine*, Autumn 2005, 21.

60. *Fort Wayne Journal Gazette*, 24 March 2009. There is some discussion if President Obama's speech might have caused a pocketbook boycott of Notre Dame that continues to the present.

61. Riley, *God on the Quad*, 53–69; Walton Collins, "The Pastoral Presidency of Monk Malloy," *Notre Dame Magazine* (Winter 2004–2005), 23.

62. Joel A. Carpenter, *Revive Us Again*, 3, 16–22, 86; Riley, *God on the Quad*, 33–52, 215–19; Sheler, *Believers*, 142, 147. For other examples, see Wheaton College, http://www. wheaton.edu/, 27 October 2009; Patrick Henry College, http://www.phc.edu/, 27 October 2009. Others on this list include Liberty University and Regent University. "Liberty University," http://www.liberty.edu, 31 October 2009; "Regent University," http://www.regent. edu, 31 October 2009.

63. George M. Marsden, *The Evangelical Mind and the New School Presbyterian Experience* (New Haven, CT: Yale University Press, 1970), xi, 2.

64. George M. Marsden, *Fundamentalism and American Culture: The Shaping of Twentieth-Century Evangelicalism, 1870–1925* (New York: Oxford University Press, 1982), 130.

65. Mark A. Noll, *The Scandal of the Evangelical Mind* (Grand Rapids, MI: William B. Eerdmans Publishing, 1994).

66. Edward J. Larson, *Summer for the Gods: The Scopes Trial and America's Continuing Debate Over Science and Religion* (New York: Basic Books, 2006), 271; Noll, *Scandal of the Evangelical Mind*; Lee Strobel, *The Case for a Creator* (Grand Rapids, MI: Zondervan, 2004); Marsden, *Fundamentalism and American Culture*, 212–14; Cimino and Lattin, *Shopping for Faith*, 42; Francis S. Collins, *The Language of God: A Scientist Present Evidence for Belief* (New York: Free Press); "High-tech Museum Brings Creationism to Life," http:// www.MSNBC.com, 4 August 2006; C. S. Lewis, *The Weight of Glory* (New York: Touchstone, 1996), 104–6.

67. Their silence on political issues may be changing. The Episcopal Church (along with other members of the Seven Sisters) routinely issues statements on the federal budgetary process. For what the Methodists have been up to, see Steven M. Tipton, *Public Pulpits: Methodists and Mainline Churches in the Moral Argument of Public Life* (Chicago: University of Chicago Press, 2008).

68. Sheler, Believers, 38, 59–61; George Marsden, "The Sword of the Lord," *Books and Culture*, March/April 2006, 11; "Fuller Theological Seminary," http://www.fuller.edu, 31 October 2009; D. G. Hart, *That Old Time Religion in America: Evangelical Protestantism in the Twentieth Century* (Chicago: Ivan R. Dee, 2002), 115–17.

69. Hart, *That Old Time Religion*, 79–81.

70. Blumhofer, *Restoring the Faith*, 160, 180–97; Adam Laats, "The Quiet Crusade: Moody Bible Institute's Outreach to Public Schools and the Mainstreaming of Appalachia, 1921–1966," *Church History* 75 (September 2006): 565–93.

71. Philip Jenkins, *The New Faces of Christianity: Believing the Bible in the Global South* (New York: Oxford University Press, 2006), 4–7, 18–19, 40–41, 156, 178.

72. John Micklethwait and Adrian Wooldridge, *God Is Back: How the Global Revival of Faith is Changing the World* (New York: Penguin, 2009), 87. For some examples, see Karen Armstrong, *A History of God: The 4,000-Year Quest of Judaism, Christianity, and Islam* (New York: Ballantine Books, 1993); Anthony Dancer, ed., *William Stringfellow in Anglo-American Perspective* (Burlington: Ashgate, 2005).

73. *Christianity Today*, September 2006, 116; Cimino and Lattin, *Shopping for Faith*, 145–46.

NOTES TO CHAPTER 6

1. "Christ Church," http://www.christchurchsavannah.org/index.htm, 27 January 2011; Author visit, March 2010.

2. Jason VanHorn, correspondence with author, 24 January 2011; Jayson Hartman, correspondence with author, 24 July 2011.

3. Thomas S. Kidd, *The Great Awakening: The Roots of Evangelical Christianity in Colonial America* (New Haven, CT: Yale University Press, 2009).

4. "Praying Indians," http://www.bio.umass.edu/biology/conn.river/praying.html, 4 January 2011.

5. See for example the "Carlisle Indian Industrial School," http://www.historicalsociety.com/ciiswelcome.html, 16 January 2011.

6. "Reconstruction, Prosperity, and New Issues: 1866–1913," http://www.umc.org, 25 August 2010; George C. Rable, *God's Almost Chosen Peoples: A Religious History of the American Civil War* (Chapel Hill: University of North Carolina Press, 2010), 332–33; Derek Chang, *Citizens of a Christian Nation: Evangelical missions and the Problem of Race in the Nineteenth Century* (Philadelphia: University of Pennsylvania Press, 2010); *American Missionary*, January 1878, January 1901 as examples.

7. William R. Hutchison, *Errand to the World: American Protestant Thought and Foreign Missions* (Chicago: University of Chicago Press, 1987).

8. R. Lawrence Moore, *Touchdown Jesus: The Mixing of Sacred and Secular in American History* (Louisville, KY: Westminster John Knox Press, 2003), 169–71.

9. Christopher Harding, *Religious Transformation in South Asia: The Meanings of Conversion in Colonial Punjab* (New York: Oxford University Press, 2008), 179.

10. "Presbyterians in Mission: An Historic Overview," from *A Guide to Foreign Missionary Manuscripts in the Presbyterian Historical Society* by Frederick J. Heuser Jr. (Online version, 1988).

11. "Commissioners for Foreign Missions," http://globalministries.org, 24 September 2010.

12. Gale L. Kenny, *Contentious Liberties: American Abolitionists in Post-Emancipation Jamaica, 1834–1866* (Athens: University of Georgia Press, 2010); "Reconstruction, Prosperity, and New Issues: 1866–1913," http://www.umc.org, 25 August 2010; "Methodist Church Grows in China," http://www.wfn.org/1998/01/msg00019.html, 15 December 2010; Heather J. Sharkey, *American Evangelicals in Egypt: Missionary Encounters in an Age of Empire* (Princeton, NJ: Princeton University Press, 2008); Elias B. Sanford, ed, *Federal Council of the Churches of Christ in America: Report of the First Meeting of the Federal Council, Philadelphia, 1908* (New York: Revell Press, 1909), 352.

13. David Killingray, "The Black Atlantic Missionary Movement and Africa, 1780s–1920s," *Journal of Religion in Africa* (February 2003): 3–31.

14. James T. Yarsiah, *Early Missionary Work of the Protestant Episcopal Church (DFMS) in Liberia and Their Differential Effects, 1821–1871* (New York: CreateSpace, 2010).

15. *Time*, 27 August 1951.

16. "Reconstruction, Prosperity, and New Issues: 1866–1913," http://www.umc.org, 25 August 2010; "Mary and Joseph Gomer," http://gbgm–umc.org/umhistory/sierra–leone/gomer.html, 23 December 2010.

17. One need only consider Ruth Bell Graham, the wife of Billy Graham, who was born to missionary parents in China, or the author Pearl Buck who was largely raised in China while her parents were missionaries there, sparking a lifelong interest in East–West relations. See Ian Tyrrell, *Reforming the World: The Creation of America's Moral Empire* (Princeton, NJ: Princeton University Press, 2010), 28–35, 49–89, 98–119, 23–165, 182, 191–208.

18. Joel A. Carpenter, "Fundamentalist Institutions and the Rise of Evangelical Protestantism, 1929–1942," *Church History* 49 (March 1980): 62–75.

19. David Killingray, "The Black Atlantic Missionary Movement and Africa, 1780s–1920s," *Journal of Religion in Africa* (February 2003): 4.

20. Paul Hutchinson, "The Conservative Reaction in China," *Journal of Religion* 2 (July 1922): 337–61.

21. *Time*, 23 April 1934; Robert Hastings Nichols, "Fundamentalism in the Presbyterian Church," *Journal of Religion* 5 (January 1925): 28.

22. Sanford, ed, *Federal Council*, 358, 361; "One Hundred Years of Missionary Activity," *America*, 10 June 2010.

23. Sanford, ed., *Federal Council*, 351–52.

24. Ibid., 352, 354, 356.

25. William H. Swatos Jr., "On Latin American Protestantism," *Sociology of Religion* 55 no. 2 (1994): 197–205.

26. Charles M. Good Jr., *The Steamer Parish: The Rise and Fall of Missionary Medicine on an African Frontier* (Chicago: University of Chicago Press, 2004), 12. Some of this is also reflected in a 1932 report funded by John D. Rockefeller Jr., "Re-Thinking Missions: A Laymen's Inquiry After One Hundred Years."

27. Christopher Harding, *Religious Transformation in South Asia: The Meanings of Conversion in Colonial Punjab* (New York: Oxford University Press, 2008), vii.

28. Gerald H. Anderson, "A Moratorium on Missionaries?" *Christian Century* 16 (January 1974).

29. One can see the beginning of this trend in the creation of relief-centered organizations, such as the United Methodist Committee on Relief. See "History," http://new.gbgm–umc.org/umcor/about/history/, 16 January 2011.

30. "International Ministries," http://www.internationalministries.org, 27 January 2011.

31. "Global Ministries—About General Board of Global Ministries," http://new.gbgm–umc.org, 27 January 2011.

32. Sam Dixon, "To the Ends of the Earth: Mission Papers 2008—Global Ministries of the United Methodist Church," author's collection.

33. *USA Today*, 7 November 2010.

34. "About Us," http://www.themissionsociety.org/go/about, 19 November 2010; "Role Reversal," *Unfinished*, Fall 2010, 10–15. Originally named the Mission Society for United Methodists, the denominational affiliation, which was never official, was eventually dropped in order to be more ecumenical.

35. "IMB—Home," http://www.imb.org/main/page.asp, 27 January 2011.

36. "Southern Baptist Convention—Mission Work," http://www.sbc.net/missionswork. asp, 27 January 2011.

37. "The Assemblies of God: Our Heritage in Perspective," http://www.ifphc.org, 27 September 2010.

38. "Heritage," http://www.ntm.org/about/heritage.php?page=heritage&io=1, 23 December 2010; *Time*, 27 August 1951.

39. "SEND," http://www.send.org/, 4 January 2011; "SEND International Missions—History," http://www.send.org, 27 January 2011. Both Joel Carpenter and William Martin have estimated that some 90 percent of American missionaries are now affiliated with either fundamentalist, evangelical, or Pentecostal organizations or churches.

40. Jason VanHorn, correspondence with author, 24 January 2011; Jayson Hartman, correspondence with author, 24 July 2011. Of course, members of the Seven Sisters also use short-term mission trips as well.

41. Kevin Xiyi Yao, *The Fundamentalist Movement among Protestant Missionaries in China, 1920–1937* (New York: University Press of America, 2003); "Methodist Church Grows in China," http://www.wfn.org/1998/01/msg00019.html, 15 December 2010.

42. "Fastest Growth," http://www.christianpost.com/article/20050228/fastest-growth-of-christianity-in-africa/, 7 February 2011.

43. Episcopal News Service, 8 January 2007.

44. Allen C. Guelzo, "Bonfire of the Sacristies: To the 2006 General Convention," *Anglican and Episcopal History* 75 (March 2006): 99–103.

45. N. J. Demerath III, "Cultural Victory and Organizational Defeat in the Paradoxical Decline of Liberal Protestantism," *Journal for the Scientific Study of Religion* 34 (December 1995), 458–69.

46. Dave Shiflett, *Exodus: Why Americans Are Fleeing Liberal Churches for Conservative Christianity* (New York: Sentinel, 2005), 12, 39.

47. Elizabeth Adams, *Going to Heaven: The Life and Election of Bishop Gene Robinson* (Brooklyn, NY: Soft Skull Press, 2006).

48. Stephen Bates, *A Church at War: Anglicans and Homosexuality* (New York: I. B. Tauris, 2004), 191.

49. Shiflett, *Exodus*, 3, 5, 12, 20, 28, 117; Episcopal News Service, 23 February, 28 February, and 3 March 2007; Pope Benedict XVI and Marcello Pera, *Without Roots: The West, Relativity, Christianity, and Islam* (New York: Basic Books, 2006), 77; C. S. Lewis, *Mere Christianity* (New York: Touchstone, 1996), 90–96; N. T. Wright, *Simply Christian: Why Christianity Makes Sense* (New York: HarperSan Francisco, 2006), 129; Episcopal News Service, 16 February 2007; Radner and Sumner, *Reclaiming Faith*, 1, 13; Terry Mattingly, "Cracks in the Anglican Communion," http://www.gospelcom.net/tmattingly/col.07.16.97. html, 4 September 1998 and "Lambeth '98—The Americans are coming!" http://www. gospelcom.net.tmattingly/col.10.29.97.html, 4 September 1998; Philip Jenkins, *The Next Christendom: The Coming of Global Christianity* (New York: Oxford University Press, 2003), 196–204; Philip Jenkins, *The New Faces of Christianity: Believing the Bible in the Global South* (New York: Oxford University Press, 2006), 1, 16; Grant LeMarquand, "African Responses to New Hampshire and New Westminster: An Address," *Anglican and Episcopal History* 75 (March 2006): 21–29; Bates, *Church at War*, 5, 31; *Episcopal Life*, 24 October 2010.

50. Guelzo, "Bonfire of the Sacristies," 105–6, 110–11; Philip Jenkins, *The Next Christendom: The Coming of Global Christianity* (New York: Oxford University Press, 2003), 121–24; LeMarquand, "African Responses to New Hampshire," 30–35. For historic perspective, from the 1998 Lambeth Conference, see Anglican Communion News Service, Note 1643, 20 July 1998; Note 1718, 5 August 1998; Note 1723, 5 August 1998; Note 1763, 14 August 1998; Note 1792, 30 November 1998; Episcopal News Service, 19 February, 20 February, 22 February, 23 February, 20 March, 21 March, 22 March 2007.

51. Episcopal News Service, 13 November, 15 November 2006, 18 April, 1 May 2007; Guelzo, "Bonfire of the Sacristies," 103–4; Philip Turner, "An Unworkable Theology," *First Things* (June/July 2005): 10–12.

52. Episcopal News Service, 27 March 2007; Petersen, "Tensions," 427, 452; Jacqueline Field-Bibb, *Women Towards Priesthood: Ministerial Politics and Feminist Praxis* (New York: Cambridge University Press, 1991), 85–175.

53. Timothy F. Sedgwick and Philip Turner, eds., *The Crisis in Moral Teaching in the Episcopal Church* (Harrisburg, PA.: Morehouse Publishing, 1992), 15, 24–32, 35–36, 56, 65 137–38, 144; Roof, *Community and Commitment*, 6; Jeffrey K. Hadden, *The Gathering Storm in the Churches* (New York: Doubleday, 1969), 67; Rev. Gordon Chastain, interview with author, 2 October 1998; Paul Moore, *Presences: A Bishop's Life in the City* (New York: Farrar, Straus, and Giroux, 1997), 255–60; Alfred Tsang, correspondence with author, 2 March 1999; Bishop Edward Jones, interview with author, 8 April 1999.

54. *Christianity Today*, August 2006, 52; Episcopal News Service, 14 June, 20 June, 21 June, 15 September 2006, 8 October 2009.

55. Guelzo, "Bonfire of the Sacristies," 111–15; Bates, *Church at War*, 3.

56. Concerned Clergy and Laity of the Episcopal Church, "Concerned Clergy and Laity of the Episcopal Church (CCLEC)," http://www.episcopalian.org/cclec/index.htm, "About CCLEC," http://episcopalian.org/cclec.about-us.htm, 24 September 1998. For more on Episcopalians United, see their website at http://www.episcopalian.org/EU/about.htm. For more on the American Anglican Council, see http://www.episcopalian.org/aac/narra.htm.

57. Douglas Bess, *Divided We Stand: A History of the Continuing Anglican Movement* (Riverside, CA: Tractarian Press, 2002); Guelzo, *Union*, 334; A. Donald Davies, ed., *The Episcopal Synod of America: Speeches, Sermons, Documents, and Pictures from the Founding Meeting* (Wilton, CT: Morehouse Publishing, 1990); The Episcopal Missionary Church, "The Episcopal Missionary Church: Defend the Historic Faith," http://emc-holycross.org/emc_info. html, 11 September 1998; *South Bend Tribune*, 21 March 1999; Rev. Mary Campbell, interview with Polis Center, 7 July 1998; Stephen Neill, *Anglicanism* (London: Mowbray, 1977).

58. *Christianity Today*, 7 July 2009.

59. Episcopal News Service, 28 June, 31 July, 18 September, 2 October 2006, 24 October 2009; *Living Church*, 25 October 2009; "Christ Church Savannah," February 2010 newsletter in author's collection.

60. Episcopal News Service, 28 June 2006.

61. Episcopal News Service, 7 July, 11 August, 18 August, 13 September 2006, 3 January 2007.

62. Episcopal News Service, 20 November, 4 December 2006.

63. Episcopal News Service, 15 September, 20 October 2006, 17 December, 18 December, 19 December 2006, 18 January, 19 January, 31 January, 12 February, 27 March, 1 May, and 7 May 2007; *Economist*, 23 December 2006, 43; *Episcopal Life*, 16 September 2010.

64. *Episcopal Life*, 27 October 2010.

65. Episcopal News Service, 29 March, 1 May, 3 May, 7 May 2007, 3 December 2008, 20 October 2009; *Los Angeles Times*, 23 October 2009.

66. The Confessing Movement, 2 May 2007; Episcopal News Service, 12 July, 13 July 2009.

67. Episcopal News Service, 30 November, 1 December 2006.

68. *Living Church*, 22 May 2007; Episcopal News Service, 17 April 2007; *Washington Post*, 1 August 2009.

69. Episcopal Life Online, 28 May, 8 June 2010; Episcopal News Service, 15 May 2010.

70. Philip Jenkins, *The New Faces of Christianity: Believing the Bible in the Global South* (New York: Oxford University Press, 2006), 2–4; *Indianapolis Star*, 4 November 2006.

71. Harvey Hill and Jennifer Watson, "In Christ There Is No Gay or Straight? Homosexuality and the Episcopal Church," *Anglican and Episcopal History* 75 (March 2006): 67–68.

72. *Social Principles of the United Methodist Church, 2005–2008* (Washington, DC: United Methodist Church General Board of Church and Society, 2004), 9–11; Adam Hamilton, *Confronting the Controversies: Biblical Perspectives on Tough Issues* (Nashville: Abingdon Press, 2005), 129–55; Milton J. Coalter, John M. Mulder, and Louis B. Weeks, eds., *The Presbyterian Predicament: Six Perspectives* (Louisville, KY: Westminster/John Knox Press, 1990), 27–30; Richard Cimino and Don Lattin, *Shopping for Faith: American Religion in the New Millennium* (San Francisco: Jossey-Bass, 1998), 143; *Christianity Today*, August 2006, 17; The Confessing Movement, "Happenings Around the Church," 7 December 2006 and 1 October 2009; Episcopal News Service, 14 November 2006, 20 August and 21 August 2009.

73. "Message from the Dean," *News from the Hill: Virginia Theological Seminary* (June 2010), 2; Jason VanHorn, correspondence with author, 24 January 2011.

NOTES TO CHAPTER 7

1. Richard Cimino and Don Lattin, *Shopping for Faith: American Religion in the New Millennium* (San Francisco: Jossey-Bass, 1998), 2.

2. "Top Twenty Religions in the United States, 2001-ARIS," Largest Religious Groups in the United States, http://www.adherents.com, 27 August 2010; "Pew U.S. Religious Affiliation, 2002," Largest Religious Groups in the United States, http://www.adherents.com, 27 August 2010; "Gallup Religion Poll," http://www.gallup.com/poll/1690/religion.aspx, 29 April 2011. Gallup found that an additional 26 percent of Americans rated religion as "fairly important" to their lives, putting the combined total at 80 percent.

3. "Largest Denominational Families in the United States, 2001-ARIS," Largest Religious Groups in the United States, http://www.adherents.com, 27 August 2010; "Religious Bodies which are the Largest Church in One or More U.S. States, 1990," Largest Religious Groups in the United States, http://www.adherents.com, 27 August 2010.

4. "Religious Bodies which have the Most Congregations of any Denomination in One or More States, 1990," Largest Religious Groups in the United States, http://www.adherents.com, 27 August 2010; John C. Green, *The Faith Factor: How Religion Influences American Elections* (Westport, CT: Praeger, 2007), 181–83. States in which there are more of the Seven Sisters and evangelicals are Connecticut, Iowa, Maryland, Massachusetts, Minnesota, Nebraska, New Jersey, New York, North Dakota, Ohio, Rhode Island, South

Dakota, and Vermont. States in which the Seven Sisters are at least 20 percent of the population are Alaska, Delaware, Indiana, Iowa, Kansas, Kentucky, Maine, Minnesota, Missouri, Montana, Nebraska, New Hampshire, North Dakota, Ohio, Oregon, Pennsylvania, South Dakota, Tennessee, Vermont, West Virginia, Wisconsin, and Wyoming. States in which there are at least evangelicals are at least 20 percent of the population are Alabama, Alaska, Arizona, Arkansas, Colorado, Delaware, Florida, Georgia, Idaho, Illinois, Indiana, Iowa, Kansas, Kentucky, Louisiana, Maine, Michigan, Minnesota, Mississippi, Missouri, Montana, Nebraska, Nevada, New Hampshire, North Carolina, Ohio, Oklahoma, Oregon, Pennsylvania, South Carolina, South Dakota, Tennessee, Texas, Virginia, Washington, West Virginia, Wisconsin, and Wyoming. States in which there are more Catholics than Protestants are Connecticut, Massachusetts, New Jersey, New Mexico, New York, Rhode Island, and Vermont. States in which the population is at least 20 percent Catholic are Arizona, California, Colorado, Connecticut, Florida, Hawaii, Illinois, Indiana, Iowa, Kansas, Louisiana, Maine, Maryland, Massachusetts, Michigan, Minnesota, Montana, Nebraska, Nevada, New Hampshire, New Jersey, New Mexico, New York, North Dakota, Pennsylvania, Rhode Island, South Dakota, Texas, Vermont, Washington, and Wisconsin.

5. Robert Bruce Mullin and Russell E. Richey, eds., *Reimagining Denominationalism: Interpretive Essays* (New York: Oxford University Press, 1994).

6. Robert E. Webber, *The Younger Evangelicals: Facing the Challenges of the New World* (Grand Rapids, MI: Baker Books, 2002); Jeffery L. Sheler, *Believers: A Journey into Evangelical America* (New York: Viking, 2006), 297.

7. *Indianapolis Star*, 27 June 2004.

8. Thomas S. Kidd, *The Great Awakening: The Roots of Evangelical Christianity in Colonial America* (New Haven, CT: Yale University Press, 2007), xii–xiv.

9. D. G. Hart, *That Old Time Religion in America: Evangelical Protestantism in the Twentieth Century* (Chicago: Ivan R. Dee, 2002), 170–71; D. Michael Lindsay, *Faith in the Halls of Power: How Evangelicals Joined the American Elite* (New York: Oxford University Press, 2007), 216–18.

10. Lindsay, *Faith in the Halls of Power*, 6.

11. Joel A. Carpenter, *Revive Us Again: The Reawakening of American Fundamentalism* (New York: Oxford University Press, 1997), 3, 8–11; John Pollock, *Billy Graham: Evangelist to the World* (New York: Harper and Row, 1979); John Micklethwait and Adrian Wooldridge, *God Is Back: How the Global Revival of Faith is Changing the World* (New York: Penguin, 2009), 99–100; "Billy Graham Center," http://www.billygrahamcenter.com/, 1 November 2009; Billy Graham, *Just as I Am: The Autobiography of Billy Graham* (New York: HarperOne, 2007); Alister E. McGrath, *Christianity's Dangerous Idea: The Protestant Revolution–A History from the Sixteenth Century to the Twenty-first* (New York: HarperOne, 2007), 395–96.

12. For example, the First Presbyterian Church in Nappanee, Indiana, left PCUSA, joined the Evangelical Presbyterian Church, and is now known as Grace Point. Rev. Matt Price, email correspondence with author, 17 August 2009.

13. Christine Leigh Heyrman, *Southern Cross: The Beginnings of the Bible Belt* (Chapel Hill: University of North Carolina Press, 1997); Micklethwait and Wooldridge, *God Is Back*, 170–172; David Dockery, ed., *Southern Baptists and American Evangelicals: The Conversation Continues* (Nashville: Broadman and Holman Publishers, 1993), 2; Mark New-

man, *Getting Right with God: Southern Baptists and Desegregation, 1945–1995* (Tuscaloosa: University of Alabama Press, 2001), 210.

14. Shiflett, *Exodus*, 112–13.

15. Dockery, ed., *Southern Baptists and American Evangelicals*, 63–65, 88, 91; Mark Oppenheimer, *Knocking on Heaven's Door: American Religion in the Age of Counterculture* (New Haven, CT: Yale University Press, 2003), 173.

16. Arthur Emery Farnsley II, *Southern Baptist Politics: Authority and Power in the Restructuring of an American Denomination* (University Park: Penn State University Press, 1994), xi, 38, 61; Walter B. Shurden, ed., *The Struggle for the Soul of the Southern Baptist Convention: Moderate Responses to the Fundamentalist Movement* (Macon, GA: Mercer University Press, 1993); Dockery, *Southern Baptists and American Evangelicals*, 113; Daniel K. Williams, *God's Own Party: The Making of the Christian Right* (New York: Oxford University Press, 2010), 156–58.

17. Darren Dochuk, *From Bible Belt to Sunbelt: Plain-Folk Religion, Grassroots Politics, and the Rise of Evangelical Conservatism* (New York: W. W. Norton, 2011), xv, 39–40.

18. Shiflett, *Exodus*, 128; *Christianity Today*, August 2006, 19–20.

19. "The Saddleback Story," http://www.saddleback.com/flash/story.asp, 5 April 2006.

20. Sheler, *Believers*, 114–41; Micklethwait and Wooldridge, *God Is Back*, 127–28; *Christianity Today*, 16 February 2007; Daniel K. Williams, *God's Own Party: The Making of the Christian Right* (New York: Oxford University Press, 2010), 270–76; Dochuk, *From Bible Belt to Sunbelt*, 402.

21. Cimino and Lattin, *Shopping for Faith*, 56–59; *Seattle Post-Intelligencer*, 18 March 2002.

22. Barry Hankins, *God's Rascal: J. Frank Norris and the Beginnings of Southern Fundamentalism* (Lexington: University Press of Kentucky, 2010); David Stokes, *Apparent Danger—The Pastor of America's First Megachurch and the Texas Murder Trial of the Decade in the 1920s* (New York: Bascom Hill Books, 2010). It should be pointed out that Norris was a colorful figure, often at odds with the SBC, tried for perjury and arson (related to a fire at his church), and then a murder trial (after killing a man in his office).

23. Stephen Ellingson, *Megachurch and the Mainline: Cultural Innovation, Change, and Conflict in Mainline Protestant Congregations* (Chicago: University of Chicago Press, 2007); Micklethwait and Wooldridge, *God Is Back*, 144; Geoff Surratt, Greg Ligon, and Warren Bind, *The Multi-Site Church Revolution: Being One Church in Many Locations* (Grand Rapids, MI: Zondervan, 2006).

24. Scott Thumma, Dave Travis, and Warren Bird, "Megachurches Today 2005: Summary of Research Findings," Hartford Institute for Religion Research, 2005; "Church Growth Today: 2010," http://churchgrowthtoday.wordpress.com/2010/12/13/church-growth-today-100-largest-churches-2010-megachurches-double-in-size/, 29 April 2011.

25. Sheler, *Believers*, 114–41.

26. "The Business of Faith," *Black Enterprise*, May 2006; *Christianity Today*, October 2006, 24–25; Micklethwait and Wooldridge, *God Is Back*, 183–93; "Willow Creek," http://www.willowcreek.org, 31 October 2009.

27. Shayne Lee, *T. D. Jakes: America's New Preacher* (New York: New York University Press, 2005). One might also look at the drama that has unfolded at the Crystal Cathedral as well. See *New York Times*, 23 October 2010.

28. James Hudnut-Beumler, *In Pursuit of the Almighty's Dollar: A History of Money and American Protestantism* (Charlotte: University of North Carolina Press, 2007).

29. Ronald J. Sider, *The Scandal of the Evangelical Conscience: Why are Christians Living Just Like the Rest of the World?* (New York: Baker Books, 2005).

30. David W. Wells, *The Courage to be Protestant: Truth-lovers, Marketers, and Emergents in the Postmodern World* (Grand Rapids, MI: William B. Eerdmans, 2008).

31. Edith L. Blumhofer, *Restoring the Faith: The Assemblies of God, Pentecostalism, and American Culture* (Chicago: University of Chicago Press, 1993), 268; Ruth A. Tucker, *Left Behind in a Megachurch World: How God Works Through Ordinary Churches* (Grand Rapids, MI: Baker Books, 2006); Hartford Institute for Religion Research, "The National Congregations Study by Dr. Mark Chaves," http://hirr.hartsem.edu/org/faith_congregations_research_ncs.html, 17 February 2005.

32. Author visit to St. John's Catholic Church, 15 March 2007.

33. Shiflett, *Exodus*, 60.

34. Jay P. Dolan, *In Search of an American Catholicism: A History of Religion and Culture in Tension* (New York: Oxford University Press, 2002), 14, 58.

35. Philip Gleason, *Keeping the Faith: American Catholicism Past and Present* (Notre Dame, IN: University of Notre Dame Press, 1987); John T. McGreevy, *Catholicism and American Freedom: A History* (New York: W. W. Norton, 2003), 293–95; John T. McGreevy, *Parish Boundaries: The Catholic Encounter with Race in the Twentieth-Century Urban North* (Chicago: University of Chicago Press, 1996), 264.

36. Jay P. Dolan, *The Immigrant Church: New York's Irish and German Catholics, 1815–1865* (Notre Dame, IN: Notre Dame University Press, 1987).

37. *Western Christian Advocate*, 9 January 1850, 23 February 1870, 23 October 1895; *Indianapolis Star*, 4 April, 6 April 1910; *Indiana Catholic*, 4 March, 8 April 1910, 22 September 1911; Dolan, *Immigrant Church*, 161–69; Dolores Liptak, ed., *A Church of Many Cultures: Selected Historical Essays on Ethnic American Catholicism* (New York: Garland Publishing, 1988), 33, 38; Charles Yrigoyen Jr., "Methodists and Roman Catholics in Nineteenth-Century America," *Methodist History* 28 (April 1990): 172–86.

38. *Indiana Catholic*, 3 March, 10 March, 5 May, 10 November 1911, 9 November 1917, 21 November 1919, 27 February, 19 March, 16 April 1920, 9 September 1927, 2 November 1928.

39. *Hamilton County Ledger*, July and August 1903; *South Bend Tribune*, 16 September 1907; Mary J. Oates, *The Catholic Philanthropic Tradition in America* (Indianapolis: Indiana University Press, 1995).

40. *Indianapolis News*, 12 November, 28 November 1910; *Indiana Catholic and Record*, 16 May 1919; Francis G. Couvares, "Hollywood, Main Street, and the Church: Trying to Censor the Movies Before the Production Code," *American Quarterly* 44 (December 1992): 589; Gregory D. Black, *The Catholic Crusade Against the Movies, 1940–1975* (New York: Cambridge University Press, 1998); Stephen Vaughn, "The Devil's Advocate: Will H. Hays and the Campaign to Make Movies Respectable," *Indiana Magazine of History* 101 (June 2005): 125–152.

41. Mark S. Massa, *Catholics and American Culture: Fulton Sheen, Dorothy Day, and the Notre Dame Football Team* (New York: Crossroad Publishing, 1999); Dolan, *In Search of an American Catholicism*, 173, 180–85. St. Augustin Roman Catholic Church in Brooklyn, New York, founded in 1870, is one early example of this suburbanization trend.

42. St. Francis Chapel–Prudential Center Boston, Author's visit, 8 January 2011.

43. "Study: Hispanics Transforming U.S. Religion," http://www.washingtonpost.com, 7 May 2007; Philip Jenkins, *The Next Christendom: The Coming of Global Christianity* (New York: Oxford University Press, 2003), 61, 66–67, 74–75, 156–59, 194, 197–98, 213.

44. McGreevy, *Catholicism and American Freedom*, 153, 163.

45. Scott Mainwaring and Alexander Wilde, eds., *The Progressive Church in Latin America* (Notre Dame, IN: University of Notre Dame Press, 1989); McGreevy, *Catholicism and American Freedom*, 270–73.

46. Kevin McNamara, *Vatican II: The Constitution on the Church, A Theological and Pastoral Commentary* (Chicago: Franciscan Herald Press, 1968); Dolan, *In Search of an American Catholicism*, 192–95.

47. McGreevy, *Catholicism and American Freedom*, 289–93; Donald Cozzens, *Sacred Silence: Denial and the Crisis in the Church* (Collegeville, MN: Liturgical Press, 2002); David France, *Our Fathers: The Secret Life of the Catholic Church in an Age of Scandal* (New York: Broadway Books, 2004); Thomas P. Doyle, A. W. Richard Sipe, and Patrick J. Wall, *Sex, Priests, and Secret Codes: The Catholic Church's 2000-year Paper Trail of Sexual Abuse* (Los Angeles: Volt Press, 2006); Karol Jackowski, *The Silence We Keep: A Nun's View of the Catholic Priest Scandal* (New York: Harmony Books, 2004); Paul R. Dokecki, *The Clergy Sexual Abuse Crisis: Reform and Renewal in the Catholic Community* (Washington, DC: Georgetown University Press, 2004); Philip Jenkins, *Pedophiles and Priests: Anatomy of a Contemporary Crisis* (New York: Oxford University Press, 1996); Donald L. Boisvert and Robert E. Goss, eds., *Gay Catholic Priests and Clerical Sexual Misconduct: Breaking the Silence* (New York: Harrington Park Press, 2005); Thomas Cahill, *Mysteries of the Middle Ages: The Rise of Feminism, Science, and Art from the Cults of Catholic Europe* (New York: Nan A. Talese, 2006), 314–17; "Catholic League" letter in author's collection, 2006; *Fort Wayne Journal Gazette*, 17 March 2007.

48. *Boston Globe*, 21 June 2007; McGreevy, *Catholicism and American Freedom*, 228–81.

49. Peter Feuerherd, *Holyland USA: A Catholic Ride Through America's Evangelical Land-scape* (New York: Crossroad Publishing, 2006).

50. Lindsay, *Faith in the Halls of Power*, 96–97.

51. "The Call To Holiness," *First Things*, March 2005, 23–26; Samuel Pufendorf, *Of the Nature and Qualification of Religion in Reference to Civil Society* (Indianapolis: Liberty Fund, 2002), 80–81, 116; Mark A. Noll and Carolyn Nystrom, *Is the Reformation Over? An Evangelical Assessment of Contemporary Roman Catholicism* (Grand Rapids, MI: Baker Book House, 2005); "The Papal Court," *Economist*, 28 January 2006, 34.

52. Shayne Lee, *T. D. Jakes: America's New Preacher* (New York: New York University Press, 2005).

53. Harvey Cox, *Fire from Heaven: The Rise of Pentecostal Spirituality and the Reshaping of Religion in the Twenty-first Century* (New York: Addison-Wesley Publishing Company, 1995), 46, 57, 71. In light of later developments, it should be noted that Azusa Street did not happen in a Pentecostal vacuum but rather was one of several such revival moments around the world in the opening decade of the twentieth century, all of which occurred (more or less) independently of one another. See McGrath, *Christianity's Dangerous Idea*, 422.

54. Cox, *Fire from Heaven*, 48–50.

55. Blumhofer, *Restoring the Faith*, 56, 60–61, 71–72, 92–93, 116–19; Micklethwait and Wooldridge, *God Is Back*, 17, 81–83, 213–37; "History," http://ap.org/top/about/history.cfm, 31 October 2009; McGrath, *Christianity's Dangerous Idea*, 417.

56. Cox, *Fire from Heaven*, 74–75; "The Assemblies of God: Our Heritage in Perspective," http://www.ifphc.org, 27 September 2010; Blumhofer, *Restoring the Faith*, 12–30, 49, 222–23.

57. "The Assemblies of God: Our Heritage in Perspective," http://www.ifphc.org, 27 September 2010; Blumhofer, *Restoring the Faith*, 1–2, 242; Micklethwait and Wooldridge, *God Is Back*, 17, 81–83, 213–37; N. T. Wright, *Simply Christian: Why Christianity Makes Sense* (New York: HarperSan Francisco, 2006), 122; *Christianity Today*, September 2006, 86–89; *Economist*, 23 December 2006, 48–50; Michael S. Stephens, *Who Healeth All Thy Diseases: Health, Healing, and Holiness in the Church of God Reformation Movement* (Lanham, MD: Scarecrow Press, 2008).

58. Randall J. Stephens, *The Fire Spreads: Holiness and Pentecostalism in the American South* (Cambridge. MA: Harvard University Press, 2008); Blumhofer, *Restoring the Faith*, 100–107, 128–35; George M. Marsden, *Fundamentalism and American Culture: The Shaping of Twentieth-Century Evangelicalism, 1870–1925* (New York: Oxford University Press, 1982), 93–101; "History," http://ap.org/top/about/history.cfm, 31 October 2009.

59. Lee, *T .D. Jakes.*

60. "National Baptist Convention," http://blackandchristian.com, 27 August 2010.

61. Ronald J. Sider, *Rich Christians in an Age of Hunger: Moving from Affluence to Generosity* (New York: Thomas Nelson, 2005); *Christianity Today*, 14 September 2006.

62. *Christianity Today*, 15 January 2009.

63. *Atlantic*, December 2009, online edition.

64. Blumhofer, *Restoring the Faith*, 1–2, 242; Micklethwait and Wooldridge, *God Is Back*, 17, 81–83, 213–37; N. T. Wright, *Simply Christian: Why Christianity Makes Sense* (New York: HarperSan Francisco, 2006), 122; *Christianity Today*, September 2006, 86–89; *Economist*, 23 December 2006, 48–50; M. Stephens, *Who Healeth All Thy Diseases*.

65. "The Assemblies of God: Our Heritage in Perspective," http://www.ifphc.org, 27 September 2010.

66. "History," http://ap.org/top/about/history.cfm, 31 October 2009.

67. T. S. Eliot, *Christianity and Culture* (New York: Harvest, 1976), 17; "Pilgrim's Progress," *Newsweek*, 14 August 2006, 36–43; David Hempton, *Methodism: Empire of the Spirit* (New Haven, CT: Yale University Press, 2005), 192; Rodney E. Wilmoth, *How United Methodists Share Their Faith* (Nashville: Abingdon Press, 1999), 11–12, 57.

Index

Adams, John, 25
Adams, Samuel, 25
African Methodist Episcopal Church, 30
Allen, Richard, 30
Allin, John M., 56
American (Northern) Baptist Convention, 54, 58, 122. *See also* Baptists
American Civil Liberties Union, 68
American Council of Christian Churches, 103
American Revolution, 23, 24, 25, 27
Americans United for the Separation of Church and State, 72, 76, 99
Andrew, James, 33
Anglican Church. *See* Church of England
Anglican Communion, 50, 80, 94, 95, 113, 114, 115, 116, 117, 118, 119
Anti-Catholicism, 4, 28, 130
Anti-Protestantism, 130
Anti-Saloon League, 40, 77
Anti-slavery, 32
Arch Street Presbyterian Church (Philadelphia, PA), 44
Asbury, Francis, 29
Assemblies of God, 93, 112, 136
Azusa Street Revival, 133, 134, 136

Baptists, 29, 31, 33, 37, 44, 106. *See also* American (Northern) Baptist Convention; Southern Baptist Convention
Baylor University, 100
Beecher, Henry Ward, 32, 34, 91
Beecher, Lyman, 31, 32, 69, 106
Biggs, John, 68, 162n17
Black Manifesto, 52, 53, 54, 55, 57, 155n33

Book of Common Prayer (Episcopal Church), 51, 58; and changes to it, 59, 62; as source of denominational unity, 61
Boyd, Malcolm, 57, 156n43
Bush, George H. W., 81
Bush, George W., 82
Bushnell, Horace, 38, 88, 89
Bryan, William Jennings, 43, 44, 45, 78, 79

Calvin, John, 10, 11
Campolo, Tony, 79
Campus Crusade for Christ, 75
Carnegie, Andrew, 37
Carroll, Colleen, 81
Carter, James, 73, 74, 75
Cauthen, Baker James, 112
Christ Church Episcopal (Philadelphia, PA), 65
Christ Church Episcopal (Savannah, GA), 105
Christ Church United Methodist Church (New York, NY), 49
Christian Coalition, 77
Christian Endeavor, 108
Christian Science, 4
Church and State, 11, 65, 67, 70, 71, 78, 96
Church growth, 125, 127
Church of England, 7, 15
Church of Jesus Christ of Latter-day Saints, 4, 31
Church of the Incarnation Episcopal Church (Santa Rosa, CA), 113
Civil rights movement, 51, 52, 53, 63
Civil War, 27, 33, 34, 39, 52, 86, 106, 124
Clinton, William Jefferson, 81, 82
Coffin, Henry Sloane, 45

Cold War, 50, 56, 67, 81, 111
Colonization, 12, 13, 22; and England, 13, 18, 21; and Spain, 9, 12
Columbus, Christopher, 8, 9, 10
Congregational Church, 27, 28, 29, 30, 46, 54, 58, 73, 76, 82, 86, 101, 107, 163n37
Consumerism, 86, 87, 88, 96, 123
Convocation of Anglicans in North America, 117, 118
Coughlin, Charles, 92
Covenant theology, 16, 17
Craine, John, 60, 158n61
Crystal Cathedral (Garden Grove, CA), 179n27
Culture wars, 66

Darwinian evolution, 43, 44, 45, 46, 47, 78
Deism, 20, 21, 22, 24, 73
Denominational bureaucracies, 43, 57, 58, 89, 90, 113, 114, 115, 118, 123, 124
Disciples of Christ, 31, 37, 46, 54, 58, 75, 122
Ditter, J. William, 72
Dixon, A. C., 42, 81, 101
Dollar, Creflo, 93, 135

Edwards, Jonathan, 21
Eisenhower, Dwight, 50
Elizabeth I, 14, 15
Elizabeth II, 7
Enlightenment, 19, 20, 21, 22
Episcopal Church, 27, 28, 29, 46, 50, 52, 56, 57, 63, 64, 74, 85, 86, 95, 114, 115, 118, 125, 132, 172n67; and Black Power movement, 54, 55, 56; as example of Mainline decline, 49, 51; and female ordination, 59, 60, 61; and homosexual ordination, 80, 114, 115, 116; and internal divisions, 61, 62; and liturgical movement, 62; and Roman Catholics, 59, 117; and splinter churches, 89, 116, 117
Episcopal Society for Cultural and Racial Unity, 51, 52, 53, 55
Erdman, Charles R., 45
Establishment clause. See Church and State
Eugenics, 43

Evangelicals, 29, 30, 31, 33, 37, 38, 42, 45, 77, 78, 92, 97, 102, 107, 108, 122, 123, 124, 129, 132, 136; and anti-intellectualism, 101, 102; and Cold War, 56; and diversity of, 79, 80, 123; and reforms, 32, 37; and strength of, 123; and voting, 82
Evangelical Lutheran Church, 36, 54, 58, 119, 147n39

Falwell, Jerry, 75
Federal Council of Churches, 4, 35, 39, 40, 41, 50, 51, 92, 103, 109, 147n36. *See also* National Council of Churches
Finney, Charles, 30, 88
First Presbyterian Church (Nappanee, IN), 178n12
First World War, 44
Ford, Gerald, 74, 81
Forman, James, 54, 55
Fosdick, Harry Emerson, 44
Franklin, Benjamin, 21, 24
Fundamentalists, 41, 42, 44, 45, 46, 47, 49, 56, 76, 81, 92, 96, 97, 101, 102, 103, 104, 108, 109, 111, 112, 123, 125, 126, 134

Gladden, Washington, 38
Global Christianity, 89, 103, 104, 105, 106, 113, 114, 116, 117, 119, 136, 137; and missionary activity, 105, 108; and Pentecostalism, 134, 136
Global South. *See* Global Christianity
Graham, Billy, 69, 81, 82, 89, 91, 123, 124, 133, 174n17
Great Awakening, 21, 22, 23, 77
Great Depression, 41, 49
Greek Orthodox Church, 3, 7

Hamilton, Alexander, 25
Heitzig, Skip, 127
Henry, Patrick, 24, 25
Henry VIII, 13, 14
Hines, John, 53, 54, 56
Higginbotham, A. Leon, 71
Hutchinson, Anne, 17, 18

Immigration, 35, 36, 40, 41, 98, 129, 130, 131

Indianapolis Church Federation, 155n33
Internet, 94, 95
Islam, 7, 8, 9

Jakes, T. D., 93, 128, 133, 135
Jefferson, Thomas, 24, 96
Jefferts Schori, Katharine, 117, 118
"Jesus Movement," 90
Johnson, Lyndon, 58
Judaism, 50, 98

Kelly, Dean, 63, 66, 86
Kennedy, John F., 131
King, Martin Luther, Jr., 52
King James Version of the Bible, 141n27
Kingdom of God theology, 29, 35, 37, 38, 39, 40, 42, 44, 128

Lemon cases, 70, 71, 72
Liberation theology, 131
Lincoln, Abraham, 33
Locke, John, 20
Luther, Martin, 8, 10, 90

Macartney, Clarence, 44
Machen, J. Gresham, 42, 44, 109
Madison, James, 23, 24
Mainline, 3, 19, 25, 34, 35, 38, 39, 41, 47, 51, 61, 64, 74, 78, 81, 88, 92, 96, 97, 104, 110, 111, 113,119, 121, 123, 125, 137, 140n10; decline of, 1, 49, 50, 64, 65, 66, 80, 83, 85, 89, 96, 98, 104, 119, 121, 122; and education, 70, 71; formation of new Mainline, 5, 122, 132, 137; origin of term 1, 139n2
Marshall, John, 25
Mather family, 17
McIntire, Carl, 103, 109
McPherson, Aimee Semple, 36, 92
Meek case, 71
Megachurches, 93, 126, 127, 128; and business model, 127,128; and evangelicals, 122
Membership, 1, 87, 88, 122, 177n4; and megachurches, 127, 128; and mobility, 87, 88
Meridian Street United Methodist Church (Indianapolis, IN), 85

Methodist Church, 20, 29, 31, 33, 34, 37, 46, 54, 73, 81, 86, 89, 94, 106, 111, 122, 163n37, 172n67; and 2009 Membership, 1; decline, 85, 86; and mergers, 73; renewal movements in, 119
Millennialism, 37, 152 n86
Missionary activity, 12, 34, 105, 106, 108, 112; and American Baptists, 111; and denominational boards, 107, 108, 109, 110, 111; and education, 107; and Methodists 111, 112, 174nn29, 34; and Presbyterians, 109; and short-term trips, 112; and women, 108
Means, Jacqueline, 60
Moderates, 42, 46, 47, 78, 79, 123, 125
Modernists, 41, 42, 44, 45, 46, 47, 73, 76, 78, 79, 97, 102, 103, 108, 113, 114, 115, 132
Moral Majority, 75, 77
Moody, Dwight, 36, 38, 42, 108; and Moody Bible Institute, 92
Moore, Paul, 57, 59
Moore, Peter C., 80

National Association of Evangelicals, 77, 103, 123, 136
National Baptist Church, 135
National Council of Churches, 51, 57, 77
New Deal, 50
New Tribes Mission, 112
Niebuhr, H. Richard, 50, 51, 153n8
Niebuhr, Reinhold, 50, 51
Non-denominationalism, 90, 91, 112, 122, 128
Norris, J. Frank, 126, 127, 179n22

Obama, Barack, 82, 101, 126
Ockenga, Harold, 103
Oneness theology, 134, 135
Osteen, Joel, 127, 135

Parham, Charles Fox, 133
Park Street Congregational Church (Boston, MA), 102
Peale, Norman Vincent, 50, 51
Penn, William, 18

United Church of Christ. *See* Congregational Church

United Methodist Church. *See* Methodist Church

United States Supreme Court. *See various court cases*

University of Notre Dame, 100, 101

Urbanization, 36

Vietnam War, 51, 56, 57, 58, 63

Virtual congregationalism, 92, 93, 94, 95, 96, 127

Wallis, Jim, 79, 82

Warren, Rick, 126, 135

Washington, George, 24, 65

Washington, Paul, 55

Wesley, Charles, 20, 21, 105

Wesley, John, 20, 21, 23, 105

Whitefield, George, 20, 21, 105

Williams, Roger, 18

Williams, Rowan, 116, 118

Willow Creek Community Church (South Barrington, IL), 127

Windsor Report (2004), 115, 119

Winthrop, John, 15, 18, 21

Witherspoon, John, 23, 25

Woodbridge, Charles J., 109

World War II, 50, 57, 68, 102, 125, 131

Wright, J. Elwin, 103

Wright, N. T., 80

Wycliffe, John, 14

YMCA, 108

Youth for Christ, 75, 123

About the Author

JASON S. LANTZER is an adjunct professor of history at Butler University and Indiana University-Purdue University Indianapolis and the author of *"Prohibition Is Here to Stay:" The Reverend Edward S. Shumaker and the Dry Crusade in America.*